A bold call to recognize and respond to our responsibilities for a just society in our own backyard.

> "The obligation *l'harot et atzmo*, 'to show ourselves' … as having experienced poverty, discrimination, and inequality, means continuously working to alleviate the suffering of others."
>
> —from Chapter 1

Our increasingly globalized reality compels us to take responsibility for people around the world. But we can't let concern for places other than our own absolve us of responsibility for the places closer to home.

In this important and practical look at social justice work from a Jewish perspective, Rabbi Jill Jacobs offers a model for organizing explicitly Jewish responses to social justice issues in our communities. She addresses the key questions in crafting a social justice program, including: How do we define our community? What are our obligations to this community? How do we develop effective partnerships with other communities? How do we move toward creating a better world?

Her practical tips will help synagogues, schools and other institutions make effective and meaningful social change. Each chapter includes an exploration of related Jewish texts and secular wisdom, as well as a guide to implementing the relevant strategies in your congregation.

Also Available

There Shall Be No Needy
Pursuing Social Justice through Jewish Law and Tradition
By Rabbi Jill Jacobs
Foreword by Rabbi Elliot N. Dorff, PhD
Preface by Simon Greer

Confronts the most pressing issues of twenty-first-century America by bringing together classical Jewish sources, contemporary policy debate and real-life stories about poverty, employers and unions, homelessness, health care, the environment and more.

6 x 9, 288 pp, Quality PB, 978-1-58023-425-2
Hardcover, 978-1-58023-394-1

Building a Successful Volunteer Culture
Finding Meaning in Service in the Jewish Community
By Rabbi Charles Simon
Foreword by Shelley Lindauer
Preface by Dr. Ron Wolfson

A step-by-step guide to cultivating volunteers who thrive within the Jewish community.

6 x 9, 192 pp, Quality PB, 978-1-58023-408-5

RABBI JILL JACOBS is executive director of Rabbis for Human Rights–North America. Widely acknowledged as one of the leading voices in Jewish social justice, Rabbi Jacobs is also the author of *There Shall Be No Needy: Pursuing Social Justice through Jewish Law and Tradition* (Jewish Lights). She has been voted to the *Forward* newspaper's list of fifty influential Jews, to *Newsweek*'s list of the fifty most influential rabbis in America, and to the *Jewish Week*'s list of "thirty-six under thirty-six."

Rabbi David Saperstein is director of the Religious Action Center of Reform Judaism. A prolific writer and speaker, he has appeared on many television news and talk shows.

"An important contribution to synagogues that want to deepen their commitment to social justice work, [and] to individual Jews who want to understand the deep connection between Judaism and the commitment to repair the world."
—**Rabbi Laura Geller**, senior rabbi, Temple Emanuel of Beverly Hills

"A magnificent how-to guide for Jewish institutions that want to take social justice seriously."
—**Rabbi Sidney Schwarz**, author, *Judaism and Justice: The Jewish Passion to Repair the World*

"Masterful.... Gives voice to a broader meaning of what it means to be a 'religious' Jew.... A deeply authentic religious underpinning for a 'spiritual practice' of social justice."
—**Rabbi Elie Kaunfer**, author, *Empowered Judaism: What Independent Minyanim Can Teach Us about Building Vibrant Jewish Communities*

Also Available

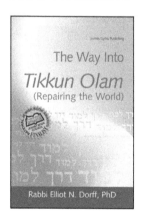

The Way Into *Tikkun Olam* (Repairing the World)
By Rabbi Elliot N. Dorff, PhD

"Lucid, clear and inspirational.... Acknowledges that the acts of *tikkun olam* that we perform have to be underpinned by a spiritual dimension as well."
—**Union of Liberal & Progressive Synagogues Newsletter**

An accessible introduction to the Jewish concept of our responsibility to care for others and repair the world.
6 x 9, 304 pp, Quality PB, 978-1-58023-328-6

JEWISH LIGHTS Publishing

www.jewishlights.com

Find us on Facebook®
Facebook is a registered
trademark of Facebook, Inc.

Praise for *Where Justice Dwells: A Hands-On Guide to Doing Social Justice in Your Jewish Community*

"Unique insights [on] repairing the world through social justice as part of the fullest expression of Jewish values."
—**Rabbi Steve Wernick**, executive vice president, United Synagogue of Conservative Judaism

"Presents more than the possibilities of Jewish social justice … a compelling road map that moves us from a place of altruism to a place of profound obligation."
—**Dr. Erica Brown**, author, *Inspired Jewish Leadership: Practical Approaches to Building Strong Communities*

"[Turns] passion and deep insights about justice into a practical and practicable guide … teaches us how we can place justice at the center and change the world."
—**Rabbi J. Rolando Matalon**, Congregation B'nai Jeshurun

"There are several publications and websites that give us the 'how-to' for doing the work of social justice and religious action. In this volume, Rabbi Jacobs also provides us with the 'why-to'—the Jewish sources and in-depth thinking about our obligation to make this work a priority in our communities."
—**Rabbi Ellen Weinberg Dreyfus**, immediate past president, Central Conference of American Rabbis

"An inspiration. I could not put it down.... In a voice of passion, wisdom and compassion … teaches us to turn our prayers into reality."
—**Rabbi Naomi Levy**, author, *To Begin Again* and *Hope Will Find You*

"Takes our hand and leads us step by step down the path of *tikkun olam*.... Pragmatic and yet lofty … a must for individuals and communities alike."
—**Rabbi Tirzah Firestone**, Nevei Kodesh, Boulder; author, *The Receiving: Reclaiming Jewish Women's Wisdom* and *With Roots in Heaven*

Where Justice Dwells

A Hands-On Guide to Doing Social Justice in Your Jewish Community

Rabbi Jill Jacobs

author of *There Shall Be No Needy:*
Pursuing Social Justice through Jewish Law and Tradition

Foreword by Rabbi David Saperstein

JEWISH LIGHTS Publishing

Where Justice Dwells:
A Hands-On Guide to Doing Social Justice in Your Jewish Community

Library of Congress Cataloging-in-Publication Data
Jacobs, Jill, 1975–
  Where justice dwells : a hands-on guide to doing social justice in your Jewish commu-
nity / Jill Jacobs ; foreword by David Saperstein.
       p. cm.
  Includes bibliographical references.
  ISBN 978-1-58023-453-5 (quality pbk.)
  1. Social justice—Religious aspects—Judaism. 2. Social service—Religious aspects—
Judaism. 3. Jewish ethics. I. Title.
  BM645.J8J34 2011
  296.3'8—dc22
                                                                        2011013917

ISBN 978-168336-491-7 (hc)

Manufactured in the United States of America

Cover Design: Jenny Buono
Cover Art: © iStockphoto.com/Andrey Volokhatiuk
Interior Design: Heather Pelham

Published by Jewish Lights Publishing
www.jewishlights.com

for Lior Brakha,

והוציא כאור צדקך ומשפטך כצהרים
תהילים לז: ו

Contents

Foreword

This is an extraordinary era in Jewish history, when social justice has emerged as an increasingly powerful force in the shaping of Jewish identity and Jewish institutions. Today, we are seeing an expansion of a long-standing pattern in American Jewish life of social justice as an organizing principle of Jewish identity. We are a community forged by the interaction of three strands of such organizing principles:

1. A God-oriented world dominated by a covenant at Sinai with its vision of ethical monotheism. In this worldview, God calls us to a task of righteousness and holiness, and sets upon us a mission to be a light to and of the nations, taking as our inspiration the prophetic idealism of what the world and humanity could be.

2. The Age of Reason, with its emphasis on ethics as the most rational and logical essence of religion—a view of ethics that promoted social justice, and that shaped Reform, Conservative, and Reconstructionist Judaism, and strands of modern Orthodoxy, as well as the Christian "social gospel" tradition.

3. An existential embrace of social justice here in America, the first nation that welcomed Jews in our historic role of speaking truth to power, creating a secular culture that reaffirmed and legitimized our embrace of civic and social justice engagement.

American Judaism has very much embodied these three organizing principles of Jewish theology and thought, each of which in its own way emphasizes the social idealism that led to social action becoming a key expression of Jewish life in the twentieth century. Reinforcing this trend was the recognition that we Jews would never be safe, never secure so long as we lived in a society in which any group could be subject to persecution, discrimination, and deprivation. The Jewish community has concretized this social justice emphasis in the broad array of social service agencies providing for the sick, the hungry, the elderly, the children, the unemployed; and in the almost universal organizational and synagogue social justice activities and programs, which have involved hundreds of thousands of Jews in local, national, and international causes of social justice including civil rights, Vietnam, Darfur, women's rights and gay rights, *bikkur cholim* programs, shelters for the homeless and food assistance for the hungry, literacy mentoring, Mitzvah Days, High Holy Day hunger collections, environmental issues, socially responsible investment practices, fund-raising for disaster and humanitarian relief, opposing anti-Semitism, and advocating for oppressed Soviet Jewry, Israel's security, and Middle East peace.

Some of these programs have been superb, others have been quite limited; some have engaged large swaths of synagogue members, others have touched only a few people; some have involved ongoing programs and others short-term engagement. (A quick look at the Reform movement's Fain Awards to innovative social action programs in synagogues over the last few years or the equivalent in other streams shows the power of the many success stories among these activities.) Nonetheless, too few of these programs have been transformative to the synagogues or their membership; too few have been sustainable over long periods of time. Too few have found ways to celebrate and embrace the achievements of synagogue members as they have served as leaders, staff, board members, and donors to social justice causes outside of the synagogue.

And that's where *Where Justice Dwells* comes in. In a compelling tour de force, Rabbi Jacobs weaves together seamlessly several kinds of books to create a work that masterfully integrates Jewish legal and narrative text, sociological research, and compelling stories of people she has met and with whom she has worked. She has created an inspiring call to arms and a practical tool for everyone interested in creating and expanding social justice work in their synagogues and larger communities. Most particularly, it is a rich repository of invaluable analysis and, drawing on best practices from across the nation, an effective guidebook for synagogues, rabbis, and lay activists that describes with clarity, insight, and creativity how to bring about real transformation in synagogue life around *tikkun olam.*

In doing so, she has laid out the two essential themes for lifting Jewish social justice to new levels and making it a powerful tool for strengthening Jewish identity and Jewish life in the twenty-first century. First, she points out that transformative Jewish social justice requires individuals and synagogues to fully integrate social justice into the educational and ritual lives of the synagogue.

As to those who say we must choose between study, spirituality, and social justice, who suggest that any one of these pillars of Jewish life must come at the expense of the others, our response—to paraphrase Leonard Fein, one of the most influential intellectual forces regarding Jewish social justice of the past two generations—would be that such a choice would offer inauthentic Jewish answers to the challenges we face. For otherwise, we would have to answer unanswerable Jewish questions:

- Which is more Jewish—wearing a *kippah* or clothing the naked?

- Which is more urgent—feeding matzah to our children on Pesach or feeding the starving children dying in Sudan?

- Which is the more religious act—welcoming with joy the Sabbath Queen or welcoming with love the refugee fleeing persecution? Praying with fervor, with *kavannah* on Shabbat or expressing our indignation in the face of injustice?

The heart of an authentic Jewish understanding is that we do not have to choose between these commitments. At the core of our precepts is understanding that serious Jewish study inevitably leads to the soup kitchen; that sincere prayer, among many valuable things, is a way of preparing to do battle with injustice; that social justice without being grounded in text and ritual is ephemeral and unsustainable. Our goal must be to weave *torah* (study), *avodah* (worship), and *u'g'milut chasadim* (acts of loving-kindness) together into a stronger tapestry of Jewish life.

We are seeing new approaches to such integration: synagogues that are downplaying separate social justice committees and assigning to *every* committee a social justice vice chair charged with integrating social justice into its work; the Conservative movement's lead work on *hekhsher tzedek*, which weaves together kashrut and social values; Mazon, which connects Jewish life-cycle ceremonies and *tzedakah* for hunger; the work of the various streams in lifting up social justice themes of holidays; congregation-based community organizing (CBCO); and the efforts of the various movements' responsa or law committees in lifting up the insights of Jewish texts to the urgent moral issues of the day.

In this latter regard, Rabbi Jacobs's book is exemplary. Indeed, *Where Justice Dwells* exemplifies the very integration for which it calls. Her choice of insightful and evocative texts smoothly integrated into the narrative of the book, the honest and detailed presentation of these texts with all their contradictions and nuances, and her powerful modeling of how to apply the moral wisdom of the halakhic and aggadic traditions of our faith to the vexing issues confronting us today would provide an invaluable study course for a synagogue high school or adult education program all on its own.

Second, she lifts up the transformative impact that true personal engagement can have among members of the synagogue, and between givers and recipients of services and charity. Her own personal stories and those of others that have inspired her provide a paradigm for the power of storytelling and the growing phenomenon of CBCO led by national entities like the Reform movement's Just Congregations initiative and Jewish Funds for Justice as well as the growing array of local-based Jewish social justice organizations. By effecting widespread buy-in by large numbers of people, developing a new cadre of trained leaders across synagogue life, and empowering people to address the real needs of their own lives and of their own communities, CBCO work has the potential to reinvigorate communities and synagogues like few approaches before it.

The success of Rabbi Jacobs's vision will require restructuring the way the next generation of rabbinic and lay leadership is trained. We have taken important steps with the service learning programs of American Jewish World Service, the CBCO training of Jewish Funds for Justice and

Just Congregations, and the Religious Action Center's Brickner rabbinic and rabbinic student training programs.

Where Justice Dwells provides a foundation for this ambitious agenda and secures Rabbi Jacobs's influence in the American Jewish community as a powerful voice on how Jewish values can truly inspire and transform our synagogues and communities.

And transform we must. For one thing is clear: if the Judaism we offer our young does not speak to great moral issues of their lives or the great moral issues of the world they will inherit, it will not capture their excitement, their inspiration, their loyalty, or their engagement. And on that challenge, the future of the Jewish community will depend.

Rabbi David Saperstein

Acknowledgments

I wrote much of this book as a Jerusalem Fellow at the Mandel Leadership Institute. I am grateful to the institute for granting me the space and time to study, write, and bounce ideas off of brilliant people. Thank you first to the Mandel faculty and staff: Dr. Zvi Beckerman, Dr. Yehuda Ben-Dor, Dr. Eli Gottlieb, Dr. Moshe Halbertal, Dr. Jen Glaser, Richie Juran, Dr. Daniel Marom, Dr. Jonathan Sarna, and Abi Dauber Sterne. I owe infinite thanks to my fellow fellows that year: Rabbi Lisa Goldstein, Andrea Hendler, Dr. Sarra Lev, Rabbi Leonel Levy, Nina Price, Rabbi Susan Silverman, and David Stoleru. Each of them read multiple drafts of several chapters and acted as cheerleaders and coaches over way too many soy lattes and bourekas.

Many other thank-yous are in order to the friends and colleagues who contributed to my thinking about this book: Aryeh Bernstein was my *chavruta* in studying the texts that became the basis for chapter 1, and our free-flowing conversations influenced my thinking on place and communal responsibility. Laura Jackson's editing was, as always, wise and sensitive. Rabbi Brent Spodek offered a helpful reading of one chapter. Carolyn Hessel and Miri Pomerantz Dauber have been generous in sharing their extensive knowledge of the world of Jewish books. Thank you to Jewish Funds for Justice for granting me a sabbatical year to write this book. Thank you to Rabbi Jonah Pesner for his feedback on the sections on community organizing. My new colleagues at Rabbis for Human Rights–North America have already proven to be inspiring partners in the quest for justice, and I look forward to our continued work together. Ayala Cohen and

Aura Sosa and her team cared for my daughter while I wrote and worked. The Fort Tryon Jewish Center community has been a warm and supportive base for my family through our many transitions of the past year. My other friends and colleagues in the worlds of social justice, Jewish education, synagogue life, and communal leadership are too many to name, but each has helped to shape this book by sharing his or her own experiences, questions, and challenges.

A special thank you to the staff of Jewish Lights, starting with Stuart Matlins, publisher and editor-in-chief, for his vision and his faith in this project. This is my second time working with Emily Wichland, vice president of editorial and production, and I remain grateful for her guidance through every step of the publishing process. Thank you to project editor Lauren Hill for shepherding this book through the final stages of editing. Jennifer Rataj and Barbara Heise have already been tremendously helpful with publicity, and I look forward to working with them even more closely in the months to come.

Thank you to my family—Paula and David Jacobs, Dan and Ziona Austrian, and Karen and Shahar Yitzhak-Austrian—for your constant support and encouragement.

I wrote most of this book during the first year of my daughter Lior's life. It will be a few years before she is able to read her mother's work. I hope that by the time she does, the world will be a much more just place than it is right now.

My deepest thanks go to Guy Austrian, my life partner and my most important social justice mentor, for editing every chapter and, more important, for his boundless love.

Introduction

The Road Ahead

I heard something remarkable, again and again, when traveling around the country to speak about my book *There Shall Be No Needy: Pursuing Social Justice through Jewish Law and Tradition* (Jewish Lights). In that book, I examined a number of current American social and economic issues through the lens of Jewish law and history. After the book came out, I set out on a speaking tour of synagogues, bookstores, and Jewish organizations from coast to coast. At each stop, someone would inevitably raise his or her hand and say, "You've convinced me that social justice is deeply rooted in Judaism. Why, then, isn't it a bigger priority in my synagogue [or school or Jewish Community Center]?"

This response was remarkable, but not actually surprising. Over the past decade, I have spent thousands of hours with rabbis, educators, and lay leaders who share some of the same complaints about their synagogue, school, or camp's social justice work. These programs often feel marginal to the life of the community. While an annual "Mitzvah Day" might attract a large crowd, leaders struggle to attract volunteers for ongoing projects that require consistent commitment and sustained effort. Many communities shy away from issue-based advocacy, for fear that such efforts might look "too political."

I intend this book to be a tool for these dedicated volunteers, rabbis, educators, and communal professionals who want to engage their institutions in meaningful and effective justice work. In the course of this book, I will share strategies for creating a communal vision for the place where you live, identifying your community's passions, finding appropriate partners and projects, and integrating Jewish text and ritual with justice work. Throughout the discussion, I will weave in lessons from my own and others' experience, as well as Jewish texts and ideas that illuminate the conversation.

I have divided this book into three parts. In part 1, "Envisioning a Just Place," I walk through a visioning process by which your community will set big-picture goals for what you hope your social justice work to achieve. In part 2, "Principles and Practice of Social Justice," I offer some general principles for effective and meaningful social justice work. In part 3, "Taking Action," I examine four modes of action and offer strategies for choosing among these and for implementing each.

There are several ways you might go about reading this book. The board, social action committee, or faculty of your institution might decide to read this book together, over the course of several months or a year. If so, you could choose one chapter to read ahead of time for each of your meetings. When you get together, talk about the ways that you might implement the lessons of this chapter in your own community. Try out a few techniques over the next month or so, and come back together to evaluate the results and to think about next steps. Or, you might read the book as an individual and pick up a few tools to bring into your own social justice work or that of your community.

Each chapter includes a set of discussion questions meant to prompt reflection and conversation. I encourage you to use these questions—as well as others of your own design—as you develop meaningful and effective social justice practices for your own community. And I look forward to my next book tour, during which I expect to hear many tales of synagogues, schools, camps, and other Jewish communities in which social justice has moved to the center.

PART ONE

Envisioning a Just Place

Jewish tradition holds out the promise of a messianic era, when the lion will lie down with the lamb, every person will have a roof over his or her head, nobody will die before old age, and all war will end. This vision challenges us to believe that incremental progress in each generation will eventually lead to a perfected world. With this vision in mind, we can never be satisfied even with major changes in policy or culture.

But this picture of the ideal world can sometimes feel too big. Few of us are optimistic enough to believe that we will achieve this vision in our own lifetime, or even in the lifetimes of our grandchildren. It's true that at a few points in Jewish history, some communities became so convinced that the messianic age waited around the corner that they picked up their belongings and followed false messiahs, with disastrous financial and emotional results. And some rabbis even spent much time calculating exactly when the Messiah would arrive.[1] For the most part, though, Jews have assumed that the messianic era will come someday, but not soon.

Thus, even as we pray for and dream of the perfected world, we also need a goal that's a bit closer at hand—perhaps five or ten years away. In sitting down with members of your own community to plan your social justice work, you might start by asking yourselves, "What do we want our city to look like a decade from now? What do we hope that our own community will look like as a result of our involvement in the place where we live?" By beginning with this question, rather than jumping into whatever projects seem readily available, you will create a collective vision that will guide your work in the years to come.

Much goes into arriving at this vision. You will need to answer some basic questions about why your community is committed to social justice, about the geographic focus of your work, and about what issues matter most to you. In chapter 1, I will dive into the question of why Jews should do social justice work at all, and what's different about doing social justice work in the context of a Jewish community. Chapter 2 will examine the role of *place* in social justice work and will consider strategies for choosing the places where you will work. Finally, chapter 3 asks what the places we touch might look like when our work is done.

These chapters are intended to guide a visioning process within your community. Read a chapter a week, and discuss the material with your team using the questions provided. Then, together, develop the vision that will inspire and guide your work for the immediate future.

1
Why Jewish Social Justice?

During rabbinical school, I spent a summer working at a labor union in New Jersey. Word spread quickly that a rabbi-to-be was in the building. In my first few days there, at least half a dozen people showed up at my desk to talk about their own Jewish identities. The son of a Jewish communal professional wondered aloud whether labor organizing constituted Jewish work. A union lawyer spoke about her commitment to public interest law as a calling rooted in Judaism. A few staff members hoped for confirmation that they were "good Jews" despite not going to synagogue or keeping kosher.

All of these union employees shared a deeply felt conviction that social justice work is inherently Jewish. But most of them struggled to define exactly what was Jewish about this work. Progressive Jews often note, as a point of pride, the number of Goldbergs and Cohens who sit at the helm of American social justice organizations. These social justice leaders may not often speak publicly about the role of Judaism in their lives; when probed, though, many describe their work as stemming from their Jewish identity. Meanwhile, virtually every rabbi, educator, and synagogue lay leader I've met brags about his or her synagogue's or school's involvement in social action.

But we Jews can hardly just pat ourselves on the back for having produced so many prominent social justice leaders or for the existence of

3

social action committees in virtually every synagogue. The Jewish community has also produced more than its share of slumlords, bosses who mistreat their workers, and corporate tax evaders. Ubiquitous as they may be, social action committees often hover on the sidelines of synagogue life.

As the American Jewish community becomes increasingly wealthy and increasingly comfortable in the United States, it is no longer fair to assume that Jews will always put aside personal financial self-interest in favor of creating opportunity for others. The vague sense that there is "something Jewish" about social justice will not be enough to sustain long-term involvement in this work. Instead, we must formulate a coherent argument for why justice must remain at the center of Jewish life.

The Jewish obligation for social justice stems from four sources: the historical experience, the legal imperative, a vision of the world to come, and practical considerations about the place of Jews in a diverse society. These four sources should inspire Jews to do social justice work not only as individuals, but also within the specific context of Jewish communal institutions.

THE HISTORICAL IMPERATIVE

Ask most Jews what they know about Jewish history, and they will recite some of the following information: We were slaves in the land of Egypt. We survived the Babylonian and Roman invasions, the Inquisition, and the Holocaust. We came to America as poor immigrants. We established some of the first labor unions in America. We marched for civil rights in Selma, Alabama. We have been at the forefront of the feminist movement, the gay and lesbian movement, and other modern liberation struggles.

Jews who are deeply involved in social justice often trace their commitment to this work to their family histories. From supporters of immigration and immigrants' rights, I have heard stories about parents and grandparents who came to the United States with nothing, found a foothold in their new country, and taught their children and grandchildren to care for vulnerable populations. Public school teachers have shared with me the role that good public schools played in propelling their own families from poverty into the middle class. Labor organizers cite the union movement as the reason their families escaped the tenements.

We tell these stories as though it is a foregone conclusion that a people that has experienced both suffering and liberation will dedicate itself to alleviating the suffering of others. But the world does not always work like that. The experience of oppression can trigger at least two types of responses. The first model is that of the proverbial playground bully who suffers abuse at home and then takes out his anger on anyone smaller than himself. After suffering through centuries of persecution, the Jewish community could decide to wage a violent attack against everyone else. The Torah even would offer some precedent for such action, in the commandment to wipe out Amalek in retribution for this tribe's attack on the Israelites on their way out of slavery (Deuteronomy 25:17–19).[1] Some Jewish extremists do advocate violence toward non-Jews. But the normative Jewish tradition rails against the instinct for revenge. The Torah itself forbids oppressing Egyptians, let alone orphans, widows, foreigners, or other vulnerable populations. In its repeated exhortation to care for the stranger because "you were strangers in the land of Egypt" (Exodus 22:20), the Bible sets a precedent that history imposes obligations.

One of the best-known lines of the Passover Haggadah comments, "In every generation, one is obligated to see oneself [*lirot et atzmo*] as though he or she, personally, had come forth from Egypt." The obligation to tell the story of the Exodus compels us not only to speak of our ancestors' slavery and liberation, but to see their story as our own.

How do we *see* ourselves as having come forth from Egypt? The most literalist readings point to another line in the Haggadah: "If God had not brought our ancestors out of Egypt, we and our children and our children's children would still be enslaved to Pharaoh in Egypt." We see ourselves as liberated slaves because, absent a miraculous series of events, we actually might have been born into slavery. More allegorical interpretations speak instead of the different kinds of emotional and spiritual slavery from which we continuously seek liberation.

The Sephardic tradition maintains a slightly, but significantly, different version of this command. The Sephardic Haggadah comments, "In every generation, one is obligated to *show oneself* [*l'harot et atzmo*] as though he or she, personally, had come forth from Egypt." In contrast to the introspective nature of the command *lirot et atzmo*—to see ourselves as having come forth from Egypt—this version of the obligation demands action.

For me, the intersection between these two commands speaks precisely to the challenge of being a Jew in America today.

The obligation of memory is twofold. The commandment *lirot et atzmo*, "to *see* ourselves" as liberated slaves, compels us to remember the suffering that has characterized much of Jewish history and to take pride in the role that Jews played in early civil rights and labor struggles.

But telling stories about the past does not suffice. The obligation *l'harot et atzmo*, "to *show* ourselves," demands action, not just introspection. *Showing* ourselves as having experienced poverty, discrimination, and inequality means continuously working to alleviate the suffering of others. And the cycle continues: the more we *show* ourselves to be people who respond to oppression, the more we and our children will see ourselves as such. And so on.

THE OBLIGATION FOR JUSTICE

When I first tell someone that I am a rabbi, I often find myself the beneficiary of an outpouring of Jewish guilt. "Rabbi," my new acquaintance says, "I'm so sorry—I haven't been to synagogue since my bar mitzvah." Or: "I'm such a bad Jew—I didn't fast on Yom Kippur." Or: "I guess I shouldn't tell you that I had bacon for breakfast."

I certainly didn't get into the rabbinate to police other people's practice. The outpouring of guilt can be a bit much when I'm just trying to enjoy a quiet airplane flight or shmoozing at a party. A rabbi friend of mine got so fed up with the guilt that she started telling strangers that she is an astrophysicist. "Nobody can ever think of another question," she explained.

While I will probably never enjoy hearing confessions of others' perceived sins, I am struck that nobody has yet apologized to me for cheating on his or her taxes, underpaying workers, or failing to give *tzedakah*. Somehow, most Jews have decided that being a "good Jew" means adhering to rituals such as Shabbat, kashrut, and prayer.

But the word *halakhah*, generally translated as "Jewish law," literally means "the way to walk." Rather than a limited set of ritual laws, *halakhah* represents an all-encompassing way of life. Classical compendiums of *halakhah* generally consist of four sections of law: *Orach Chayim* deals with prayer, holiday observance, Shabbat, and other aspects of day-to-day life; *Yoreh De'ah* addresses kashrut, *brit milah*, *tzedakah*, and other ritual practices; *Even HaEzer* focuses on marriage, divorce, and family law; and *Choshen Mishpat* tackles civil law. Traditionally, Jewish education has emphasized the first two of these sections, and to a lesser extent the third. Many more *teshuvot* (legal opinions) respond to questions about Shabbat and kashrut than to ones about the appropriate treatment of workers. And modern Jews have largely internalized the idea that the core of Jewish practice consists of prescribed ritual behaviors.

There are good historical reasons for this de-emphasis of civil law. For most of history, Jews have had little political power and have been subject to the laws of the lands in which they have lived. With Christianity as the dominant model, Jews adapted to the idea that religion governs only private life. In considering whether to grant citizenship to French Jews or to expel them, Napoleon asked representatives of the community a series of questions aimed at determining whether Judaism was a religion or a nation. The answers, all of which classified Judaism as a religion, were the right ones from the perspective of allowing French Jews to become citizens; but from the perspective of classical Jewish thought, they reduced Judaism to a shadow of itself. Much later, the founders of the State of Israel struck a deal between the religious and secular factions: British common law (with some influences from Ottoman and international law) would continue to govern the nascent state, but laws pertaining to personal status would follow *halakhah* as interpreted by the Orthodox establishment. Since 1948, Israeli courts have increasingly looked to international law as well as *halakhah* and Jewish tradition in their decisions.

The decision to base Israeli law on British common law was a logical one. During the period of the British Mandate (1923–1948), British common law ruled Palestine; maintaining existing laws was certainly easier than resuscitating ancient and medieval Jewish laws that had never been used to govern a sovereign nation. However, ceding matters of personal status to the Orthodox rabbinical establishment has caused no end of difficulties. The absence of civil marriage or divorce means that women can be trapped by husbands who refuse to grant a religious divorce. Conservative and Reform rabbis cannot perform weddings in the State of Israel, and interfaith couples or those who want no religious ritual must go abroad to marry. It seems likely that an attempt to base civil law on *halakhah* would also have resulted in a disempowerment of non-Orthodox movements and individuals.

The decision to split Israeli law between the religious sphere and the secular sphere was grounded in practical concerns. Ultimately, though, this split reinforces the notion that Judaism has nothing to say about everyday life, but serves only as a limiting (and even oppressive) factor in areas of ritual and life cycle.

But *halakhah* can make a positive contribution even to modern systems of law. One of the most exciting moments of my own career occurred when an Israeli lawyer called to ask for guidance in arguing a Supreme Court case against the "Wisconsin Plan," a controversial welfare-to-work program that cast many low-income Israelis into even deeper economic distress. Basing ourselves on classical Jewish sources, she and I crafted an argument about the responsibility of the state to care for its citizens. Using this argument—as well as precedents from Israeli and international law—she and her team won the case and secured the cancellation of the program.

Jewish communities outside of the State of Israel might not expect civil courts to take *halakhah* into consideration. But for Jews who do not want to leave their spiritual selves and their relationship with the Divine at the synagogue door, taking *halakhah* seriously requires thinking about civil law in terms of obligation, rather than altruism. Religious Jews will not spend money on Shabbat or eat a ham sandwich no matter how tempting the alternative might be. In the same way, being a religious Jew should mean being scrupulous about paying workers appropriately, giving *tzedakah* (gifts to the poor), and maintaining fair business practices.

In 2008, the Conservative movement's Committee on Jewish Law and Standards passed a *teshuvah* (halakhic opinion) that I wrote, in which I concluded that Jewish employers are obligated to pay their workers a living wage.[2] In the course of the discussion, a number of committee members objected that this requirement would cut into the profit margins of small businesses and could even force synagogues and schools to cut their program budgets. I responded that Jewish institutions think nothing of spending tens of thousands of dollars more to serve kosher food. El Al, the national airline of Israel, no doubt loses millions of dollars a year as a result of not flying on Shabbat. But Jewish institutions calculate into their budgets the costs of ritual practices commonly understood as obligatory. The demands of Jewish civil law are no less serious.

Accepting Jewish civil law as obligatory means sometimes prioritizing the needs of the larger world over our immediate desires. This approach rejects definitions of *tzedakah* or justice work as altruism, generosity, or good deeds. Instead, this work becomes something we *have* to do in the process of creating a world that reflects the divine presence.

VISIONS OF A PERFECTED WORLD

Despite all of the injustices, bloodshed, and pain to which human beings have subjected one another, Judaism maintains a belief in the possibility of a world of loving-kindness and justice. In such a world, humans will fulfill their destiny to be "very good," in the words of the creation story, and will perfect rather than destroy creation.[3]

In a column for the *New York Times*, the philosopher Peter Singer asks whether human beings should make a worldwide pact not to have children. In the end, Singer rejects this proposition, saying that he remains too much of an optimist to wish for the end of the human species. But along the way, he questions the justice of bringing a new person into the world when it is likely that this person will suffer. Singer asks, "Is life worth living? Are the interests of a future child a reason for bringing that child into existence? And is the continuance of our species justifiable in the face of our knowledge that it will certainly bring suffering to innocent future human beings?"[4]

Along the same lines, a midrash imagines the angels arguing about whether human beings should be created at all. In this midrash, God comes to the angels to ask their opinions about whether human beings should be created. The angels split into factions, representing the attributes of loving-kindness, truth, justice, and peace:

> Loving-kindness said, "Create humanity, for they will do acts of loving-kindness." Truth said, "Do not create them, for they are full of lies."

Justice said, "Create them, for they will do acts of justice." Peace said, "Do not create them, for they are quarrelsome."

Determined to break the tie in favor of creating humanity, God throws truth to the ground. In response to the other angels' pleas, God eventually restores truth, but not before human beings have been created (*B'reishit Rabbah* 8:5).

In this midrash, the angels make logical arguments for and against the creation of human beings. At the end of the discussion, the philosophical question has not been resolved. We do not know whether the authors of the midrash conclude that human beings do more harm or more good to the world. We do know that God dispenses with logic and creates humanity by fiat. This is the Jewish response to Singer: logical arguments will not solve the question of whether human beings are ultimately good or evil. Rather, the investment in human survival is a matter of faith, not philosophy.

The ancient Rabbis not only imagined the angels debating the wisdom of creating humanity, but even continued the argument among themselves. According to one Talmudic passage, the schools of Hillel and Shammai spent two and a half years debating whether it would have been better for human beings (or each individual person, according to a different reading) to be created or not to have been created (BT, *Eruvin* 13b).[5] In the end, those opposed to the creation of humanity win the argument. "But," the discussion concludes, "now that humanity has been created, let them examine their past deeds"—or, according to an alternate reading recorded in the text, "let them examine their future actions." That is, given that human existence is a fact, people should learn from the past and try to act justly in the future.

Jewish tradition promises that positive human actions have the potential to bring about a perfected world. The biblical prophets imagine a peaceful messianic era, in which every human being enjoys basic sustenance and the nations of the world live in harmony. Kabbalistic (mystical) thought proposes that individual human actions directly affect the cosmos, ultimately guiding the world back to its original untainted state.[6]

Judaism offers no conclusive description of the messianic age. The ancient Rabbis and medieval commentators argued about when and how this time will come about, about which laws will remain in effect during this time, and about the place of non-Jews in this new world. The refusal to make definite claims about the messianic era indicates an insistence on devoting our attention to the here and now. Paying too much attention to the details of a perfect age might encourage us to meditate on this future time, while ignoring the pressing needs of the moment.

But maintaining faith in the possibility of a perfected world helps us to avoid getting stuck in day-to-day concerns. When the immediate problems of the world feel intractable, the vision of a utopian future inspires and challenges us to improve upon the status quo.

PRACTICAL MATTERS

Some years ago, I was involved in a Jewish-Muslim community building project in Chicago. Over the course of a few years, a group of Jews and Muslims spent time getting to know one another, celebrating holidays together, and working together on local issues of common concern. The mainstream Jewish community publicly opposed this project. One central agency even printed a notice in its newsletter condemning any relations with the Muslim organization most involved in the project. Some prominent members of the Jewish community argued against working with any group that would not publicly affirm the right of Israel to exist as a Jewish state. On the other side, some Muslim organizations would not work with our group unless we publicly supported the Palestinians' struggle for statehood. But the Jewish and Muslim organizations that remained involved understood that personal relationships and shared work can cut through grand political rhetoric. One night, vandals spray painted swastikas on a local synagogue. The next morning, a group of Muslims involved with the community building project appeared at the synagogue to join in the cleanup and help repair the damage.

Jewish communal rhetoric often divides the world into "us" and "them," as well as into "Jewish issues" and "non-Jewish issues." We Jews must take care of ourselves, we are told, because no one else will take care of us. Therefore, this argument goes, we must prioritize donating to institutions that help Jews in need, supporting synagogues and day schools, and defending Israel's every action.

But this dichotomy between "us" and "them" is both false and dangerous. Issues and institutions rarely touch *only* Jews or *only* non-Jews. An exclusive focus on "internal" issues can lead to missed opportunities to partner with communities who might, in turn, work on issues crucial to the Jewish community. Uncritical support of the Israeli government often backfires by generating more resentment and reinforcing a belief that it is impossible to support the legitimate needs of both Israelis and Palestinians.

When I tell people that I am a rabbi who works on social justice issues, I am often asked whether I work on "Jewish issues." The question puzzles me. Is poverty a Jewish or a non-Jewish issue? Yes, some organizations mostly work with Jews, and others mostly work with non-Jews. But long-term efforts to reduce poverty will make life better for people of all religious and ethnic backgrounds. Most agencies that operate under Jewish auspices, such as the Federation system, understand the interconnection between Jews and non-Jews. Appeals for donations to these organizations tend to feature pictures of elderly and poor Jews in the United States, Israel, and the former Soviet Union, but the organizations themselves serve people of all religious and ethnic backgrounds. The Federations know that it is impossible to solve poverty for one group without addressing the circumstances that contribute to poverty in general.

What about public education? Given the communal push to enroll Jewish children in day schools, perhaps we can classify public education as a non-Jewish issue. But the percentage of Jewish children who attend day schools and other private schools remains low in comparison with the percentage in the public school system. So, if public schools struggle, Jewish children will suffer along with their non-Jewish peers.

Or we can make a different utilitarian argument. Even for those who send their own children to private schools, public education plays a large role in shaping the world in which their children will live. We are fooling ourselves if we think that sending our own children to private school will free us from the effects of a broken public education system. Graduates of the public education system will be our children's coworkers, bosses, employees, neighbors, and elected representatives. The success of the entire country depends on whether we succeed in educating our own citizens.

American Jews often look to the civil rights era as the golden age of social justice activism and wax nostalgic about the partnership between the Jewish and the African American communities. Many Jews—along with other whites—traveled south to conduct voter registration drives, to march, and to sit in at restaurants and drugstores. One of the classic images of that time shows Rabbi Abraham Joshua Heschel marching arm in arm with Rev. Martin Luther King Jr. in Selma, Alabama. Famously, two young Jewish activists—Andrew Goodman and Michael Schwerner—lost their lives to a mob of KKK members, along with their African American colleague James Chaney. We should certainly applaud those who risked their lives to end segregation. But we rarely remember that Jews also benefited directly from the enactment of civil rights legislation. Albeit to a lesser extent than African Americans, Jews had also suffered from housing discrimination, hotels that refused to accept Jewish guests, and even entire neighborhoods and towns where restrictive covenants kept Jews out altogether. I do not point out these concrete gains in order to diminish the involvement of Jews in the civil rights movement. Quite the opposite! The struggle for civil rights offers a prime example in which the Jewish community recognized the fundamental interconnection between Jewish interests and the interests of other groups.

Forging relationships with other communities provides other benefits as well. I mentioned the Muslims who appeared with paint cans ready to cover up anti-Semitic graffiti. Now imagine that the incident had been more serious, perhaps involving violence or threats of violence against Jews. The communities with which Jews already enjoyed close relations would be most likely to step up as allies in protecting the Jewish community from danger.

In her analysis of the rise of anti-Semitism in Europe, Hannah Arendt notes that late-nineteenth- and early-twentieth-century Jews made a fatal error in relying on the political elite for protection, rather than forging alliances with the masses. She writes:

> Of all European peoples, the Jews had been the only one without a
> state of their own and had been, precisely for this reason, so eager

and so suitable for alliances with governments and states as such, no matter what these governments or states might represent. On the other hand, the Jews had no political tradition or experience, and were as little aware of the tension between society and state as they were of the obvious risks and power-possibilities of their new role. What little knowledge or traditional practice they brought to politics had its source first in the Roman Empire, where they had been protected, so to speak, by the Roman soldier, and later, in the Middle Ages, when they sought and received protection against the population and the local rulers from remote monarchical and Church authorities. From these experiences, they had somehow drawn the conclusion that authority, and especially high authority, was favorable to them and that lower officials, and especially the common people, were dangerous.[7]

Twenty-first-century America is not eighteenth-century Europe or Weimar Germany. Strict laws and cultural norms protect Jews against most outward anti-Semitism. The quota system of college admissions has long disappeared, and Jews hold prominent positions in government, business, and the nonprofit sector. The rising rate of intermarriage, though much bemoaned by mainstream Jewish leaders and sociologists, also indicates the deepening acceptance of Jews by non-Jewish society. A generation ago, a Christian family might have shunned a child who married a Jew. Now, this same family is more likely to consider the new spouse a "catch."

And yet, the American Jewish establishment still often chooses to look for partners among the power elite, rather than among the masses. This strategy, aimed at securing power for ourselves, easily backfires. In cozying up to the power brokers, we sometimes abandon our own historic and halakhic commitments, our vision of what a perfect world should be, and our alliances with other minority communities. Furthermore, we make ourselves vulnerable to shifts in the attitudes of the elites. When it is convenient to allow Jews to be scapegoated, such as at the start of the Iraq War, powerful former allies stand back and allow Jews to take the blame.

DOING JUSTICE WITH OTHER JEWS

Some people suggest that if Jews are already disproportionately represented within social justice organizations and movements, there is no reason for Jews to do justice work through their own institutions as well. Perhaps Jewish institutions should be places of refuge, where members can pray, learn, explore culture, and build community without engaging with the troubles of the world.

It is true that justice work based in Jewish institutions should not and could not replace the crucial work that Jews do as staff members and volunteers of social justice organizations, as public interest attorneys, and as elected officials and civil servants. But doing justice work through our synagogues, schools, and communal organizations has the potential to be more effective and meaningful than work done by individual Jews in secular contexts:

1. Engaging our institutions in justice work creates a space in which we can live full and integrated Jewish lives. Our prayers sustain and inspire our actions, and our actions take prayers and texts off the page and into real life.

2. Justice work builds community. Through engaging in a collective project that draws on individuals' passions and talents, community members become more deeply involved in one another's lives. They celebrate victories—both communal and personal—together, and mourn personal and collective losses as one.

3. Religious institutions have power. When private individuals or community groups speak, public officials sometimes pay attention but often do not. Few public officials, however, will outright ignore prominent religious institutions or coalitions of congregations.

4. Through our institutions, we show up publicly as Jews. When I do volunteer work or activism as an individual, I might mention that I am Jewish, or even that I am a rabbi. When I write a check to an organization, it is possible that the recipient wonders whether Jacobs is a Jewish name. But when an identifiably Jewish institution takes on an issue, it is clear that this action is a Jewish response.

Such institutional action helps to build relationships with non-Jewish partners, to raise the profile of the Jewish community as one dedicated to social justice, and to define issues important to our communities as "Jewish issues."

5. Through being public Jews, we can bring Jewish wisdom into the public discourse. The centuries of Jewish discussion about interpersonal relations, the creation of a just society, and the responsibilities of the individual and the community to one another include significant wisdom about creating a better world. As Jews, we can contribute this wisdom to the public discourse, while also learning from the best of the wisdom of other religions and of secular thinkers.

The connections between Judaism and justice are not vague or ill-defined. Rather, the Jewish tradition includes specific historical, halakhic, messianic, and utilitarian imperatives to contribute to building a more equitable world.

QUESTIONS FOR CONSIDERATION

1. With which of the categories discussed above—historical, halakhic, visionary, or utilitarian—do you most identify? Why? Are there any categories with which you do not identify at all?

2. Which of these categories do you feel is most present in your institution's approach to social justice? How might you bring the other categories into the equation?

2
Place Matters

This book begins with the assumption that place matters.[1] Even in this globalized, Internet era, I believe in making long-term commitments to specific places, and especially to the places where we live. In the next few pages, I will argue that our communal social justice efforts should begin by choosing the places where we will make an impact. I will then offer guidance for undertaking a place-based visioning process within your institution.

FINDING MY PLACE

My own journey to place-based social justice began in the 1990s in Morningside Heights, a New York City neighborhood dominated by academic institutions. By far, the largest of these is Columbia University, which includes Barnard College and Teachers College. Just a few blocks north of Columbia sit Union Theological Seminary, The Jewish Theological Seminary, and the Manhattan School of Music. The local coffee shops are populated by graduate students in thick eyeglasses arguing over Derrida, rabbinical students studying Talmud, and musicians lugging cello cases on their backs. Harlem, which was then a majority low-income and African American neighborhood, borders this academic enclave to the north and east.

I moved to this neighborhood as a seventeen-year-old undergraduate at Columbia College. It was my first time living away from home and my first time living in a city. I arrived with a year's worth of soap and shampoo, lest there be no drugstore nearby. I didn't know how to take the subway. I had never been to Brooklyn and could not have found Queens on a map. But I was excited to have arrived in the big city. I imagined myself spending Saturday nights at Broadway shows, rummaging through independent bookstores, and tutoring a child who would grow up to become a Supreme Court justice.

When I arrived at school, the area had yet to emerge from the economic funk of the 1980s. Surveying the landscape from the window of my first-year dorm room, my father pointed to burnt-out buildings and boarded-up storefronts all around us. Ninety-nine-cent stores lined the streets, and homeless men huddled by the university gates. Just a few years before, the infamous "Central Park Jogger" had been raped and left for dead only ten blocks from campus.

First-year orientation included a mandatory session on safety. There, the speaker sketched the invisible boundaries of the campus: Never go north of 125th Street (the unofficial border of Harlem). Don't go into Morningside Park, just east of the university. If you accidentally get on the northbound express train to Central Harlem, don't try to walk home. Get back on the train heading south. The campus stood in the middle of New York City and yet sought to be an island of safety amid a threatening world.

For much of college, I stayed within the invisible boundaries of the campus. I took care never to miss my subway stop. I avoided parks. But slowly, I began to wonder what lay on the other side of the walls. I summoned the courage to walk through the nearby housing projects. I did start tutoring, and so I got a glimpse of the city's public school system. I discovered the beauty of Harlem brownstones.

When I began rabbinical school in 1998 at The Jewish Theological Seminary a few blocks away, I decided that I could no longer live in Morningside Heights without involving myself in the community around me. As I related in my first book, my initial impressions of JTS were of a fortress shut off from the outside world. The building stands on the corner of 122nd street, with Harlem to the north and east, and yet the only door to the school opens toward Columbia. The *beit midrash* (study hall) where I would be spending much of my time sat in a windowless basement. If I was to spend five years in this building, I resolved, I would learn something about the surrounding neighborhood. By chance, I found my way to a tenants' rights group in Central Harlem, and from there I went on to volunteer and paid work in community organizations elsewhere in New York, as well as in Chicago and Jerusalem.

Fast-forward to 2005: A few months after Hurricane Katrina hit the Gulf Coast, I sat on top of a roof in Biloxi, Mississippi, with a group of college students from the University of Michigan. As we pounded nails into fresh shingles, I asked one young man, "Would you have come on this trip if it had been going to Detroit?" His confused look served as response enough. "No, why?" he asked.

Today, social justice is hot in Jewish circles. Thousands of young people participate in Jewish service learning trips to the Gulf Coast, Latin America, Africa, Arizona, and other places usually far away from their homes. These participants return inspired to take action. In the best cases, program alumni devote themselves to raising money for the community they visited, to taking political action on an issue they learned about during their program, or to involving themselves in a local issue for the first time. But more often than not, the initial excitement dissipates with the return home. Too often, we jump from place to place in search of the next exciting cause or meaningful experience. Heartbreaking pictures of a natural disaster in New Orleans, Haiti, or Chile prompt us to empty our wallets, but we have typically forgotten about that place by the time the difficult work of long-term rebuilding gets under way. We listen to speakers talk about the human rights crisis of the moment, and we leave the hall furious. But a week later, another speaker excites our passions about a different issue in a different place.

What if, instead, individuals and communities chose a small number of places and invested heavily in a personal, financial, and political relationship with these places? One of these places should be the place we live. But another might be a place we have visited on vacation, where we have studied, or one that fascinates us from afar. For some Jews, one of these places will always be Israel. Some of us will choose the place where our grandparents were born. Parents of children adopted from abroad might continue to invest in their children's birthplace. Television images of genocide or natural disaster might prompt us to learn more about the struggles of people we may never meet.

"Our places" may change over the course of our lifetime, as we move from city to city, explore the world, and develop relationships with new people and locales. But in the course of a multiyear commitment to a place, we have the chance to develop an intimate connection to that place, and perhaps even to have an impact there. This commitment does not mean that we should never respond to a natural disaster or humanitarian crisis or should never direct our money or advocacy toward a place that is not "ours." But these contributions should supplement, not replace, our primary investments in our places.

Jews once had a word for this idea. The nineteenth-century Bundists (Jewish socialists in Eastern Europe) called investment in one's home *doykayt*, "hereness." For the Bundists, *doykayt* represented an explicit rejection of the early Zionist movement, with its belief in *sh'lilat hagolah*, "the negation of the Diaspora." That Zionist belief proposed that Jewish life, by definition, could not flourish in the Diaspora; the Bundists thought otherwise. But *doykayt* no longer has to stand in opposition to a commitment to the State of Israel or another place. Air travel, the Internet, and the common practice of living in multiple places over a lifetime all enable us to establish a long-term relationship with a distant part of the world—even while we form deep commitments to the place in which we currently live.

TO SEE OR NOT TO SEE

The conversation with the University of Michigan student reminded me how easily we avoid looking at the places where we live. Only after five years in New York did I meet an elderly woman whose landlord had turned off her hot water in an effort to force her out of the apartment in favor of new tenants who would pay more. In Chicago, I spent hours listening to the stories of public housing residents who anticipated homelessness as the city prepared to demolish their buildings. Yet at my upscale synagogue less than five miles to the north, fellow congregants insisted to me that the housing would all be replaced and the tenants rehoused, just as the mayor promised. Another time, an educator at the same synagogue asked me for help with a volunteer project for the Hebrew School students. "The kids are going to make sandwiches for the homeless," she told me, "but the parents don't want their children to be around any homeless people. Do you know where we can just drop off the food?"

And yet, I write these words while drinking a soy latte at a bustling café in West Jerusalem. Charming paintings of Paris cover the walls, and Billy Joel sings about Long Island on the radio. At the table next to me, four young mothers, all immigrants, trade stories about their children's antics. And just a few miles away, the West Bank has been closed in preparation for the Jewish holiday of Purim. I struggle to imagine the Palestinian women unable to drop in on their friends in neighboring towns. It's much easier for me to block out this anonymous woman in favor of planning my daughter's Purim costume, making plans with friends, and generally enjoying my West Jerusalem life. And I remember a chance airport conversation with a young American preparing to move to a new settlement in the West Bank. His decision, he insisted, would have no impact on the Palestinians living nearby. I think ahead to the teenage soldiers who will inevitably be sent to protect him and his family, the roads to be secured exclusively for settlers, and the farmers who risk losing access to their land where those roads cut through. Will living in the territories open the young man to learning more about the life of Palestinians? Or will he put on blinders to avoid grappling with the complicated reality around him?

It's so difficult, yet so vital, to make the effort to discover the unseen stories wherever we live. The previous time I lived in Jerusalem, during a year of rabbinical school, I volunteered with a community group that sent me door knocking in a neighborhood of North African Jewish immigrants. Drinking instant coffee and eating prepackaged cake in living rooms a short walk from my apartment, I heard from elderly women whose inability to read or write prevented them from filling out the forms necessary to access benefits. I met young men desperate for work that paid well and sat with families unable to afford medications not included in the government health-care coverage. And I also heard success stories—the single mother whose leadership in this community organization gave her the confidence to enroll in cosmetician school; the women who helped a recently widowed man learn to cook for himself; the young woman who grew up in the neighborhood then returned as a social worker. Without wandering into this unfamiliar neighborhood just a mile from my apartment, I would have returned home confident that I now knew Jerusalem, with no idea that the experiences of an entire community remained hidden to me. Encountering the residents of this neighborhood gave me a better sense of the economic and social challenges facing this slice of Israeli society, and a glimpse of some possible approaches to ameliorating the situation.

Yet more often than not, we miss the stories right in front of our eyes. On a Friday afternoon a few years ago, I made my regular pre-Shabbat visit to the fruit and vegetable stand a block away from my home on the Upper West Side of New York. On my way in, I noticed a poster alleging that the young Latina cashiers were being paid less than minimum wage and were subjected to emotional abuse by the store manager. Several of these women, the sign informed me, had lodged a complaint and had been fired as a result. Indeed, I noticed an unfamiliar face behind the counter. On Monday, I called the advocacy organization supporting the women and confirmed the details of the case. How could I not have known? How long had this gone on while I blithely shopped in that store several times a week? I had only ever exchanged brief pleasantries with the women who worked there. Neither my rudimentary Spanish nor the rush of the store lent themselves to extended conversation. Even if I had spoken at length to the workers, they would not have risked telling me about their working conditions within earshot of their boss. I learned these women's stories only because they had had the courage to challenge their manager's behavior. But for every worker who dares to tell his or her story, there are thousands more whose suffering we will not hear.

It can be easier to care about faraway places than about the suffering in our own backyards. On a daily basis, I receive breathless e-mails, tweets, and Facebook messages from friends and organizations asking me to write a letter or donate money to the latest disaster zone or to a human rights crisis halfway across the world.

In our increasingly globalized reality, we *should* take responsibility for people around the world. Our government's economic and military policies, as well as our individual consumer practices, all contribute to the suffering or well-being of people in every country. And the constant access to news about every part of the world means that we cannot feign ignorance about what happens elsewhere.

At the same time, our concern for places other than our own can sometimes serve as a convenient way to absolve ourselves of responsibility for the places closer to us. It is easy to condemn the horrific state of maternal health services in parts of Africa. But questioning the disproportionately high rates of neonatal death within the African American community in my own city may mean acknowledging the inequalities that benefit me and my family. It is easier to send money to a girls' school in Afghanistan than to vote for policies that will distribute tax dollars evenly among public schools, possibly to the detriment of my own child's school district. Worrying about global warming in the broadest sense may inspire us to recycle and to invest in energy-efficient lightbulbs. But will we also look for ways to reduce the pollution that contributes to the disproportionate rate of childhood asthma in the neighborhood next to our own? A commitment to fix problems in our own backyard should not necessarily replace concern for issues abroad. Ideally our attention to an issue in one place will sensitize us to other manifestations of this issue elsewhere. But action abroad cannot substitute for making our own communities more just.

DEFINING OUR PLACES

Think back to the last time you moved to a new place. How long did it take before that place felt like your home? Until you unpacked your boxes? Until you made new friends? Until you became involved in the community? Until you found a favorite restaurant or coffee shop? Or does this new place still feel a bit strange? Do you continue to think of the place you were born as home? Or have you chosen to move back to the place where you were born? Perhaps you have never even left.

In some areas, anyone whose family has not lived there for generations will never be considered to be "from" that place. In some places, the community is so transient that it is easy for a newcomer to feel at home and even to become a community leader within a relatively brief time. Some people move to a new place and immediately seek ways to become involved in the life of the community; others like to take their time becoming comfortable in the place before making commitments. Still others move so often from place to place that they never allow themselves to become deeply involved in any one community.

When members of your own community sit down to plan your social justice activities, begin by asking, "What is our place? And what is our responsibility to this place?" The answer may not be as simple as it seems. Your place may be the town where your synagogue, school, camp, or institution physically stands. Or it may be the place where most of the members live. Or perhaps it is the neighborhood where the institution once stood.

A look at some Rabbinic discussions about responsibility to place serves as a helpful starting point for defining our own places and our obligations to these places.

WHERE IS HOME? RABBINIC PERSPECTIVES

The Rabbis of the Talmud defined residence in a place both according to the time one has already spent there and according to the time one plans to spend there. The Rabbis ask, "How long does a person have to live in a city before being considered among the citizens of that city?" The answer is, "Twelve months. But one who buys a home there is considered to be among the citizens of the city immediately" (*Mishnah Bava Batra* 1:5). A new resident has a year to make a decision about whether he or she will stay in the new city. However, one who purchases a home signals an intention to set down roots in this new place. This person therefore must immediately take responsibility for the well-being of all of the residents of this place.

The move from being an outsider to being a full resident does not happen in an instant. Rather, a person's responsibilities to the other residents of the city increase as he or she spends more and more time there. The Talmud elaborates:

> [A person who resides in a city] thirty days becomes liable for contributing to the *tamchui* [soup kitchen], three months for the *kuppah* [*tzedakah* fund], six months for the clothing fund, nine months for

the burial fund, and twelve months for contributing to the repair of the city walls.

(BT, Bava Batra 8a)

The more time a person spends in a place, the more he or she becomes responsible for the long-term needs of the residents of that place. A person who has spent only a month in a certain place must contribute to the *tam-chui*, which provides food for those who do not have even enough food for a single day.

After three months, a resident begins contributing to the *kuppah*, which provides money for those who have enough to sustain themselves for the day, but not for the week. After six and nine months, a person assumes responsibility not only for ensuring that the poor do not starve, but also for helping the poor to preserve their dignity, by providing funds for clothing and for appropriate burials. After a year—or, according to the Mishnah, after buying a home in the new city—a person assumes responsibility for the long-term security of the place.

Based on the Talmudic text above, later rabbis identify three categories of people living in a city. Those who have been there less than thirty days are considered simply to be visitors without specific obligations toward the place. People who have lived in the place for more than thirty days but for less than twelve months are called *yoshvei ha'ir*, or "city residents," and are obligated to contribute financially according to the Talmudic guidelines. Those who stay in a place for more than a year or who purchase a home there become *b'nai ha'ir*, or "people of the city"—what we would call citizens. Some rabbis also consider a person who signs a year's lease on a rental home immediately to become one of the *b'nai ha'ir*.[2] However, a person who inherits a home in a city where he or she has no intention of living need not take on full responsibility for the upkeep of that city.[3]

But what if a person lives in a place for less than a year, with the intention of eventually returning home? For example, do students automatically become residents of the place where they are studying? The answer to this question has implications for students' financial commitments to their current and former places of residence, as well as for decisions about where to vote, do jury duty, and pay taxes.

One rabbinic opinion, cited by numerous later authorities, defines intention as the most important factor in determining residence. According to Rabbi Avraham HaLevi Gombiner (Poland, ca. 1637–1683), students who go away to study and plan to return home after graduation, or professionals who take a sabbatical in another city, do not become residents of this new home as long as they maintain the intention to return to their original city (*Magen Avraham* 468).

But not every rabbinic authority privileges intention above length of residence. Rabbi Avraham Borenstein (Poland, 1838–1910), the founder of the Sochatchov dynasty of Hasidism, writes:

> Even in the case of the [itinerant] camel or donkey driver, as it says in *Bava Batra* (8a), if they stay there thirty days, they are considered to be like the residents of the city [*yoshvei ha'ir*]. The donkey and camel drivers will eventually return to their place, but even so, they are considered residents of the city. This is the law regarding the people of a city [*b'nai ha'ir*]—if they stay twelve months, they are considered to be like the people of the city [*anshei ha'ir*] even if their intention is to return.
>
> (*Avnei Nezer*, *Orach Chayim* 424)

Borenstein, then, holds that a stay of twelve months confers the status and responsibilities of a citizen, even if the person intends to leave in the future.

While there is no clear consensus among rabbinic authorities regarding when one becomes a full citizen of a place, these opinions suggest some criteria for determining where our responsibilities lie. As individuals thinking about where to invest our time and money, some of the questions we should ask ourselves include: How long do I expect to stay in the place where I am currently living? Where do I expect to live for the long term? Do I feel pulled between two places? Do I think of one as "home" and one as temporary? If so, how do I balance my responsibilities to each? As a community, we should ask ourselves: What is our historic connection to the place where we are living? To other places? What do we envision as our future relationship to this place? To what other places might we also have a responsibility? How will we balance our relative responsibility to these places?

BALANCING OUR CITY WITH OTHER CITIES

Once I determine what my city is, do I obligate myself only or primarily to the people of that city? Jewish law traditionally demands giving *tzedakah* first to "the poor of your city" before concerning oneself with poor members of any other community (BT, *Bava Metzia* 71a). If we are to take this requirement literally, perhaps we should devote all of our *tzedakah* money and all of our volunteer energy to wiping out poverty entirely in the places where we live before even thinking about poverty elsewhere in the world. This approach might result in a vast improvement in the standard of living among poor people in Western countries, but it could have dire results for people living in developing nations.

Some rabbinic authorities recognize problems inherent in devoting all of our resources to the places where we live. For example, in the law code *Arukh HaShulchan*, Rabbi Yechiel Epstein (Lithuania, 1829–1908) rules that a person's first obligation is to support his or her poor relatives. However, he worries that *tzedakah* givers will spend all of their money on their own relatives and that "poor people without wealthy relatives will die of starvation."[4] According to Epstein, then, a person who has poor relatives should give most of his or her *tzedakah* money to them, but should reserve some money for others as well.

Rabbi Moshe Sofer (1762–1839), the German rabbi more popularly known as the Chatam Sofer, goes one step further and distinguishes between the life-and-death needs of those in other cities and the less immediate needs of members of one's own community:

> "If there is a poor person within your gates" (Deuteronomy 15:7). *Sifrei* [an ancient collection of legal midrash on the book of Deuteronomy] expounds this verse saying, "When one is starving, the one who is starving takes precedence," and then expounds, "The poor of your city take precedence over the poor of another city." That is to say, this applies if both poor people need food or clothing. However, if the poor of your city have what they need to live, but just don't have any extra money [and the poor of the other city don't have food or clothing], then the poor of the other city take precedence over the poor of your city, for the neediest takes precedence.[5]

With this comment, the Chatam Sofer upends the general principle that one should prioritize the people of one's own city. Instead, he says, the people with the greatest need always come first, regardless of where they live. Only when faced with poor people who have identical needs do we prioritize those who live closer to us.

In somewhat different ways, both the *Arukh HaShulchan* and the Chatam Sofer begin to address the challenge of globalization. These rabbis simultaneously demand that we take primary responsibility for those closest to us and that we recognize that people far outside of our own orbit may have greater needs than the people in our own families and cities.

BALANCING OUR NEEDS AND OTHERS' NEEDS

One particularly difficult Rabbinic text further grapples with the question of how to weigh the urgent needs of others against our own, perhaps secondary, needs. This text, which comes from the *Tosefta*, a second- or third-century compilation of laws, considers a case in which one city is asked to share its own water supply with another city that has no water:

> In the case of a wellspring that belongs to the people of the city: [in a choice between] them and others [from another city], they come before the others. [In a choice between] the others and the animals [of the people of the city], the life of the others come before the animals. Rabbi Yosi says that the animals of the people of the city come before the life of others.
>
> [In a choice between] their animals and the animals of others, their animals come before the animals of others.
>
> [In a choice between the life of] others and the laundry of the people of the city, the life of others comes before the laundry [of the people of the city]. [But] Rabbi Yosi says that the laundry of the people of the city comes before the life of others.
>
> (*Tosefta, Bava Metzia* 11:33–37)

When I studied this text with several colleagues, one member of the group immediately responded that sources like these turn her off from text study. How, she asked, can we possibly accept as part of Jewish tradition the view of Rabbi Yosi, who seems prepared to sacrifice the lives of those living in a neighboring town in favor of washing his clothing? Another colleague responded, "We all do this all the time. I take my kids to water parks, even though I know that there are people in the world who don't have water to drink."

My two colleagues precisely identified the contours of the debate surrounding our relative responsibilities to our own places and to other places in the world. Do we first ensure the basic survival of everyone in the world, or do we allow ourselves some luxuries—or even basic comforts like clean clothes and regular showers—before attending to the needs of others? In the context of a theoretical conversation, it is easy to say that we should always first provide drinking water to others. But if we are to be honest, we must admit that few of us are willing to accept a life in which we have little more than food, shelter, and basic items of clothing.

The friends with whom I studied this text were not the first to find it problematic. Even the ancient Rabbis struggled to understand the minority position articulated by Rabbi Yosi. Some suggest that dirty clothes cause a certain type of scab, which leads to madness. In contrast, they say, scabs that result from not bathing lead (only) to blindness, meaning that laundry is essential, while bathing is less so (BT, *N'darim* 81a). While the scientific basis of this statement may be a bit shaky, the Rabbinic claim that dirty clothes are a threat to one's sanity reflects a basic discomfort with the suggestion that anything could come before human life.[6] Although most of us would not relish the prospect of wearing the same dirty clothes for weeks on end, we would probably have trouble washing our clothes if we knew that someone in the next town would die of thirst as a result.

Even the Rabbis themselves must have felt some discomfort with this justification for prioritizing one's own laundry over providing drinking water for others. Both versions of the Talmud—the *Talmud Bavli* (Babylonian Talmud, codified around the sixth or seventh century CE) and *Talmud Yerushalmi* (Jerusalem, or Palestinian, Talmud, codified around the fourth or fifth century CE)—present a story, in similar but varying versions, of a rabbinical student who is so troubled by this text that he is unable to study for several days. I will present both versions and then discuss their differences.

According to the *Talmud Bavli*:

> Isi the son of Yehuda did not come to Rabbi Yosi's study hall for three days. Vardimus, the son of Rabbi Yosi, found him and said to him, "Why haven't you come to my father's study hall for three days?" Isi said to him, "Since I don't understand your father's reasoning, how can I come?" Vardimus said to him, "Tell me what he said, and maybe I know his reasoning." He said to him, "It is taught: Rabbi Yosi said, 'Their laundry takes precedence over the lives of others'—what is the source of this?" Vardimus said, "The Torah says, 'The open spaces shall be for their animals [*b'hemtam*] and their possessions and for all of their beasts [*chayatam*]' (Numbers 35:3). What does *chayatam* mean? Maybe it means 'their beasts.' But beasts are included in 'animals.' So what does *chayatam* mean? Maybe it really means 'their lives' [*chiyuta*]. But this would be obvious! Rather, it must refer to laundry, for [not doing laundry] leads to the misery of scabs."
>
> (BT, *N'darim* 81a)

The version of the story that appears in the *Talmud Yerushalmi* follows the same contours, but includes some significant variations:

> Yehuda of Hutzi went and hid himself in a cave for three days, trying to understand the reason that the lives of the people of this city should take precedence over the lives of people of another city. [After the three days were over,] Rabbi Yosi bar Chalafta bumped into him and said to him, "Where have you been?" He said, "I went and hid in a cave for three days, trying to understand the reason that the lives of the people of this city take precedence over the lives of people of another city." Rabbi Yosi bar Chalafta called his son Rabbi Aborodimas and said to him, "Explain the reason that the lives of the people of this city take precedence over the lives of people of another city." Rabbi Aborodimas said to him, "[The Bible says,] 'Thus shall it be with these cities, each city,' and afterwards it says, 'And the open land around it' (Joshua

21:40)."[7] Rabbi Yosi bar Chalafta said to Rabbi Yehuda, "Why didn't you consult with your friends [about this question]?"

(JT, *Sh'vi'it* 8:5)

In both of these stories, a student—not yet a rabbi—finds Rabbi Yosi's statement about laundry so difficult that he disappears from the study hall for three days. In each case, Rabbi Yosi's son (whose name varies slightly in the two versions) offers an explanation based on a biblical verse. For both Talmuds, this explanation seems to suffice. That is, in neither case does the student ask additional questions or argue with the logic presented.

While both stories refer to the same statement by Rabbi Yosi, the two students focus on different aspects of the problem. In the *Bavli*, the student is troubled by the prospect of prioritizing laundry over human life. But in the *Yerushalmi*, the student asks the more basic question of why one person's life should take precedence over another person's life at all. For this student, the fact that the wellspring in question happens to be located in one city should not necessarily mean that the lives of the people of that city should take precedence over the lives of anyone else. This student, therefore, challenges not only Rabbi Yosi—the minority opinion in the text in question—but also the Rabbinic majority, who prioritize the people of the city also in regard to drinking water.[8]

What is most striking about both versions of the story is the weakness of the eventual answer to the problem that the student presents. In the *Bavli*, the explanation rests on an unorthodox reading of the word *chayot*, which literally means "beasts." Vardimus begins with the assertion that this word is redundant, as the Torah already refers to *b'hemot*, which also means "animals." The easiest interpretation of this biblical verse would define *b'hemot* and *chayot* as referring to two different types of animals. Instead, Vardimus chooses the more improbable option of noting that the word *chayot* comes from the word *chayim*, "life," and then equating "life" with "laundry" based on an earlier assertion that dirty clothes cause painful scabs. In the *Yerushalmi*, the rabbi's son explains the reasoning by citing a biblical verse that refers first to the cities the Jews are building for themselves, and only later to the space around the city. As read here, this verse suggests that a person should first take care of his or her city, and only then worry about the space outside of this city. Both of these explanations rely on fairly improbable readings of the biblical text. It is not uncommon for the Rabbis to justify a legal detail by reference to a supposedly extraneous or difficult word or letter in a biblical text; however, in the case of a complicated moral problem, we would expect the Rabbis to engage in some amount of logical argumentation. The decision to respond to a serious ethical question through a stretched biblical interpretation effectively amounts to an admission that the problem at hand is an impossible one.

The *Yerushalmi* version of this story adds two intriguing elements not present in the *Bavli*. First, the student in question does not simply skip class; rather, he hides out in a cave for three days, presumably meditating on the problematics of the situation. Second, when he reappears, his rabbi chides him by asking why he didn't consult with his friends. There are two ways to read the rabbi's criticism here. The easiest reading would have us understand Rabbi Yosi as saying, "You just wasted three days sitting in a cave when your friend had the answer all along." But given the aforementioned difficulty of the response, I hesitate to read Rabbi Yosi in this way. Instead, I understand Rabbi Yosi as telling his pupil, "You're right. There is no easy answer to this impossible moral quandary. But difficult moral problems aren't resolved by meditating alone in a cave. These problems are resolved by talking them through with friends, in the context of a human community in which we learn from the perspectives and experiences of others."

Of course, the dilemma that the Rabbis wrestle with in the Talmud has not gone away. In various forms it preoccupies philosophers and ordinary people to this day. The clearest modern articulation of the argument against Rabbi Yosi comes from Peter Singer, an Australian philosopher. In the introduction to his book *The Life You Can Save*, he presents the following scenario:

> On your way to work, you pass a small pond. On hot days, children sometimes play in the pond, which is only about knee-deep. The weather's cool today, though, and the hour is early, so you are surprised to see a child splashing about in the pond. As you get closer, you see that it is a very young child, just a toddler, who is flailing about, unable to stay upright or walk out of the pond. You look for the parents or

babysitter, but there is no one else around. The child is unable to keep his head above the water for more than a few seconds at a time. If you don't wade in and pull him out, he seems likely to drown. Wading in is easy and safe, but you will ruin the new shoes you bought only a few days ago, and get your suit wet and muddy. By the time you hand the child over to someone responsible for him, and change your clothes, you'll be late for work....

But consider that, according to UNICEF, nearly 10 million children under five years old die each year from causes related to poverty.... By donating a relatively small amount of money, you could save a child's life. Maybe it takes more than the amount needed to buy a pair of shoes—but we all spend money on things we don't really need, whether on drinks, meals out, clothing, movies, concerts, vacations, new cars, or house renovation. Is it possible that by choosing to spend your money on such things rather than contributing to an aid agency, you are leaving a child to die, a child you could have saved?[9]

In accordance with his argument that failing to save the faraway child is as immoral as ignoring the drowning child, Singer advocates living on the amount necessary for basic subsistence—as of 2001, he suggested thirty thousand dollars for the average American family—and donating the remainder of one's income toward ending world poverty.[10] At the very least, he says, those able to provide for their own basic needs should devote 5 percent of their family income to fighting global poverty.[11] In the context of our Talmudic debate, we may understand Singer as supporting the majority Rabbinic view that the people of the city should first distribute drinking water to everyone who needs to drink, and only then use the water for less essential purposes of their own.

Singer's approach to the distribution of resources may be the most rational one, yet few of us act accordingly. As Singer points out, we can attribute some of the discontinuity between what we believe is right and what we actually do to a blindness toward those who are not in our line of sight. But there is also deep wisdom in Rabbi Yosi's position and in the Rabbinic injunction to care first for those in our own family or our own city.

Human beings are not purely rational creatures. We love our own children more than those of other people even though we may intellectually believe that all children are equal. We follow our passions in choosing careers and hobbies, rather than making calculated decisions about what the world most needs. We devote significant time to making ourselves and those closest to us happy, rather than use those hours to address the basic needs of strangers. These tendencies are not flaws to be corrected, but rather the essence of what makes human relations possible and what makes us able to find meaning in our own lives.[12]

The ancient Rabbis demonstrated an understanding of the limits of rational utilitarianism when they factored intimacy into the hierarchy of responsibility. Our primary responsibilities are toward our families, our people, and the residents of our own town because of our intimate relationship with members of these groups—and *not* because we believe certain individuals to be more worthy of saving than others.

The rabbis refuse to let intimacy trump all else. The commentators who seek to explain Rabbi Yosi's position go to great lengths to demonstrate that laundry is an essential human need. But ultimately, the *halakhah* goes along with Rabbi Yosi (*She'iltot d'Rav Ahai Parshat Re'eh* 147). Some even allow the residents of one city to cut off water flow to another city in order to take care of their own needs (Rashi, comment on *N'darim* 81a). The rabbis refuse to prioritize intimacy above *all* other needs, and therefore stop short of classifying laundry as a mere luxury. At the same time, these rabbis demand that we *do* take intimacy into account when we make decisions about allocating money, time, and other resources. And, of course, our decisions in this regard must be made in the context of a rich and nuanced debate with our friends, family members, and colleagues.

IS ISRAEL "MY CITY"?

I have already alluded a few times to the complexity that results from the Jewish framework of homeland, exile, and Diaspora. For most of Jewish history, the Land of Israel functioned more as a theoretical ideal than as an actual place. While there was always a small population of Jews living in the Land, a mass immigration there remained a political impossibility for the greater part of the past two thousand years. Jews could mourn the destruction of the Temple and pray for a return to Israel without actually facing the reality of life there.

All of this changed with the advent of Zionism, the Holocaust, and the establishment of the State of Israel in 1948. Suddenly, Jews had to grapple with the very real possibility of uprooting their lives and making a new home in the nascent state. Among those who supported the creation of a Jewish state, some argued that only an autonomous government could guarantee Jews long-term security in a world prone to fits of anti-Semitism. Certainly, the Holocaust offered grim evidence that even a state where Jews had previously prospered could turn murderous. Others based their support for the state on a belief that Jewish art and culture could best flourish in a Jewish state. Still others strove for a more full religious life, desiring to fulfill the commandments that apply only within the Land of Israel. On the other side, some opponents of Zionism embraced *doykayt*, "hereness," the ideological commitment to Diaspora life that we discussed in chapter 1. Other opponents of Zionism had more practical fears that Judaism and the Jewish people might be sullied by the exercise of power and by the politics of running a sovereign state.

In the nineteenth and early twentieth centuries, competing ideological fervor made the choice between Israel and the Diaspora a stark one. Today, rather than falling into an either/or debate, we can ask ourselves how to balance a commitment to the place we live (for those of us in the Diaspora) with a concern for sustaining a safe, stable, and just Jewish state.

Generations of rabbis have debated whether the obligation to care first for the people of "your city" should also include the people of Israel. Rabbi Moshe Sofer (Germany, 1762–1839), for example, ruled that the poor of the Land of Israel should take precedence over the poor of one's own city. Worrying that the poor might migrate to Israel only in the hopes of collecting *tzedakah*, he restricted this preference to the poor who have lived in Israel for some length of time.[13] For him, the demand to support the poor of Israel, and especially the poor of Jerusalem, is based both in a belief in the sanctity of Jerusalem and in a practical acknowledgment that those living in Israel (in the late eighteenth to early nineteenth century) had little access to well-paying jobs.[14] This latter assumption, of course, is no longer precisely true. While Israeli Jews, on average, earn less and have a higher poverty rate than Jews in the United States, Israel has also produced its share of millionaires and billionaires.

Instead of making a blanket choice between "my city" (New York) and the State of Israel, I choose to accept both as "my city." The bulk of my family's *tzedakah* money goes to these two places, though we also reserve a smaller percentage of our giving for projects in the rest of the United States and the rest of the world.

QUESTIONS FOR CONSIDERATION

1. What places feel like *your* places? Why?

2. Do members of your community feel connected to different places? Do some members feel connected to the same places for different reasons?

3. Has your communal social justice work focused on the city or town where you live? On the state where you live? On your country? On Israel? On the rest of the world? How have the choices about where to focus been made in the past? How might a deliberate discussion of place affect these decisions?

3

The Ideal City

Some years ago, while considering job opportunities in a few unfamiliar cities, I spent some time playing with a then-popular website called "FindYourSpot." Users of this site would respond to a survey on subjects ranging from favorite leisure activities to weather preferences to transportation options, and then receive a list of the places that best fit these specifications. I dutifully answered the questions: Yes, I want easy access to theater and museums. Yes, I prefer public transportation. No, I don't mind winter. The answer popped up: Charlotte, North Carolina. Since I had no job prospects in North Carolina, I tried again: No, I don't like football. Yes, I like hiking outdoors. Again: Charlotte, North Carolina.

After a few tries at this exercise, I began to suspect that the site was sponsored by the chambers of commerce of Charlotte, North Carolina, and a small number of other cities; no matter how I answered the questions, I always received the same list of cities, albeit in a slightly different order. Or perhaps, I wondered, were some cities, in fact, ideal for everyone?

Regardless of what a given website might claim, I doubt that there is any one perfect place for anyone. That said, there may be certain basic qualities that make a place more or less fit for human life. In the last chapter, we talked about starting your community's visioning process by identifying the place or places where you will focus your social justice efforts. Now that you have identified these places, the next questions to ask yourselves are: What is our vision for this place or these places? What would need to change in order to transform this place or these places into this ideal?

Jewish texts can help us to identify the basic qualities that make a place ideal. In this chapter, we will explore some of these Jewish perspectives, starting with biblical portrayals and moving on to Rabbinic conceptions of creating livable communities.

BIBLICAL PLACES: THE GOOD, THE BAD, AND THE UGLY

The Torah begins in an idyllic place. The Garden of Eden is a lush paradise, abounding with water, fruit trees, and other vegetation.

> Adonai planted a garden in Eden, in the east, and placed there the man whom God had formed. And from the ground Adonai caused to grow every tree that was pleasing to the sight and good for food, with the tree of life in the middle of the garden, and the tree of knowledge of good and bad. A river issues from Eden to water the garden, and it then divides and becomes four branches…. Adonai took the man and placed him in the Garden of Eden, to till it and tend it.
>
> (Genesis 2:8–10, 2:15)

In Eden, Adam and Eve can fulfill all of their bodily needs with only minimal effort. God does all of the initial planting; the human inhabitants need only sustain the trees and other vegetation. According to the early Rabbis, Adam and Eve actually did no physical labor whatsoever. In the text above, Adam and Eve are described as working and protecting the land. The Hebrew verbs that the Bible uses are *la'avod* (to work) and *lishmor* (to protect). One midrash uses alternative translations of these verbs to suggest that Adam spent his time studying Torah, praying, and observing *mitzvot*, not doing agricultural work. As the rabbis who wrote this midrash noted, the verb *la'avod* ("to work") can also mean "to worship," and *lishmor* (to protect) can also mean "to observe." In other words, according to this text, Adam and Eve lived a purely spiritual existence in the Garden of Eden. Another Rabbinic passage further develops the picture of Eden as a paradise of leisure by imagining Adam and Eve lounging around the garden as angels serve them food and pour them wine.[1]

But this paradise is too good to last. While it is easy to read the story of Adam and Eve as a tragic tale of a sin that ended the possibility of a utopian human existence, Rabbinic readings of the story lend a certain inevitability to the transgression. In fact, one midrash asserts that Adam and Eve spent less than one hour in the garden before their expulsion.[2] Other Rabbinic traditions imagine God looking into the future, seeing the evil of which humans are capable, and choosing to create these flawed creatures anyway (B'reishit Rabbah 8:4).

This paradise of leisure is ultimately not sustainable. From the beginning, at least according to Rabbinic interpretations, God understands that human beings will eventually need to live in a world governed by law, where good and evil are equally possible, and where human work is necessary for the preservation of the world. Thus, various midrashim portray God as writing the Torah before creating the world. Even before the world exists, God plans to create human beings to preserve this world and also anticipates that these humans will need law to guide their actions. Other texts declare that human beings are obligated not only to rest on Shabbat, but also to actually work for the six days of the week.[3]

After Eden, biblical living takes a decidedly urban turn, often with disastrous results. An examination of these early—and unsuccessful—biblical cities will offer us some clues toward constructing a city that may not approach the perfection of Eden, but that comes as close as possible to an ideal living environment.

When human beings first show their capacity for wickedness, God responds by nearly destroying the world through flood. Some time after this catastrophe, the remaining people decide to build a tower that will reach into heaven. By their own description, they fear dispersal and wish to stay close to one another in order to protect themselves. God responds by playing directly into their fears; as punishment for constructing this tower, God scatters the people throughout the earth and gives them different languages such that they can no longer understand one another and do not take on any more joint projects.

The biblical account of the Tower of Babel offers few clues about what the people did to warrant such an extreme divine punishment. We might expect God to congratulate the people for undertaking a cooperative project aimed at maintaining unity among all human beings. Instead, God reacts with alarm, saying, "If, as one people with one language for all, this is how they have begun to act, then nothing that they may propose to do will be out of their reach" (Genesis 11:6).

In explaining this response, the Rabbis suggest that the people wish to build a tower to heaven in order to declare war on God (*B'reishit Rabbah* 38:6). Whereas Eden offered at least the possibility of a lasting human-divine partnership, the story of the Tower of Babel sets up an animosity between human beings and God. In this story, human beings concern themselves exclusively with their own self-preservation, perhaps to the exclusion of any concern about the environment or even the long-term stability of humankind.

Other Rabbinic interpretations of this story portray the people of Babel as becoming so absorbed in building the tower that they cease to care for each other's needs. According to one midrash, the workers would methodically lift each brick up to its appropriate position. So focused were the people on this laborious effort that "if a person fell and died, they would not pay attention to him. But if a single brick fell, they would sit and cry and say 'Woe to us; when will we lift up another one in its place?'" (*Pirkei d'Rabbi Eliezer* 24).

The next major city mentioned by the Torah proves guilty of a similar callousness to human suffering. The book of Genesis several times describes the city of Sodom as "evil," but we get an up-close look at the nature of this evil only when God sends messengers to warn the inhabitants of the city of its imminent destruction. Lot, Abraham's nephew, invites these messengers to stay with his family. While the messengers take shelter in Lot's home, a gang of townspeople show up at the door and demand that Lot send the visitors out so that the townspeople can rape them. Lot refuses (though he does offer his virgin daughters instead) (Genesis 19:1–9).

Lot's hospitality to these messengers contrasts sharply with the behavior of his neighbors, who seek to gang-rape the strangers. But even Lot, who appears more righteous than the other residents of his town, is prepared to allow his daughters to be raped. God does eventually save Lot from the burning city. But, in the process, Lot loses his wife and is seduced into having sex with his daughters. Lot merits being saved by virtue either of his hospitality or of his relationship to Abraham, but he does not emerge unscathed from his connection with the wicked city.[4]

Rabbinic interpretations of this story expand on the biblical portrayal of the city residents as excessively inhospitable to strangers. The Talmud describes the people of Sodom inviting visitors to sleep in a special bed. If the guest turned out to be too long for the bed, the residents would cut off his legs; if the guest was too short, they would stretch him. The city residents, according to the Talmud, so disliked strangers that they even enacted a law that anyone who invited a stranger to a banquet would be humiliated by being stripped naked (BT, *Sanhedrin* 109b). This behavior appears even worse in contrast to the story that immediately precedes this one, in which Abraham and Sarah warmly welcome three strangers into their tent and are rewarded when these strangers turn out to be divine messengers.

In Rabbinic lore, Sodom appears as a lawless city where residents rob one another in the middle of the night, impose forced labor on the poor, and refuse to give *tzedakah*. Corrupt judges force the victim of a violent crime to pay damages to the perpetrator, and they permit a man who has physically assaulted a woman to rape her as well. In one grotesquely imagined scene, the Rabbis describe a young woman in Sodom who sneaks some bread to a poor person. When her neighbors learn of her action, they dip her in honey and leave her to be eaten by bees (BT, *Sanhedrin* 109b). The Bible itself identifies the sin of Sodom as "pride, fullness of bread, and careless ease ... she did not strengthen the hand of the poor and needy" (Ezekiel 16:49).

With cities like Babel and Sodom, one might easily read the book of Genesis as an argument for solitary living. As long as Adam and Eve live alone in the Garden of Eden, they enjoy a peaceful existence in harmony with nature. As soon as additional people enter the picture, chaos begins. Cain kills his brother Abel. Humanity eventually becomes so evil that God destroys the entire world with a flood, saving only Noah and his family. The hubris of the residents of Babel results in their dispersal. Abraham and

Sarah's tent is a warm and welcoming place, but in the large city of Sodom, strangers fear for their lives. Abraham's descendents eventually make their way to Egypt only to endure oppressive slavery at the hands of this majestic empire.

Even in Jerusalem, theoretically the "city of peace," the Jews succumb to idol worship, abandonment of the poor, and the prioritization of wealth over the care of others. Accordingly, the biblical prophets spend the bulk of their time berating the people for such sins and pleading for repentance. The prophet Jeremiah, for example, offers a vivid picture of Jerusalem as a place overrun by transgression prior to the destruction of the First Temple. "Roam the streets of Jerusalem," he writes, "search its squares, look about and take note: you will not find a man, there is none who acts justly, who seeks integrity—that I should pardon [the city]" (Jeremiah 5:1).

Yet there is hope for such cities. From the book of Genesis, we learn that even a small number of righteous people can redeem a city from punishment. Upon hearing of the imminent destruction of Sodom and Gomorrah, Abraham bargains with God on behalf of these cities. "What if there are fifty righteous people there?" he asks. "Forty-five?" "Forty?" "Thirty?" Eventually, God agrees to spare the city for the sake of even ten innocents (Genesis 18:24–32). But only Lot and his family measure up. And Jerusalem is even worse off: according to the biblical account, Jerusalem in the years preceding the Babylonian conquest boasted not a single righteous person capable of saving the city.[5]

What could the Jewish people have done so wrong as to merit such a harsh divine response? Chief among their sins is idol worship—the elevation of human-made objects to divine status. This disregard for God manifests itself also in an inattention to the needs of human beings, who are created in the image of God. In explaining what the people will need to do in order to avoid punishment, Jeremiah tells the people that God promises:

> If you really mend your ways and your actions; if you execute justice
> between one person and another; if you do not oppress the stranger, the
> orphan, and the widow; if you do not shed the blood of the innocent
> in this place; if you do not follow other gods, to your own hurt—then

only will I let you dwell in this place, in the land that I gave to your
ancestors for all time."

(Jeremiah 7:5–7)

We moderns may not often attribute military victories to divine will. We
are all too aware of the damage of claiming that God takes sides in human
conflict or of blaming one people's suffering on their sins. Even so, the
biblical text teaches us what sins are considered sufficiently atrocious to
warrant a near-complete rupture in the human-divine relationship, as sym-
bolized by the fall of the Temple and the exile from the Promised Land.
From Jeremiah's rebukes, we learn that the worst sins involve murder,
abandoning the weakest residents, and worshiping idols. This list corresponds with the biblical descriptions of Babel and Sodom as cities characterized by a general disregard for either God or humanity. Vulnerable
strangers visiting Sodom fared no better than the abandoned orphans and
widows of Jerusalem. The people of Babel became so absorbed in their
tower that they began to prioritize this "idol" over either God or human
life. In thinking about how to make our own cities the best places possible
for human life, we can begin by thinking about whether the laws and
norms of these places prioritize human life or idols, such as money, status,
or beauty.

CITIES AND SMALL TOWNS: DANGERS AND PROTECTIONS

Growing up in suburban America in the 1980s, I knew about cities only
from the evening news and from a few family visits or school field trips to
New York or Boston. I therefore absorbed two competing notions of city
life: on the one hand, I imagined cities to be dens of violence, filled with
crack dealers shooting one another in the streets; on the other hand, my personal experience of cities was of art museums, theaters, and historical sites.
On television, I saw only the most frightening images of the perils of city life;
with my family, I saw only the areas that had been cleaned up for tourists.

Of course, neither of these stereotypes captures the reality of most
cities. For all the hype, cities can be as mundane as the smallest small town.

In general, people in cities spend most of their time working, going to school, taking care of their families, running errands, and otherwise tending to everyday tasks. As for social life, cities contain two extremes at the same time. On the one hand, cities enable alienation and anonymity; a person might easily live in the same apartment building for years without ever knowing the names of most of his or her neighbors. On the other hand, the presence of so many people of different backgrounds allows those with even the most unusual interests or personalities to find a welcoming subgroup.

The *Tosefta*, a second- or third-century Rabbinic text, captures the fear often associated with cities by instituting a series of prayers to be said upon entering or leaving a large city:

> One who enters a large city prays twice: once upon entering and once upon leaving. Rabbi Shimon said: [One prays] four times: twice upon entering and twice upon leaving.
>
> Upon entering, what does one say? "May it be Your will, Adonai, my God, to bring me into this city in peace." One who has entered safely says, "I give thanks to You, Adonai, my God, that You have brought me into this city in peace. Similarly, may it be Your will to bring me out in peace." One who leaves safely says, "I give thanks to You, Adonai, my God, that You have brought me out of this city in peace; similarly, may it be Your will that You will bring me home safely."
>
> (*Tosefta*, B'rakhot 6:16)

With this prayer, the Rabbis depict cities as so dangerous that one enters and leaves only through divine intervention. According to Rabbi Shimon, the danger is sufficiently extreme as to warrant two prayers in each direction. In the Rabbis' anxiety, I hear the voice of a family friend who, upon learning from my parents that I planned to attend college in New York City, replied, "I'll pray for her."

But the Rabbis do not dismiss the city as an unredeemably perilous place. One Talmudic text qualifies the *Tosefta*'s general instruction to pray on the way in and out of a city. According to this text, the requirement to pray may only apply to certain types of cities:

Rav Mattena said: This applies only to a city in which criminals are not tried and sentenced, but in a city where criminals are tried and sentenced, this is unnecessary. Some report: Rav Mattena said: Even in a city where criminals are tried and sentenced, for sometimes one may happen not to find anyone who can plead in one's defense.

(BT, *B'rakhot* 60a)

This text defines a dangerous city as one lacking an effective and fair criminal justice system. A city that lacks any criminal justice system whatsoever poses obvious dangers, both to residents and to visitors. But even in a city with a seemingly functional criminal justice system, the possibility remains that no one will come to the defense of an unknown visitor. As was the case in Sodom, the residents of a city may actively prey on defenseless strangers. And it is even more likely that longtime residents will defend even the most abominable actions by one of their own over the claims of a victimized stranger.

In one of the most infamous examples of this phenomenon, the Mississippi courts in 1964 refused to try the accused murderers of civil rights workers Andrew Goodman, Michael Schwerner, and James Chaney. The desire to protect respected members of the community—including a minister and several members of the police force—proved much stronger than any concern for Jewish and African American strangers. This episode demonstrates that strangers may fare no better in small towns than in big cities. In a large city, there is a risk of anonymity. The foreigner may suffer harm without anyone noticing or taking action. In a small town, the danger is not anonymity but visibility. The foreigner sticks out and may be viewed as a threat to the status quo. If the visitor suffers any harm, the close-knit nature of the community may lead residents to maintain silence about what has happened.

The treatment of the visitors to Sodom and of the young civil rights workers in Mississippi was, no doubt, extreme. Most of us probably cannot imagine looking away while even the closest friend or family member assaults or murders another. But it is easier to imagine a less nefarious inattention to those who differ from us. In describing Rome, seen by the Rabbis as the epitome of the evil city, the Talmud reports:

> Rabbi Yehoshua ben Levi said, "When I went to Rome, I saw pillars of
> marble that were covered with blankets so that they would not crack
> from the heat or freeze from the cold. I also saw a poor man with only
> a thin reed mat below him and a thin reed mat on top of him."
>
> *(Vayikra Rabbah* 27:1)

According to this account, in Rome as in Babel, the people had become so
absorbed in building impressive edifices that they neglected the health and
safety of their own citizens. We can imagine the citizens of Rome failing
even to notice the shivering poor man as they rushed about their daily
business. But as easy as it may be to condemn the citizens of Rome for their
lack of sensitivity, our own society is also guilty of often prioritizing buildings and monuments over the lives of human beings. We might also
imagine that the citizens of Rome had seen so much poverty that they
became desensitized to the pain of others. Those of us who live in cities
where the homeless regularly beg for money on the street will have little
trouble imagining the compassion fatigue that can result from seeing so
much poverty on a daily basis. The possibility that continuous exposure to
poverty will result in less generosity, not more, prompted the Rabbis to
demand that we give even one hundred times to the same person (*Midrash
Tannaim*, Deuteronomy 15:8).

Similarly, the anonymous author of the fifteenth-century ethical work
Orchot Tzaddikim commented:

> One who gives to a deserving person one thousand gold pieces at once
> is not as generous as one who gives one thousand gold pieces one by
> one, each gold piece to an appropriate recipient. For one who gives one
> thousand gold pieces at once is seized with a fit of generosity that after-
> wards departs.[6]

When a catastrophic natural disaster hits, as was the case with the
Southeast Asian tsunami in 2004, Hurricane Katrina in 2005, the earthquake in Haiti in 2010, or the earthquake and tsunami in Japan in 2011,
a worldwide outpouring of gifts generally follows. Individuals write
checks, schools and religious institutions take up collections of money and

goods, and foreign governments send food and relief workers. This immediate response is necessary; in the wake of a major disaster, there is generally a small window of time to rescue survivors and to fend off disease and
starvation. But as the *Orchot Tzaddikim* points out, it is much more difficult to maintain a generous stance in the face of ongoing and less dramatic
suffering. In the worst cases, wealthier residents will literally step over the
homeless, left on the street to freeze.

From the examples of Babel, Sodom, Rome, and the cities without a
functional or fair criminal justice system, we can identify a few characteristics that contribute to making a city an unhealthy place to live. These
include the prioritization of buildings over human beings, antagonism
toward strangers, and an inability or unwillingness to notice the most vulnerable. In the next few pages, we will examine some of the ingredients
necessary for creating an ideal living environment.

ASPECTS OF THE IDEAL CITY

From the harsh biblical and Rabbinic descriptions of large cities, we might
conclude that human beings are meant to live in small family groups, or—
at most—in small towns. But the eventual progression toward communal
life in the Land of Israel belies any claim that the Bible favors a solitary
existence. God does not give the Torah to Adam and Eve, to Abraham and
Sarah, to Isaac and Rebecca, or to Jacob, Rachel, Leah, and their children.
Only when the Jewish people constitute themselves as a community do
they merit a covenantal relationship with God.

Central to this covenant is the promise that the fledgling Jewish community will eventually have a place to call their own. In the biblical conception, this homeland will be a utopia, where the people no longer need
worry about hunger, war, or persecution.

While the biblical land of Israel turns out to be less than ideal, the
prophets hold out hope for a better future. Isaiah, for instance, describes a
time when

> the voice of weeping shall be no more heard in [Jerusalem], nor the
> voice of crying. There shall be no more there an infant of days, nor an

old man who has not filled his days.... And they shall build houses, and inhabit them; and they shall plant vineyards, and eat the fruit of them.

(Isaiah 65:19–21)

This passage amounts to a comprehensive social service agenda. In the rebuilt Jerusalem, neither war nor disease takes people before their time. Every person enjoys adequate housing and a reliable food source. Weeping ceases, presumably because people are able to live in comfort and without fear. We might also assume that the absence of audible pain speaks to a city in which residents hear and respond to the needs of others.

To this idyllic vision, the Rabbis add a few specifics about how best to construct places that nurture human life. The Talmud and some later sources present lists of ten (or in some versions, nine) elements necessary for a city to be an appropriate place for a Torah scholar to live. According to the Talmud:

> A Torah scholar may not live in a city that does not have the following ten things: a court that enacts punishments, a *tzedakah* fund collected by two people and distributed by three people, a synagogue, a bath- house, an outhouse, a doctor, an artisan, a scribe, (a butcher), a teacher for children. Rabbi Akiva adds, "Also many types of produce, as these brighten the eyes."[7]
>
> (BT, *Sanhedrin* 17b)

We can divide this list into two basic categories: physical well-being and religious fulfillment. The physical health of residents depends on the pres- ence of hygiene facilities such as bathrooms and bathing facilities, on the availability of fresh food, and on access to a doctor. As we saw earlier, the mark of a safe city is a court with the power to try and punish criminals. Rabbi Akiva's addition of produce that benefits the eyes can be understood as a requirement that medicine or other health necessities be available.

Elsewhere, the Talmud also prohibits Torah scholars from living in towns where certain types of vegetables are unavailable. This statement prompts the Rabbis to launch into a discussion of which vegetables are beneficial for one's health and which cause bodily harm. While the Rabbis differ on which vegetables should be considered nutritious, the bottom line is that Torah scholars should take their health into account when choosing a place to live (BT, *Eruvin* 55b–56a).

The category of religious fulfillment begins with the synagogue, scribe, and teacher, who contribute to the flourishing of Jewish life. The synagogue serves as a place for prayer and study. The scribe makes sacred texts available for use in the synagogue. The teacher ensures that the tradition in those texts is transmitted to children.

We can place the *tzedakah* fund in both categories. On the one hand, the *tzedakah* fund supports the physical needs of the poor of the city. On the other hand, the *tzedakah* fund serves a spiritual purpose in conditioning the other residents of the city to take responsibility for the poorest among them.

The one item that seems out of place on this list is the artisan. In general, when the Talmud refers to artisans, the person in question is a craftsperson, such as a woodworker or builder. However, "artisan" can refer to any type of skilled worker. Presumably in response to this apparent incongruity, Rashi (France, 1040–1105), in his commentary on this list, defines "artisan" as a bloodletter, the ancient version of a doctor; he then redefines the "doctor" in the list as a *mohel* (one who performs circumcisions). Accordingly, most later commentaries on the Talmud, as well as most modern English translations of the passage, read "a mohel and a surgeon."[8] In this reading, the doctor becomes a religious worker, and the artisan becomes one who cares for the physical health of residents (putting aside the dubious medical efficacy of bloodletting).

In his own commentary on this Talmudic passage, Rabbi Menachem Meiri (Provence, 1249–1310) stresses the importance of religious institutions. He specifies that the butcher mentioned is a *shochet uvodek*, a ritual slaughterer capable of certifying that the meat is kosher, and he substitutes a *beit midrash* (study hall) for an outhouse.[9] In a world without indoor plumbing, we can assume that the Meiri would not want to live in a city lacking an outhouse; regardless, the desire to highlight religious needs without lengthening the list requires dropping another element, in this case a basic hygienic need.

In contrast to the Meiri, one tenth-century midrash emphasizes the physical well-being of residents over religious practice. In *Seder Eliyahu Zuta*, we find the following list:

> A Torah scholar may not live in a city that does not have the following ten things: a synagogue, an outhouse, a bathhouse, a schoolhouse for children, a court that enacts punishments, a *tzedakah* fund, a spice fund, a *tamchui* fund. Rabbi Akiva adds, "Also many types of produce, as these brighten the eyes."
>
> (*Seder Eliyahu Zuta* 16)

A poor person living in the city described by this text can be certain of having his or her physical needs met. The *tamchui*, a kind of soup kitchen, distributes meals to those who do not have even enough food for the day. The *tzedakah* fund offers longer-term monetary support. Most commentators understand the "spice fund" to refer to perfume or makeup that women would use to make themselves attractive to their husbands. According to this interpretation, the spice fund aimed to maintain happy marital relations by providing poor women with perfume and spices.[10] Alternatively, the need for such a fund may respond to the tendency of spice dealers, according to the Rabbis, to chase after women in inappropriate ways. The fund would make it possible for women to avoid these menacing spice dealers altogether.[11]

Most of us will find offensive the idea that women must wear perfume or makeup for their husbands to find them attractive. That said, the requirement to maintain a spice fund acknowledges that the community bears responsibility for the emotional well-being, and not only the physical survival, of its members. The text responds to a reality (or an assumed reality) in which women suffer when they cannot afford perfume and makeup or when they must fend off the unwanted advances of traveling spice dealers. Our modern equivalent of a spice fund might be community-supported mental health services, educational campaigns about sexual harassment, or clothing pantries that provide school and work outfits to those who might otherwise be embarrassed by their dress.

We have seen a number of versions of the list of the ten elements that make a city an appropriate home for a Torah scholar. Despite their variations, all of these lists require the city to be hygienic and physically safe, to care for the physical (and perhaps emotional) needs of the poor, and to support learning, prayer, and other central Jewish practices.

On one level, these texts worry about the personal and religious life of the scholar himself. In order to study Torah and live a full Jewish life, the scholar will need a place to pray, a place to study, books to read, kosher meat to eat, and perhaps a *mohel* to circumcise his son. Appropriate care of his body—itself a creation in the image of God—and respect for Torah require that he bathe regularly and defecate in a designated and out-of-the-way place. The presence of a court and a doctor (or bloodletter) will help him to avoid victimization or illness. If the scholar falls into poverty, perhaps because he spends all of his time studying rather than working, the *tzedakah* fund will support him and his family.

But even beyond these concerns, the laws governing the lifestyle choices of a scholar point to a commitment to connect the world of the *beit midrash* (study hall) with the world outside its walls. Inside the *beit midrash*, the students spend time debating the finer points of Jewish law, including questions of responsibility toward the poor, appropriate forms of criminal justice, and even the specifics of where to locate an outhouse and what blessing to say upon emerging. It would be hypocritical for students to talk about these issues theoretically without guaranteeing that the world outside of the *beit midrash* meets the requirements of *halakhah*. In fact, we might read the restrictions on where a Torah scholar may live as demanding that the student either move to a place that already meets the requirements or move elsewhere and create such institutions.

In thinking about improving our own cities, we can begin by asking the extent to which the places where we live care for the physical and spiritual needs of all residents. Those of us living in the Western world can safely assume that all of our cities and towns have hospitals, doctors, indoor plumbing, religious institutions, and even soup kitchens and other social services. On one level, then, we can dismiss the Rabbinic list of the ten necessary elements as dated or inapplicable to the Western world. However, the Rabbinic discussion should also force us to ask whether these basic necessities are available to everyone in the places where we live or the other places we support. Does everyone have access to medical services? Does everyone have access to social services? Do all people feel safe walking down the street? Is anyone hungry? Is sexual harassment a problem? If we find our places to be lacking in any of these areas, we need not move—instead, we should assume responsibility for turning these places into the Rabbinic ideal.

OPENING AND CLOSING THE GATES

As we have seen, a scholar thinking of moving to a new city must first do significant research about the hygiene facilities, social services, and religious institutions in that place. In the course of these explorations, the scholar will probably learn a significant amount about the lives of the residents of that city. Even if the scholar has enough money to support himself, learning about the available *tzedakah* funds will force him to develop an appreciation of the experiences and needs of the poor of that city.

Often, the lives of the urban poor are invisible. In the worst-case situation, cities can be alienating places where, as in Babel and Sodom, no one looks out for strangers or vulnerable citizens. Yet even in a typical place, it is common for people of different socioeconomic statuses to have very little knowledge about each other's lives, even if they live within a few blocks of one another. A Los Angeles resident recently told me that when her car broke down, she was forced to take the bus to work. To her shock, she learned that her usual five-minute commute takes an hour and a half on the city bus. Of course, this fact would come as no surprise to the half a million people—90 percent of whom are people of color—who rely daily on LA's notoriously slow bus lines to get to work, school, the grocery store, and medical appointments.[12]

The lack of information goes the other way as well, with the poor shut out of knowledge shared by the affluent, often with serious negative consequences. For example, among my friends and colleagues with young children, the topic of schools and education is a big deal. Members of this group trade tips on public and private schools, share information about new charter schools, and learn from each other how to negotiate New

York's complicated kindergarten application process. Those who do not have access to such informal networks find themselves at a disadvantage in securing the best educational options for their own children.

In the best-case scenario, however, cities provide opportunities for encounter between people with very different backgrounds and experiences. Even in the Rabbinic description of Rome, the presence of a homeless man lying on a reed mat has the potential to stir compassion within some of the passersby. At the very least, Rabbi Yehoshua ben Levi is forced to imagine the pain of another when he comes into contact with a man freezing on the street. This is not the only time Rabbi Yehoshua ben Levi notices poverty; the Talmud and midrash describe him as a frequent companion of Elijah the Prophet, known as the savior of the poor.[13]

In my own experience, growing up in an ethnically and economically diverse suburb exposed me early on to some of the struggles of immigrants, as well as to the different experiences of those with more or less money than my own family. Most people who donate money, volunteer, or take part in political advocacy report that their commitment to a certain issue or organization stems either from personal experience or from an encounter with an individual affected by the issue in question.

What is it about cities that enables these kinds of encounters? One essential is public space—but what is that, and how can we ensure that it exists? In the *Shulchan Arukh*, the most authoritative code of Jewish law, Joseph Caro (Spain/Israel, 1488–1575) classifies public space as an area that facilitates interaction among people:

> [The streets and markets of a public space] do not have walls, and even if they have walls, these are interrupted by gates. (Rabbi Moshe Isserles adds: and [the gates'] doors are not locked at night.) And there are some who say that any space through which sixty myriads of people do not pass each day is not considered public space.
>
> (*Orach Chayim* 345:7)

This text partially defines public space according to the number of people who pass through the area on a daily basis—after all, the more people, the more encounters are possible! But the primary characteristic of public space, according to the *Shulchan Arukh*, is its accessibility to everyone. Public spaces do not have walls to keep out "undesirables." Rabbi Moshe Isserles, a younger contemporary of Caro whose glosses appear within printed editions of the *Shulchan Arukh*, adds that the gates of public spaces are not locked even at night, when residents might be especially scared of intrusion.

This definition of public space challenges the modern obsession with segregating ourselves into more and more private spaces in the name of protecting our safety. During my time in Chicago, I witnessed an effort on the part of residents of the predominantly white and wealthy Lincoln Park neighborhood to evict a shelter housed in a local church and occupied primarily by African American men. I even heard one neighborhood resident comment, "I want my children to be exposed to city life—just not in our backyard."

Public space is not just a meeting hall or club for like-minded people. By its very nature, public space forces people from different backgrounds and different walks of life into contact with one another. For me, the New York City subway exemplifies this ideal of public space. Virtually everyone, from Wall Street bankers to middle managers to janitors, rides the subway. On an average daily commute, I may see rambunctious high school students gossiping about their teachers, a sleeping homeless man sprawled over two seats, lawyers in suits comparing notes about a new case, and Jewish women in long skirts whispering morning prayers. Of course, a minority of the population travels exclusively or primarily by taxi or private car; still others, myself included, periodically jump in a taxi to save time or to avoid multiple transfers. Still, for the vast majority of city residents, the subway remains a daily means of encountering New Yorkers of all ages, ethnic backgrounds, and income levels. Subway riders not only encounter one another, but also share in one another's fate, whether this fate consists of service delays, breakdowns, surprise skip-stops, or terrorism threats. Of course, most subway trips are silent, as people try to respect each other's privacy and avoid the possibility of unpleasant encounters. But the chance of a real, authentic outburst of human interaction is always there, and sometimes it really happens.

In cities where most people drive, such encounters are less common. While living in Chicago, I was often surprised to hear upper-middle-class parents remark that it was "impossible" to bring children on the El train. I know from my own experience the difficulty of lugging a stroller up and down subway stairs, but I also know that this task is not impossible and that sympathetic fellow passengers are always ready to help. The blanket rejection of subway transport as "impossible" for people with children results in the self-segregation of those who can afford to drive in their own private cars. They then fail to recognize the day-to-day reality of those who cannot afford to drive, and they lose an opportunity to encounter people whose lives differ from their own.

Why are such encounters necessary? Meeting people different from ourselves gives us a broader perspective on the world. From those with different life experiences, we can expand our sense of what is true or possible. Such encounters also help us to recognize our own place in the world and to make more conscious decisions about the direction of our own lives.

The growing trend toward gated communities secludes Americans within small neighborhoods whose residents belong to the same socioeconomic class. The gates protect residents from chance encounters with those different from themselves. In her study of the experiences of residents of gated communities, sociologist Setha Low comments:

> Gated community residents use gates to create the community they are searching for. But their personal housing decisions have had unintended social consequences. Most important, they are disruptive of other people's ability to experience "community": community in the sense of an integration of the suburb and the city, community in terms of access to public open space, and community within the American tradition of racial and ethnic integration and social justice.... The gated community contributes to a geography of social relations that produces fear and anxiety simply by locating a person's home and place identity in a secured enclave, gated, guarded, and locked.[14]

The separation among people of different racial, ethnic, religious, and economic backgrounds negatively affects everyone, and not only those who occupy lower rungs on the socioeconomic ladder. Most of us can probably name times when a person with a different life experience helped us to gain a new perspective on a current political issue, a piece of literature, or a means of navigating the world. In the course of writing her book, Low interviewed her own sister, a resident of a gated community in Texas, who complained about how long it takes to drive out of the neighborhood. Low's sister reflects, "The irony is that we are trapped behind our own gates ... unable to exit. Instead of keeping people out, we have shut ourselves in."[15]

Emmanuel Levinas, a twentieth-century French Jewish philosopher, has taught us that the encounter with the other should provoke a feeling of infinite responsibility. When we come face-to-face with another person, he writes, we are struck by the vulnerability of the naked face. The awareness of this vulnerability simultaneously forces us to take responsibility for the other and allows us to recognize ourselves as distinct individuals.[16]

This is a scary concept. It is enough for most of us to assume infinite responsibility for ourselves without also taking on so much responsibility for others. Integral to Levinas's grandiose demands is the promise that looking at another's face holds out the possibility of encountering God. When we see someone else as a creation in the image of the Divine and act accordingly toward that person, we have the chance to deepen our own relationship with divinity.

In the ideal city, ordinary day-to-day encounters will force people who are very different from one another to see and to take responsibility for each other. If I pass a person begging for money every morning on my way to work, I may begin by giving her my loose change. But eventually I may investigate the causes of homelessness in my city or state and advocate for better housing policies. In fact, the first living-wage campaign in America is said to have begun when ministers and volunteers in Baltimore's church soup kitchens and food pantries noticed that a majority of clients were actually employed but were still unable to afford enough food for their families.[17] Since the passage of that initial living-wage law, in 1994, more than one hundred other cities, municipalities, and states have passed legislation that aims to ensure that a person working full-time earns enough to provide for the basic needs of his or her family. This radical change in economic policy would not have been possible if Baltimore churches had not opened their doors to hungry residents, and if the churches and laity of these churches had not allowed themselves truly to encounter those in need of food and to take responsibility for these clients.

By their very nature, large cities force people into contact with others of different backgrounds. I believe that the ideal encounters described above are most likely to take place in the context of a city. In nonurban areas, it is too easy to move from one sealed container to another—from home to car to workplace to car again—without meaningful contact with anyone whose experiences differ greatly from one's own.

That said, suburban dwellers who make an effort to seek out meaningful interactions with others, through diverse community organizations or through interfaith efforts, will be able to create for themselves a public space that encourages interaction. And urban dwellers who wish to seal themselves off in their own penthouses, town cars, and private schools can pat themselves on the back for living in a city, without actually allowing themselves to live in the city. Ultimately, it is not the nature of the place that determines the relationships among residents, but the way in which these residents choose to live with each other.

TAKING RESPONSIBILITY FOR OUR NEIGHBORS

At this point, we have taken some steps toward defining our place(s) and toward envisioning what these places would look like in an ideal world. Now, we turn our attention to our own responsibility in transforming these places.

In chapter 1, we examined the various conditions—including duration of residence and intention to stay—that define a person as a member of *b'nai ha'ir*, the "people of the city." As we have seen, the *b'nai ha'ir* must contribute to the city's various *tzedakah* funds, as well as to the establishment of infrastructure such as city walls and other means of security. In this way, *b'nai ha'ir* help to guarantee both the short-term well-being of other residents and the long-term sustainability of the city as a whole.

The Talmud and other early sources describe the *b'nai ha'ir* as a sort of co-op, the members of which make collective decisions that become binding on all members of the group. In order to protect the city from intruders, the *b'nai ha'ir*, for example, can force each other to contribute to the construction of "a wall, doors, and a bolt" and to pay the wages of a security guard (*Mishnah Bava Batra* 1:5).

The *Tosefta*, a Rabbinic text from the second or third century CE, offers a laundry list of decisions that the *b'nai ha'ir* may make and enforce:

> The people of a city compel each other to build a synagogue for themselves, and to purchase for themselves a Torah scroll and scroll of Prophets. The people of the city are also permitted to determine prices, weights, and workers' wages. They are permitted to establish penalties. The people of the city are permitted to say, "Anyone who is seen at so-and-so's home will give such and such amount," or "Anyone who is seen with governmental officials will give such and such amount." Or "Anyone who lets one's cow graze in the vineyards will give such and such amount." Or "Anyone who brings such and such an animal out to graze will give such and such amount." They are permitted to establish fines.
>
> (*Tosefta, Bava Metzia* 11:23)

This text grants the *b'nai ha'ir* both authority and responsibility for the religious, political, and economic health of the city. Through their enactments, the *b'nai ha'ir* may ensure that the people have a place to pray, as well as scrolls for the Torah and Haftarah readings; that prices and wages are fair; that no member of the city compromises the safety of the others vis-à-vis the presumably hostile government;[18] that city residents do not have contact with people shunned for one reason or another; and that animals do not run wild over the property of city residents. In all of these cases, the *b'nai ha'ir* may exercise their power by enforcing penalties on anyone who does not abide by the agreed-upon conditions. Medieval Jewish communities regularly enacted *takkanot hakahal*—new communal legislation—that either addressed an issue not covered by older Jewish law or, at times, even circumvented existing law. These *takkanot* covered areas ranging from the distribution of *tzedakah* to criminal justice to employment practices.[19] For city residents, the force of these *takkanot* was equal to that of biblical or Talmudic *halakhah*.

Some writers use the language of partnership (*shutafut*) to describe the relationship among the *b'nai ha'ir*.[20] As partners, the city residents have the power to make joint decisions about resources and to force a minority to comply with the decisions of the majority. The city residents also benefit equally from the sale of public property and share equally in any debts related to public resources.

There is no question within Jewish legal texts that all city residents must contribute toward certain basic elements of the public infrastructure.[21] There is a question, however, about whether each person should contribute the same amount, or whether assessments should depend either on personal wealth or on the extent to which an individual will benefit from a particular institution. In considering the fairest way to distribute tax responsibility for the construction or repair of city walls, the Talmud weighs three possible factors: the number of household members, wealth, and proximity to the walls:

> Rabbi Elazar asked Rabbi Yochanan: When the people of the city collect [for walls and other security infrastructure], do they collect according to the number of people or according to wealth? He said to him, "They collect according to wealth. Elazar, my son, fix this ruling firmly." Some say that Rabbi Elazar asked Rabbi Yochanan: When the people of the city collect [for walls and other security infrastructure], do they collect according to the number of people or according to proximity to the walls? He said to him, "They collect according to proximity to the walls. Elazar, my son, fix this ruling firmly."
>
> (BT, *Bava Batra* 7b)

Despite Rabbi Yochanan's reported insistence that the law concerning the allocation of tax burden be, literally, "fixed with nails," the Talmud can't seem to remember exactly what the law is. It is clear that we do not collect the same amount of money from each household. But do we collect according to household wealth or according to the extent to which a particular household benefits from the infrastructure project?

Most of the early commentators on the Talmud, beginning with Rabbenu Tam (Jacob ben Meir, France ca. 1100–1171), try to reconcile the two versions of Rabbi Yochanan's statement by suggesting that money should first be collected according to wealth, and only then according to proximity to the walls of the city.[22] That is, the wealthiest people give the most, regardless of where they live, and the poorest people give the least. The question of who benefits most from the infrastructure comes into play only in the case of two people whose household wealth is identical.

These rulings constitute the ideological basis of a progressive tax. We can imagine that the wealthiest people might choose to live as far as possible from the city walls, leaving those who cannot afford to live farther from the perimeter more vulnerable to bandits and burglars who might infiltrate gaps in the walls. The wealthy people in the city center might then argue that they should not be forced to pay for infrastructure repair from which they are unlikely to derive any direct benefit. Instead, Jewish law responds, each of us must contribute according to our ability, regardless of our personal need for a certain public works project. In modern contexts, this means that even people without children in public school are expected to pay taxes that support the school system, and even people who live in housing developments with private security or trash collection services are responsible for ensuring adequate policing and sanitation for the entire city or town.

In defining our relationship to the places where we focus our social justice work, we need to be clear about our own position and interests. Do we approach these places as *b'nai ha'ir*—as residents who consider ourselves obligated regarding the well-being of the community? Or are we outsiders who will never take on the status of community members? How do our own financial and other interests figure into our communal activities? When will pursuing a communal ideal also serve our personal material interests? When will our immediate interests conflict with what is best for the community? How will we navigate any conflicts that might arise?

QUESTIONS FOR CONSIDERATION

When you sit down with members of your own synagogue, school, or community organization to think about the impact that you hope to make on your own city, town, state, or region, you may begin by envisioning the place that you hope to create. Below are some questions to guide your discussion:

1. When you think about the place(s) where you have chosen to focus your social justice efforts, what adjectives come to mind?

2. Look at the vision of a perfected society in Isaiah 65:17–25. In what ways do the places you have selected already reflect this vision? In what ways do these places fail to live up to this vision?

3. Look at the discussion of the ideal encounter in this chapter. In what ways do your places already allow for such encounters? In what ways do these places fail to encourage such encounters?

4. What would need to change in order for your places to reflect both Isaiah's vision and the ideal encounter?

5. What is your relationship to the places you have selected? Do you consider yourself a member of *b'nai ha'ir*? Why or why not? How does the way in which you classify yourself in this regard affect your responsibility to this place?

6. What contribution do you think that you, personally, can make toward helping the city, town, region, state, or country where you are focusing your efforts progress toward this ideal? What contribution do you think that your synagogue, school, or community organization can make? In answering this question, think both about the needs of your place and about the particular talents and resources that you and your institution can offer.

PART TWO

Principles and Practice of Social Justice

The pursuit of social justice consists of more than a series of service projects or advocacy campaigns. It is a practice, a spiritual discipline, and a way of being and walking in the world. Transforming our communities into communities of justice will require much more than adding more volunteer programs or taking on new issues. Rather, we will need to integrate social justice concerns into the ways in which we speak with one another, into the partnerships that we develop with other communities, into our budgets and personnel practices, and into the ways in which we pray and study our source texts.

In this section, I will consider some of the core principles and essential practices for creating communities of justice. Chapter 4 explores storytelling as a means of identifying passions and building a community grounded in these passions. Chapter 5 envisions ways of integrating social justice into every area of communal life and institutional practice. Chapter 6 discusses principles for developing strong and mutually beneficial partnerships with other communities. Finally, chapter 7 focuses on the most meaningful and effective ways to apply Jewish source texts to contemporary life.

As you read these chapters alone or with members of your community's social justice team, think about whether your current social justice work reflects these principles and practices. What changes might you make to bring these principles and practices to life in your community? What effect do you anticipate that these changes will have?

4

Storytelling for Social Justice

Several years ago, a suburban synagogue asked me to consult with them about how to strengthen the community's social action work. During our first meeting, the two chairs of the social action committee, both of whom had held these positions for more than a decade, complained that no one in their synagogue cared about social action. "How do you know?" I asked. They explained that their meetings were badly attended, as were the "Mitzvah Days" that they organized. In an attempt to ramp up the community's social action work, the committee planned more and more events—with the result that each event was less attended than the last. These two dedicated volunteers had become increasingly frustrated, to the point that each was seriously considering quitting the work altogether.

From what I knew about the synagogue, I doubted that no one in the community cared about social action. The congregants, I knew, included several public interest lawyers, as well as numerous nonprofit professionals. The rabbi often gave sermons encouraging the community to take action on various political issues, and congregants relished their rabbi's outspokenness.

And so I probed a bit more. I learned that most of the synagogue's social action programs consisted of one-time events: a blood drive, a dinner shift in a soup kitchen, or a food or clothing collection drive. This assortment of activities revealed little internal coherence; the chosen issues did not necessarily represent the passions or commitments of the community, nor did the various volunteer opportunities contribute to any unifying vision of change. The synagogue's social action agenda therefore failed to capture the imagination of many congregants. This situation led to a frustrating cycle: The two chairs struggled to recruit volunteers, and so they ended up doing most of the work themselves. They concluded that no one else cared about social action, and so they continued to choose activities and issues that fit their own interests and needs. As a result, few new people joined the committee, and congregants who might have been valuable additions to the group lost the opportunity to help determine the community's social justice agenda. When I spoke with other members of the congregation, they simultaneously expressed feelings of guilt for not joining the existing service opportunities, and frustration at the absence of a coherent agenda.

The situation that these women described to me is a typical one. In many synagogues, social action work consists of one-time service projects, chosen because a member of the community has a personal connection to the partner organization, because the project can be done on Sunday afternoons or at other convenient times, or because the synagogue has always done that particular project. Or synagogues stick to collecting clothes, toys, food, or other items, because such drives do not require a time commitment on the part of community members. For most congregants, synagogue social justice activities simply do not inspire the passion necessary to devote a free afternoon or evening to volunteering or attending meetings.

Dedicated leaders become burnt out by the challenge of recruiting others, and long-term volunteers become frustrated by doing the same service projects year after year without seeing any measurable decrease in the number of people seeking emergency food or shelter. Furthermore, the social action committee often feels like a marginal add-on to the life of the synagogue. Staff members devote far less time to this committee than to worship services, adult education, or youth programs; few board members sit on the committee; and committee members are rarely active in other parts of congregational life.

One crucial element lacking in these floundering efforts is a powerful narrative that places social justice at the center of communal life and that inspires members to action. In this chapter, I will explore why stories can be powerful agents of social change. I will then offer guidelines for developing communal narratives within our own institutions. These narratives can give meaning and drive to synagogues' social justice efforts and can involve many dozens of members who had previously watched from sidelines.

THE POWER OF STORIES

Rashi (Rabbi Shlomo Yitzchaki, France, 1040–1105), the most famous of biblical interpreters, asks the following question at the beginning of his commentary on the book of Genesis: Why does the Torah begin with an account of the creation of the world? If the Torah is primarily a book of law, it should start with the first command given to the Jewish people, namely the instructions regarding the establishment of a new calendar. But that command does not appear until the book of Exodus, midway through the story of the redemption from slavery (Exodus 12:2).

Rashi asks his question to make a rhetorical point. The Torah, he says, begins by telling us that God created the world in order to establish God's authority to designate part of this world—namely, the Land of Israel—for the Jewish people. The argument about who, if anyone, possesses a divinely given claim to the Land of Israel has, of course, sparked centuries of political and religious conflict. I am not entering into that discussion here—I am more interested in Rashi's question than in the answer he provides.

Why shouldn't the Torah begin with law? The text would certainly be clearer and more concise if we removed all of the narrative. As it stands, a person who picks up a copy of the Torah hoping to find straightforward instructions about how to live his or her life will be disappointed. Though the Torah contains many laws—613 according to the traditional count—these laws appear within a larger narrative context.

Could we—or Rashi for that matter—really imagine the Torah as a dry compendium of law? For many of us, our first encounters with Torah involved childhood stories about Abraham and Sarah, Noah and his ark, and Joseph and his brothers. These stories invite us to place ourselves within the text, to see ourselves as players in a story spanning multiple millennia, and to learn from both the successes and the missteps of the biblical

figures. The laws that begin to appear in the book of Exodus are best understood as an element of the story of the Jewish people's evolving relationship
with God. As in any relationship, the two parties make demands on one
another and accept obligations toward each other. But the relationship
cannot begin with these demands and obligations. Rather, the relationship
begins with shared experiences and an extended getting-to-know-you
period before progressing into commitments.

In his influential work on the relationship between law and narrative,
the American Jewish legal scholar Robert Cover argues that law should be
understood as part of an all-encompassing system in which individual laws
interact with social and cultural forces. According to Cover, the acceptance
of a law "entails a narrative—a story of how the law ... came to be, and
more importantly how it came to be one's own."[1] He elaborates:

> No set of legal institutions or prescriptions exists apart from the narra-
> tives that locate it and give it meaning. For every constitution there is
> an epic, for each decalogue a scripture. Once understood in the context
> of the narratives that give it meaning, law becomes not merely a system
> of rules to be observed, but a world in which to live. In this normative
> world, law and narrative are inseparably related. Every prescription is
> insistent in its demand to be located in discourse—to be supplied with
> history and destiny, beginning and end, explanation and purpose.[2]

Through the stories of creation, of God's evolving relationships with
humanity, and of the Exodus from Egypt, the Torah establishes a normative world in which certain laws make sense. The demand for fidelity to a
singular God requires a backstory in which God alone creates the world.
The institution of Shabbat—a day of rest from work—is justified through
reference to the stories of creation and of slavery in Egypt. This day serves
as a reminder both that God stopped creating the world on the seventh day
and that free people—unlike slaves—have the power to take a break from
work. Even laws that do not have a specific narrative precedent, such as
the laws of kashrut (keeping kosher) or of blessings, can be understood
best within the context of an affirmation that the resources of the world,
like the world itself, ultimately belong to God. According to this world-

view, God has given us stewardship of creation, with the stipulation that we must always be mindful of the Source of this creation.

The centrality of narrative for religious life is perhaps most apparent in the popularity of the Pesach seder. In the United States, the seder is one of the most widely observed Jewish rituals, second only to lighting Chanukah candles. The seder appeals to Jews (and non-Jews) of all backgrounds for many reasons. First, the seder takes place in the home, rather than in the synagogue, where many Jews do not feel comfortable. Second, leading the seder requires neither Hebrew skills nor expertise in Judaism. The unusual symbolic foods involved, including matzah, *charoset*, and bitter herbs, heighten the seder's interest for children of all ages.

But the most important reason for the seder's popularity is that the centerpiece of the ritual is a powerful story. This story is simultaneously particularistic and universalistic; it forms the core narrative of the Jewish people, but it also resonates with the past and present stories of other peoples. On the one hand, the story allows Jews to experience a sense of connection to their grandparents, great-grandparents, and all previous generations. On the other hand, the story refuses to become frozen in the past. The Haggadah's statement that "all who expand on the story of the Exodus are to be praised" invites application of the themes of the holiday to contemporary liberation struggles, personal triumphs, and spiritual searches. Indeed, the trend of applying the story of the Exodus to other areas of life has sparked the publication of thousands of Haggadot, on issues as varied as feminism, vegetarianism, the Holocaust, addiction and recovery, the modern state of Israel, and the environment.

My family and I often invite seder guests to bring an object that, to them, represents liberation. In past years, one guest with limited sight brought a magnifying glass that allows him to read; another brought pictures of grandparents who survived the Holocaust; still another brought a flyer from an immigrants' rights campaign for which she volunteered. Beyond allowing seder guests to get to know one another better, this exercise deepens our understandings of liberation. In learning about the freedom that a magnifying glass can provide, or in hearing new stories about past or present political struggles, we gain new insight into the many ways that individuals feel constrained or free.

The philosopher Hannah Arendt wrote that "storytelling reveals the meaning without committing the error of defining it."[3] Whereas a definition limits the meaning of a word or concept or experience, a story invites multiple interpretations and allows room for more stories. If, instead of inviting stories at our seder, we were simply to go around the table and solicit abstract thoughts about liberation, the resulting conversation would be far less engaging. We might find ourselves with a working definition of liberation, but we would lose the personality and emotional impact that individual stories contribute to the discussion.

The seder reveals the power of story to help us define ourselves, to understand the other, and to challenge assumptions and accepted norms. In the next few pages, I will explore the ways in which these functions of the Exodus and other stories can guide us toward social change.

DEFINING THE SELF THROUGH STORYTELLING

Stories equalize. Not everyone can write a legal brief, draft legislation, or argue the finer points of political theory, but anyone can tell a story. Most of us tell dozens of stories a day. These stories can be funny or sad, can relate an incident that we have just witnessed or a memory of long ago, and can be either shared publicly or reserved for only those closest to us.

With each of these stories—no matter how short or seemingly insignificant—we simultaneously define our own identity and control the way that others see us. With every story we tell, we determine what events are important enough to share with others, whether to define ourselves as active or passive players in our own narrative, and how to make meaning from our experiences.

For example, when I speak of my involvement in social justice, I generally tell a story inscribed in space. As I did in the introduction of this book, I typically speak about my first days as an undergraduate at Columbia University, when I learned about the invisible boundaries around the campus. While Columbia stands at the edge of Harlem—then a majority African American and low-income area—the administration passed on a clear message not to wander too far into that neighborhood. I then speak of noticing more visible boundaries, during my first week as a rabbinical student at The Jewish Theological Seminary, just a few blocks north of Columbia. The only entrance into JTS, I saw, faced Columbia, Barnard, Union Theological Seminary, and the Manhattan School of Music. The other sides of the building—which faced Harlem—lacked entry points. For me, this architecture represented an attempt to define the institution as belonging entirely to the academic sphere, and to deny any connection to the neighborhood in which the building stood. I responded by seeking out ways to break through the invisible and visible boundaries by involving myself in a tenants' rights struggle in Harlem. Only later did I discover a vast Rabbinic discourse on the relationships between tenants and landlords and begin to see my own work within a Jewish framework.[4]

In telling this story the way that I do, I define myself as someone who is deeply connected to the places where I live. I also declare myself to be a person with agency, who refuses to accept the limits that others set on me. By ending the story with my discovery of the many generations of Rabbinic discussions about housing issues, as well as other civil law concerns, I establish my commitment to integrating social justice work into other parts of my Jewish life.

I could easily choose an entirely different story to tell. I could talk about the frustration I felt when, as a first-year student in college, I volunteered to tutor a third-grader at a local elementary school, only to realize how little difference I could make in the context of all of the challenges that conspired to keep her family in poverty. I could speak of growing up in a multiethnic, mixed-income school as my first introduction to differences in opportunity. These experiences certainly contributed to my commitment to pursuing social justice, but they did not help me to construct an identity that integrates social justice with Jewish belief and practice.

The story that I most often choose to tell about my own social justice journey is one that connects me to my physical environment and that explicitly links social justice work with Judaism. In telling this story, I define myself—both for my own ears and for my listeners—as someone committed to creating an integrated identity. Rather than describing my Judaism as something that happens in the synagogue or through ritual practices alone, I use this story as a way of explaining that Judaism drives all of my actions in the world. I also aim to convey this message to others and to influence their own self-conceptions and actions.

Some thinkers have gone so far as to say that the self exists only insofar as we define it through storytelling. According to Jerome Bruner:

> There is no such thing as an intuitively obvious and essential self to know, one that just sits there ready to be portrayed in words. Rather, we constantly construct and reconstruct our selves to meet the needs of the situations we encounter, and we do so with the guidance of our memories of the past and our hopes and fears for the future. Telling oneself about oneself is like making up a story about who and what we are, what's happened, and why we're doing what we're doing.[5]

As Bruner points out, we all tell stories about ourselves constantly. Through the choice of these stories and through the way that we tell these stories, we perpetually create and re-create ourselves. Through these stories, we define ourselves to others, and we also establish the sense of self that will determine how we respond to future situations and the many choices we will make through the course of our lives.

HEARING THE STORIES OF OTHERS

Even while making room for personal stories at our seder table, my husband and I do not throw away the Haggadah in favor of just telling our own stories. The power of the Exodus narrative lies not only in its universal themes, but also in its specificity. Slavery shares some characteristics with other oppressions and limitations, but it cannot simply be equated with disability, addiction, or even with other discriminatory experiences. Jews and non-Jews alike can appreciate the message of the story, and yet the story remains one about the early Israelite community. This simultaneous universality and particularity is a common feature of stories. While your story and my story may share some common elements, my story can never be yours, and your story can never be mine. At our seder, when one person explains the liberation he feels when he looks through a magnifying glass, another person may notice a similarity with the way she feels when she works on an immigrants' rights campaign. But she cannot understand the sensation of living with limited sight, nor can he understand fully her feelings about immigration work. The feminist thinker Adriana Cavarero writes:

> No matter how much the larger traits of our life-stories are similar, I still do not recognize myself *in* you and, even less, in the collective *we*. I do not dissolve both into a common identity, nor do I digest your tale in order to construct the meaning of mine.[6]

Rather than accept Cavarero's caution, we often try to make sense of other people's stories by drawing parallels to our own experience or to the experiences of others we know. Let's say that I start telling a friend about my experience at The Jewish Theological Seminary trying to balance study with community involvement. She interrupts to tell me that she knows how I feel—as a law student, she *also* worried about her relationship with the surrounding neighborhood. But does she really know how I felt? Maybe or maybe not. Perhaps if we take the time to listen to and to absorb each other's stories, we will find common ground and deepen our friendship as a result. But it is also possible that I will feel that she has entirely misunderstood me and hijacked my story in order to focus on her own. As a result, I may abandon the attempt to explain myself, and we will miss the opportunity to get to know one another better.

On a one-to-one level, we generally brush off such botched attempts at communication. Most likely, I will feel a bit put off by my friend's inattention to my story, but our friendship will proceed as usual. If I am truly invested in her hearing this particular story, I may try again to tell it. If I feel that she constantly misunderstands me, I may let our friendship trail off. But our communication breakdown will primarily affect only our own relationship or perhaps the relationships among our circle of friends.

Large-scale failure to hear other people's stories, however, can have major negative implications for public policy. For example, when the topic of immigration reform arises, American Jews—especially those descended from Eastern European immigrants—tend to bring up their own families' journey to the United States. We fondly tell stories about the Lower East Side of Manhattan and recall our parents' and grandparents' endeavors to rise from low-wage workers to company owners, or from illiterate immigrants to college graduates. These stories are important ones, as they link us to our past and may even help us to empathize with immigrants of the present. Too often, though, our own stories constitute a barrier to hearing the stories of others. By viewing the situation of current immigrants through the lens of our own families' stories, we can easily drift into wondering why so many of today's immigrants come illegally and fail to "pull themselves up by their bootstraps." But these questions ignore the changed conditions that make immigration today so different from immigration a hundred years ago. To mention just a few differences: the current visa system, in place since 1924, makes it virtually impossible for most would-be immigrants to secure legal visas; most of today's immigrants cannot pass as white, as most Jewish immigrants eventually did; the decline of the union movement, the rise of the service industry, and the disappearance of manufacturing jobs have resulted in low wages and a lack of job security; and public education no longer carries the same promise of career advancement.

In the previous chapter, I spoke about encounter as a first step toward social justice work. But encounter alone does not necessarily compel us to action. In the course of our everyday lives, we may meet dozens of people whose experiences differ from our own. Most of these interactions never proceed beyond the surface level. I say hello to the woman cleaning the floor of my office, but I do not take the time to learn about the family she supports on her wages. I drop money in the hand of the homeless man on the street, but I do not stop to learn how he became homeless.

STORIES THAT INSPIRE ACTION

Hearing the connection between my own story and that of another once unexpectedly landed me in the front yard of a Chicago alderman's home in the pouring rain. My own story begins with learning to drive as a seventeen-year-old. From the moment I got behind the wheel, I hated driving. I couldn't figure out how to parallel park. I always got lost. I had no patience for sitting in traffic. And so, when I applied to college, I looked only at city schools. Naturally, when I was offered a job in Chicago after graduating from rabbinical school, my first question was, "How's the public transportation?" Only when I learned that I could easily commute from home to work on the El train did I agree to move. I did, eventually, accept a hand-me-down car, but I allowed myself to drive it only when leaving the city limits.

During my first year in Chicago, I attended a community meeting in Pilsen, a Mexican neighborhood just west of downtown. I sat in a church social hall listening to resident after resident bemoan the lack of adequate public transportation to that part of the city. At the time, the Blue Line—the train branch serving Pilsen—ran neither on weekends nor late at night, following an abrupt city cutback. A fifteen-year-old told of her inability to access the main public library on weekend afternoons, the time she had available to do research for her school papers. An elderly woman described taking three buses to a Saturday appointment with a doctor whose office was only a few train stops away. A young factory worker shared the difficulties of getting home after working the night shift. As someone who also depended on public transportation most of the time, I recognized the frustration that inadequate train service can bring. I was lucky to be able to afford to live in a neighborhood with excellent train service. I also had a car of my own, albeit one I avoided driving, and—in a pinch—could take a cab. What would it be like, I asked myself, to be completely dependent on a transportation system that failed to meet my basic needs?

I had come to this meeting only to listen and to learn. To my surprise, when the meeting ended, I instead joined the delegation headed to the home of the local alderman, who had reneged on his promise to attend the meeting. The moment we arrived at his home, the skies opened up; we stood in the pouring rain until the police arrived to disperse us. The following week, I found myself riding the El at seven in the morning, as part of an organized effort to speak to other riders about the campaign to extend service on the Blue Line. When, more than a year later, the city agreed to restore weekend service, I thought immediately of the faces of the high school student, the elderly patient, and the factory worker. I can only guess how the changes in train service have affected their lives. But their stories will forever force me to see public transportation as a matter of social justice, and not just of convenience.

My interactions with the people running this campaign started as shallow encounters. I heard a few stories from a stage. But these few stories compelled me to learn more and to do more. As I got to know more of the stories of the Pilsen community, I became even more willing to pass out petitions during the early-morning commute and to speak out in favor of extending public transportation to the neighborhood.

It would be unreasonable to expect every casual interaction to become a storytelling session. If so, we would never get to work in the morning, and we'd never let anyone else get their work done either! But when appropriate, seeking out the stories of others will grant us a broader understanding of the world we inhabit, and it will challenge us to take action to improve this world.

STORYTELLING FOR SOCIAL CHANGE

Stories change us by challenging our assumptions about ourselves, our communities, other communities, and the world as a whole. Ultimately, these stories affect our personal and professional relationships, as well as our political beliefs and actions. Beyond their effect on individuals, stories also have the power to change laws and, by extension, to transform entire societies.

The Torah tells the following story: A man named Tzelophechad dies, leaving no sons to inherit his property. He does have five daughters, but according to the laws of the time, women cannot inherit property. Therefore, Tzelophechad's land is destined for more distant male relatives. But this state of affairs does not sit well with Tzelophechad's strong-willed daughters. Instead, they summon the chutzpah to approach Moses and to tell their story. The most powerful Jewish leader in history listens to their tale—and is stumped. The law clearly forbids the women to inherit their father's property. But how can Moses respond to the daughters simply by repeating the law whose injustice their story highlights? Moses turns to God for help. In an astonishing turn of events, God changes the law in accordance with the women's request: from now on, when a man dies leaving no sons, his daughters will inherit his property (Numbers 27:1–11).

The story of the daughters of Tzelophechad reminds us that laws, when made in a vacuum, may turn out to have negative effects when put into practice. But human stories can challenge and, ultimately, refine these laws. Along these lines, the contemporary legal thinker Martha Minow argues that stories provide a necessary check on the tendency of law to speak in logical generalities:

> Modes of analysis and argument that maintain their exclusive hold on the truth are suspect.... Stories disrupt these rationalizing, generalizing modes of analysis with a reminder of human beings and their feelings, quirky developments, and textured vitality.... A story also invites more stories, stories that challenge the first one, or embellish it, or recast it. This, too, is a virtue to be copied.... The revival of stories in law is welcome, not as a replacement of legal doctrine, economic analysis, or philosophic theory but as a healthy disruption and challenge to them.[7]

In other words, a law that may be expected to operate reasonably may turn out to be inadequate or even destructive when applied to specific individual cases. Lawmakers who are not aware of the stories of individuals or groups may create laws that do not adequately address the needs of these individuals. In the biblical story, the existing laws of inheritance may have sounded appropriate to Moses, who had never experienced the economic fragility of being a woman with no property of her own. In telling their story, the daughters of Tzelophechad force Moses to recognize the discriminatory nature of this law. God, who is neither male nor female, ultimately accommodates the story of the daughters into a reformulation of the law.

In a modern-day case of a story forcing a change in law, the Supreme Court ruled in 2009 that an Arizona school violated the rights of thirteen-year-old Savana Redding when school officials strip-searched her on suspicions that she was hiding ibuprofen in her underwear. In the course of trial arguments, a number of the male justices wondered aloud why strip-searching a young girl should be any different from requiring students to change for gym class. For example, Stephen Breyer, a member of the court's liberal wing, mused, "I'm trying to work out why is this a major thing to, say, strip down to your underclothes, which children do when they change for gym. How bad is this?" In contrast, Ruth Bader Ginsburg—then the only female justice—remarked, in an interview with *USA Today*, that the other justices "have never been a 13-year-old girl…. It's a very sensitive age for a girl. I didn't think that my colleagues, some of them, quite understood."[8] Ultimately the court's decision did note the indignity that a teenage girl would feel at being forced to strip down to her underwear in front of the school nurse. This decision presumably reflects the other justices' willingness to hear Ginsburg's story about the experience of being a thirteen-year-old girl.

In Judaism, the two poles of law and narrative are termed *halakhah* (law) and *aggadah* (narrative). The halakhic and aggadic modes of conversation are often seen as two separate endeavors. According to the classical understanding, *halakhah* determines law, and *aggadah* remains a set of nice stories used for enlightenment and inspiration. In some traditional yeshivot, students reading Talmud even commonly skip over the *aggadah*, so as not to waste any time that should be devoted to law.

But upon closer examination, *halakhah* and *aggadah* turn out not to be so separate after all. Each tends to be written in its own literary style, and in some cases, both approaches appear in a single text. The Talmud often veers seamlessly from legal conversation to story and back again. Within the Talmud, stories can both elucidate and challenge law. In some cases, rabbis puzzled by a legal conundrum decide to "go out and see" what the people are doing.[9] This real-life evidence casts the deciding vote in the argument.

Stories sometimes even have the power to overturn legal conclusions. In one instance, the Rabbis formulate a blessing to be recited by a person who happens upon the site of a communal miracle: "One who sees a place where a miracle happened to the Jewish people says, 'Blessed is the One who did miracles for our ancestors in this place'" (BT, *B'rakhot* 54a). In the wake of this discussion, a story challenges the assumption that the blessing should be recited only at the site of a communal miracle:

> [The anonymous narrator asks,] Does one say a blessing only on miracles that happened to the public, and not on miracles that happened to an individual? For, behold, a certain man was walking in Ever Yemina [a place] when a lion attacked him. A miracle happened and he was saved from it. He came before Rava [an important rabbi], who said,

"Every time you come to that place, you should say, 'Blessed is God, who did a miracle for me in this place.'"

(BT, *B'rakhot* 54a)

While the Talmud does not tell us what this man said to Rava, we might imagine the conversation going something like this:

UNNAMED MAN: Excuse me, rabbi, I hear that you have instituted a blessing to be recited in a place where a miracle happened to the Jewish people.

RAVA (*looking up from his papers*): Yes, that's right.

UNNAMED MAN: Well, I was wondering whether there's also a blessing to say in a place where a miracle happened to an individual.

RAVA: No, we didn't write anything like that. We decided that it's the important historical places—you know, like the Red Sea—that deserve blessings. (*Goes back to reading.*)

UNNAMED MAN: (*Coughs.*) Well, it's just that something amazing happened to me a couple months ago. I was walking home through Ever Yemina, just minding my own business, when a lion jumped out of nowhere and started chasing me.

RAVA (puts down his papers): *Oy gevalt!* What did you do?

UNNAMED MAN: I didn't know what to do! I just started running as fast as I could—but the lion ran faster. And then—unbelievably—the lion tripped over a fallen tree branch, fell, and broke his leg. While he was lying on the ground howling in pain, I managed to escape.

RAVA: Wow. That's really miraculous.

UNNAMED MAN: Yeah, tell me about it. Anyway, I've been avoiding Ever Yemina ever since. But yesterday, I finally gathered the courage to walk back through there. When I got to the place where the lion tripped, I felt like I should say something, but I didn't know what to say. So I just said, "Thank you God for protecting me from the lion."

RAVA: That's an amazing story. You're right—we need a blessing that people like you can say. Let's write one.

The exchange between Rava and this man may or may not have sounded anything like this imagined dialogue. Regardless, the man's individual lived experience prompted Rava—like the Supreme Court justices in the case of Savana Redding—to see the law's inadequacy and to adjust the law to accommodate the story of the ordinary person standing before him.

Conversations about social justice can have a tendency to remain in the realm of theory. We speak in general terms about Jewish obligations toward the stranger or argue the legal merits of a certain provision of a health-care bill. Ultimately, though, every policy decision has an impact on real people. In our own justice work, we should challenge ourselves to keep front and center the stories of real people—both those inside and outside of our own communities.

In some cases, the stories provide the inspiration for our work. During the heaviest week of editing this book, I learned that New York City planned to cut more than sixteen thousand day-care subsidies. Two parents in my daughter's day-care center told me that they had already received letters informing them that their subsidies would end in June. If the cuts went through, these mothers might have no alternative but to quit their jobs. I heard that a new coalition was forming to organize parents to oppose the changes. Going to the meeting would require missing my daughter's bedtime, taking three trains to get to the East Side, and—as it turned out—venturing out in a sleet storm. And I had hundreds of pages to edit. But I dragged myself to the meeting because I couldn't stop thinking about my daughter's two friends who might not be able to come back to day-care in a few months.

In other cases, stories challenge a seemingly logical law. For example, in August 2005 a federal court upheld an Iowa law that prevents former sex offenders from living within two thousand feet of a school or day-care center. In some counties, this restriction has made up to three-quarters of the available housing off-limits to sex offenders.[10] While this law emerged from a desire to protect children, the stories of individuals suggest that the law might actually have the opposite effect. Barred from living in whole swaths of the state, sex offenders find themselves isolated far from family members or friends who might provide the necessary support for reintegrating themselves into society. While it would be inappropriate and impractical to base cases—either in Jewish law or in secular society—only on personal stories, these stories provide a necessary corrective to generalized legal systems.

DEVELOPING A NARRATIVE OF PLACE

Are there places that you will forever associate with a particular event or moment in your life? Are there places that have taken on new meaning for you because of an experience you had there? For me, two events—one tragic and one joyful—have forever changed my relationship to the city where I live.

On the morning of September 11, 2001, I was sitting in a classroom at Hunter College in New York City, where I was studying for a master's degree in urban affairs. My classmates and our professor waited, perplexed, for a guest speaker who was inexplicably late. When our speaker finally arrived, she apologized; for some reason, she said, the subway had stopped running. A few minutes later, another professor stuck his head into the classroom to let us know that a plane had hit the World Trade Center. The fifteen of us crammed into our professor's tiny office where, by craning our necks out the window, we caught glimpses of the smoke coming from Lower Manhattan. Dazed, I wandered out of the building and started the hour-long trek home. A nauseating burning smell wafted through Central Park, which had filled with thousands of others similarly trying to get home. Strangers hugged and cried on each other's shoulders. We traded information, most of it mistaken: two more planes had been lost; the Eiffel Tower had been hit, or maybe the White House. For a moment, the collective fear and confusion cut through the usual New York City barriers between people.

Almost eight years later, I gave birth to my daughter at St. Luke's–Roosevelt Hospital, on the far west side of Manhattan. After fifty-five hours of labor, a falling heart rate, and the impending threat of a cesarean section, she finally emerged at 6:30 in the morning, breathing normally—to the surprise of the neonatal specialist who had rushed in to deliver oxygen. At that very moment, from the window of the delivery room, we could see the sun emerge over the Hudson River. Through this dramatic appearance, she earned the name Lior—Hebrew for "there is light for me."

These are two very different stories: one of death and terror, the other of birth and hope. One is a national narrative, and one is the most personal of stories. Yet in both cases, New York City not only serves as a backdrop for the story but also is forever changed—in my eyes at least—as a result of what happened. After September 11, I will always think of this powerful city as ultimately fragile and in need of protection. After the birth of my daughter, I will not be able to look at the Hudson River without seeing it as a place where miracles happen. Like the unnamed man miraculously saved from being devoured by a lion, I also now believe that a personal experience can forever mark a place as worthy of blessing.

This intrinsic connection between place names and stories is the profound subject of Keith Basso's study of the Western Apache living in Arizona. Traveling through the region with an Apache guide, Basso learns that place names both recall old stories and evoke new ones. At each stop, his guide relates the story encapsulated within the colorful name. But when the received story feels inadequate, or when he has not inherited a story about the place, the guide elaborates or even spins an entirely new tale. In one case, an older Apache man muses:

> I think of that mountain called Tsee Ligai Dah Sidile (White Rocks Lie Above In A Compact Cluster) as if it were my maternal grandmother. I recall stories of how it once was at that mountain. The stories told to me were like arrows. Elsewhere, hearing that mountain's name, I see it. Its name is like a picture. Stories go to work on you like arrows. Stories make you live right. Stories make you replace yourself.[11]

Stories, as this Apache man observes, simultaneously tie people to places, infuse places with meaning, and even have the power to change the way individuals live their lives. After September 11, I feel more connected to New York City than ever. The mention of Ground Zero evokes painful memories of that day. And when I get too caught up in the hectic pace and self-important attitude endemic to the city, I remember volunteering at the New York University Medical Center in the days after September 11. There, I answered painful call after call from parents, children, and friends desperately hoping that their loved ones would turn up in a local hospital. I remember seeing total strangers hug in the street, and I recall the spontaneous memorial gatherings in Union Square. Taking a page from the Apaches, we might attribute to New York an honorary place name such as "Caring for Each Other After Terrible Attack." Such a place name might nudge individuals there to assume the benevolent stance and sense of responsibility to others so prevalent in the weeks following September 11.

Seeking to learn the history of Apache place names, Basso is at first a bit indignant when his guide gives him a new explanation, rather than the original version. Soon, Basso realizes that these improvisations carry no less weight than received traditions:

> Whenever these constructions are accepted by other people as credible and convincing—or plausible and provocative, or arresting and intriguing—they enrich the common stock on which everyone can draw to muse on past events, interpret their significance, and imagine them anew. Building and sharing place-worlds, in other words, is not only a means of reviving former times but also of *revising* them, a means of exploring not merely how things might have been but also how, just possibly, they might have been different from what others supposed.[12]

As Basso recognizes, naming and recalling are not objective acts. Rather, the names we call a place and the stories we tell about a place are subjective decisions that determine the way we understand the past and the way we act in the present and future. In the previous two chapters, we talked about identifying the places where we will focus our social justice work and about envisioning what these places could look like in a utopian future. Another crucial component of this process of linking our social justice work to place will be creating a narrative of our connections to these places. This means crafting a story of our historical relationship to these places and bringing that story into considerations of our current and future engagement in this place.

THE NEED FOR A COMMUNAL NARRATIVE

Groups and nations, as well as individuals, define themselves through the stories they tell. The Jewish people have selected the Exodus story as our core narrative. In doing so, we define ourselves as a people committed to toppling, or at least escaping from, oppressive structures. The Torah itself refers to the Exodus dozens of times in the context of commandments to protect the most vulnerable, to love God, and to establish a homeland in Israel.

In contrast, the Torah never again speaks of the *Akedah*—the incident in which Abraham almost sacrifices his son in response to a divine command—after its initial telling. Nor does the Torah refer a second time to the sin of Adam and Eve or their expulsion from the Garden of Eden. Choosing one of these two stories as the core narrative of the Jewish people could have produced a self-identity rooted in submission or guilt, rather than in empathy with the oppressed and a commitment to freedom. At the same time, we do choose specific times and places to tell these other stories. The Torah reading for the second day of Rosh Hashanah includes the text of the *Akedah*, and the liturgy of Rosh Hashanah and Yom Kippur mentions this episode multiple times. The repeated references to the near sacrifice of Isaac highlight the theme of submission to the divine will that is central to these two holidays—but this story does not become the basic narrative frame for the tradition as a whole.

Communal narratives do not emerge out of thin air. Rather, the community—or representatives of the community—make specific choices about what stories to tell and about how to tell these stories. These choices are not always conscious and are not necessarily vetted through a committee or a formal process. More often, the people with power and authority begin telling a story, and others repeat the story until it acquires the force of truth.

What are your community's stories? Are there certain tales of your institution's founding that are told again and again? How do your institution's materials and website present your core narrative? Are there parts of the story that you choose to leave out? None of these decisions are right or wrong—they simply illustrate your community's decisions about the narrative that you wish to present to the world. These narratives are essential, in that they offer a unifying purpose and push you to action. For example, a school that defines itself as diverse will actively embrace initiatives to become more queer-friendly. A synagogue that prides itself on a history of intellectualism will focus money and time on learning programs. In the next section, we will start to get practical and will explore how to create a communal narrative for your social justice work.

CREATING A COMMUNAL NARRATIVE: ONE-TO-ONE CONVERSATIONS

The creation of a communal narrative begins with soliciting the stories of individual members of the congregation. This process, developed by the field of community organizing (see chapter 11), generally takes place through a series of one-to-one conversations, generally combined with "house meetings"—small group discussions that take place in members' homes. Through eliciting members' own narratives, these one-to-one conversations create closer relationships among congregants, help people to connect more personally to social justice work, and identify shared passions and concerns. In the course of these one-to-one meetings, you will elicit the issues that can drive your social action and social justice work for the future.

Why Do One-to-One Meetings?

One-to-one meetings take up a lot of time and energy on the part of staff and lay leaders. It often seems much easier just to take a survey about the community members' interests and passions or to hold one large community meeting to determine what issues to prioritize. But investing the time to do one-to-one meetings brings the following benefits:

- **Community building.** How many times have you sat behind the same person in synagogue week after week or year after year without knowing much more about this person than his or her name? Are there other parents at your child's school with whom you regularly chat, without the conversation ever moving beyond small talk about teachers and fund-raising? One-to-ones offer a structured means for community members to get to know each other's backgrounds and passions. These conversations can fundamentally change the quality of interactions among community members, who may now begin to connect with each other on a deeper level than before.

- **Involvement of a broader range of community members.** Some community members rarely attend meetings, either because of family or work commitments, because of impatience with meetings, or because they just don't feel a sense of belonging to the whole. But almost everyone will agree to a coffee date, arranged at a mutually convenient time. These one-to-ones will elicit the voices of people who would not show up or speak up at an open meeting.

- **Leadership development.** Through learning to tell one's own story and to elicit the stories of others, community members may develop new skills and take greater responsibility for the community as a whole. Many members of Jewish communities worry that they do not know enough or do not donate enough money to take on a leadership role. But neither Hebrew competence nor a large bank account has any bearing on a person's ability to tell a story or to conduct a one-to-one conversation. This process allows individuals to try on new leadership roles. In addition, the process of conducting one-to-one conversations with a broad segment of the community may turn up new potential leaders who had until then remained untapped.

- **Identification of the real passions of community members.** In a survey or in a large meeting, individuals might indicate that they care about affordable housing or the future of the State of Israel or the war in Afghanistan. But such responses do not indicate the depth of these passions. Caring about an issue enough to check off a box on a survey or to vote in favor at a community meeting is not the same as caring enough to show up on a volunteer day, to call one's senator, or to spend a day taking a bus to the state capitol to lobby on the issue. Through one-to-one conversations, you will probe the roots of the passions that community members profess.

ALTRUISM AND "SELF-INTEREST"

Community organizers often speak about "self-interest" as a motivating factor in social justice work—people are more likely to devote time to a campaign if they, personally, stand to benefit from this work. In one sense, this proposition is obvious. Workers on strike will stand on a picket line for days, or even months at a time; their community supporters might visit once or twice but are unlikely to show up daily in the rain and snow. Parents of children with autism will spend hours lobbying for educational accommodations both for their own children and for others, but people who don't have children in the public schools sometimes find it hard even to vote for basic public funding for education.

But many of us bristle at the suggestion that social justice work should serve our self-interest. What about responsibility to others? What about *tzedakah* as the selfless sharing of our own resources? What if my own economic self-interest as a business owner would dictate fighting living-wage laws, even though I understand that my workers could not support their families if I paid them only the minimum wage?

The concept of self-interest does not mean that we should work only on issues that will bring us material benefit. Rather, the concept of self-interest attempts to break down the us-them power dynamic prevalent in social justice and service work. In the traditional understanding of service, the "haves" altruistically provide for the "have-nots." But this paradigm is both false and destructive. In fact, low-income communities boast high levels of volunteerism. For evidence, we need look no further than the dizzying array of ministries in inner-city churches, to say nothing of the workers who forfeit their own salaries to participate in solidarity strikes for workers striking in other companies or industries. The assumption that people at the bottom of the income scale cannot take care of themselves becomes a self-fulfilling prophecy. Rather than partner with low-income communities to change policies that limit economic advancement, upper-middle-class communities focus on serving these communities without learning much about how these communities envision and build their own futures.

So while our social justice work ought indeed to benefit the communities with whom we partner, that should not be the sole motivation. When we begin by asking about our own self-interest as well, we start with the assumption that we have something to gain from our social justice work. Critically, we must broaden our notion of self-interest beyond the material. It's true that in some efforts, we will gain materially: a new health-care bill might result in better health care for our own families, legalizing same-sex marriage may allow us or our loved ones to marry, and a raise in the minimum wage will directly increase the salaries of those of us working in service jobs.

In other cases, the gains may be less material but no less powerful. For some of us, working on immigration reform may be a means of paying tribute to our immigrant parents and grandparents. Even if we have no children or send our children to private schools, we may view improvements in public education as an investment in a successful future for the city in which we live and work. We might fight for shorter prison terms for nonviolent offenders in order to feel a sense of integrity when we bless God for freeing captives. We might involve our children in a housing campaign because we want them to develop gratitude for what they have.

Self-interest also includes working on behalf of those we love. This may mean taking on issues that affect people in our family or our community. Those of us who identify as straight may choose to fight for same-sex marriage so that our friends and relatives can legally marry. Those of us who have health care through our jobs may be inspired to work for a better health-care system when we learn that other members of our community lack insurance. In this framework, partnerships with other communities may also lead to self-interest based in love. My personal commitment to worker justice emerged from getting to know low-wage workers. Even though no one in my family works a low-wage job, I consider my own self-interest to encompass protecting the rights of others I have come to care about.

In addition to breaking down the us-them paradigm, identifying our own self-interest also provides us the inspiration to continue our work. Let's say I wake up on a beautiful Sunday morning thinking about all of the ways I might spend the day. I can take my daughter to the park, go for a run, or tackle a few loads of laundry. But then I remember that I promised to spend the afternoon at a planning meeting for my synagogue's Mitzvah Day. I'm not that excited about Mitzvah Day, but I feel guilty that

I haven't attended a single social action event this year. If I can put my guilt aside, I am likely to look for an excuse to skip the meeting.

But let's say that I have spent the better part of the year getting to know a group of domestic workers who are fighting for state legislation that would guarantee a minimum wage and labor protections for domestic workers. I have come to care about these women, and I feel inspired by their dedication to the work. In addition, I am thinking about hiring a nanny for the coming year. From talking with the domestic workers, I have learned much about how to be a good employer. I also have come to realize that the proposed legislation will benefit me as an employer, as it sets clear and reasonable boundaries and responsibilities for both parties in what is often a confusingly intimate work situation. Today, the group will be staging a major rally. No matter what else I have to do, I would not think about skipping the rally—I'm excited to see a woman I have gotten to know through this work give her first public speech, and I believe that this rally has the potential to get the attention of some key legislators.

In the latter scenario, I will not receive direct financial benefit from the passage of the legislation (and I might even end up required to pay a wage higher than some of my peers pay their nannies now). I am not a domestic worker myself, and I am unlikely to become one in the future. But my relationship with the leaders of the campaign, along with my potential status as an employer, give me a stake in the success of this endeavor. When I participate in this campaign, I am not doing *for* others; rather, I am participating in a joint action from which I feel myself to derive some benefit, whether this benefit be material or spiritual, in addition to that which the workers will receive.[13]

My involvement in this campaign may have stemmed from a one-to-one process that unearthed a shared story about the conflicted feelings that many community members have about employing domestic workers. After determining that enough people felt passionately about this issue, the community may have decided to get involved with an advocacy group tackling this concern. Through this group, I would have had the chance to meet domestic workers, as well as other employers trying to do the right thing.

Now, let's take a look at how to go about instituting the one-to-one conversations that identify these passions.

STARTING THE PROCESS

The one-to-one process begins with creating a team of leaders who represent different sectors of the congregation, such as Hebrew school parents, seniors, Shabbat morning regulars, and members of the board and social action committee. Members of this group should be people with a reputation for getting things done and who have many relationships within the community. When I speak with rabbis about creating such a team, I often ask them, "If you want to make some change in the synagogue, whom do you ask for help?" Every rabbi has an immediate answer to this question—the names that come to mind may be board members or committee leaders, but just as often they are influential and respected people without any official title or role.

These leaders should begin by practicing telling each other about their own Jewish journeys and justice awakenings. These stories may draw on formative experiences, passions, fears, and hopes for the future. For example, one person might talk about the experience of being a child of Holocaust survivors as his inspiration for opposing genocide. Another might talk about the importance of education in her own life and express concern that she may not be able to afford college tuition for her children. Another might recall the magic of Passover seders at his grandparents' home and wonder how to pass that experience and those values on to his grandchildren.

Leaders should strive to tell these stories in the most effective and accessible way possible. This means choosing a story with some dramatic tension (or finding the dramatic moment in the story), avoiding tangents or unnecessary details, and telling the story clearly and passionately. In the practice sessions, leaders can try out different stories and critique each other's modes of telling. It helps to have three to four such stories well in hand for making different impacts on different listeners. I recommend working with a professional community organizer in training leaders to tell their own stories and to elicit the stories of others.

Some of the questions that you may ask in order to draw out these stories include:

- What was a key moment in your life that led to your involvement in this community? What do you hope to gain from your involvement in this community? What do you hope to contribute to this community?

- What issues in the world keep you up at night? About what issues are you so passionate that you would devote a Sunday to working on them? Why do you care so much about these issues? What experiences in your life have led you to these passions?

- What kind of world do you want to leave to the next generation? What are your hopes and dreams for your own Jewish community? For your city? Your state? Your country? The world? What impact would you like to see this institution make in the world?

Once members of this group feel comfortable telling their own stories, they should each commit to holding a certain number of one-to-one meetings—perhaps between five and ten—with other members of the community. Many synagogues have found it helpful to announce ahead of time a goal for the number of conversations that will take place within a specific time period. Whatever number you choose should be ambitious but achievable. These conversations should take place within a short, defined time period—one to three months—so that you do not lose momentum. Some of these conversations may take place over coffee; others may happen at collective "house meetings." Each one-to-one should last thirty to forty-five minutes and should move quickly from icebreaking small talk to the storytelling at the heart of the meeting. In these meetings, you should be clear that you are having these conversations as a way of figuring out what types of social action and social justice the community should tackle. If you are open to pursuing a range of types of work, possibly including service, investment, advocacy, and organizing, you should articulate this openness from the beginning. (Part 3 will discuss more about each of these modes of social change.)

After each conversation, leaders should fill out and turn in to the organizing team a form that records the essential content of the meetings (see "Sample One-to-One Reporting Form" on page 95). These reports will provide the basis for identifying the institution's communal narrative at a later stage.

You have probably already begun to notice that this one-to-one process will likely take a lot of time, energy, and logistics management. One person will need to be the point person for collecting reports, holding leaders accountable for completing their one-to-one meetings, and managing any issues that arise in the course of the process. This person may be a staff member, an organizer with a local congregation-based community organizing (CBCO) network (if you choose to work with such a group), or a lay leader who can devote at least ten hours a week to the process. Ideally, someone trained as an organizer will lead the process. Because this one-to-one process generally requires a complete change in the way that business is usually conducted in the community, it is easy for the process to fail if it is not done well and led by someone with organizing expertise. If you find that your first attempt at a one-to-one process does not succeed, consider hiring an organizer, asking a local CBCO organizer to work with your group, or sending lay leaders and staff to an organizing training.

In some cases, your institution will do one-to-ones just among your own members. In other cases, you may take part in a larger process conducted by an interfaith network. In chapter 11, I will talk more about CBCO networks and other potential partner organizations.

Tips for Effective One-to-One Conversations

- When inviting a person to a one-to-one meeting, state the purpose clearly, and set your meeting within the context of a larger effort. This framing helps the person to understand the expectations and to be ready to get beyond small talk. Explain that your synagogue, school, or other institution is engaged in a process of determining the social justice issues in which to get involved. Tell this person that the community is aiming to conduct a certain number of one-to-one conversations in order to understand better the backgrounds, interests, and passions of members of the community. Don't try to "sell" the project. Stating the purpose clearly can also help eliminate any confusion or suspicion about being invited to a social or romantic encounter. Men on organizing teams should be especially careful to avoid such confusion when initiating a one-to-one meeting with a woman (in particular when both are presumed to be heterosexual).

- Be clear that you are asking only for a single conversation over coffee (or tea, but think twice about meeting over alcohol). There is no further commitment, though the person will be welcome to become more involved if he or she wishes.

- Arrive on time, or a bit early, to the meeting.

- Keep small talk to a minimum. In order to get comfortable, spend a couple of minutes chatting about children, work, or other topics. But move quickly from this small talk to the storytelling that is the purpose of the meeting.

- Begin by restating the purpose of the meeting. Explain that you would like to share the content of your conversation with the leadership team (that is, this is a public meeting that is part of a communal process, not a private conversation or therapy session).

- Ask questions that will draw out the other person's story. You may begin with one or more of the questions listed earlier, but you should also probe deeper as the other person tells his or her story. You might ask, for example, "Why did you do that?" "How did you feel when that happened?" "Did that experience have any effect on decisions you made later?" Focus on essence, not extraneous facts. Your questions should help the person to expand on and reflect on his or her story and should not be pushy or invasive. Before each question, ask yourself, "Do I want to know this because it is necessary to understand this story or this person, or am I asking out of voyeurism?" If the person seems put off or defensive as a result of your questions, take a step back.

- At an opportune moment, tell your own story. You are not interviewing this person but establishing a relationship, which must be mutual (30:70 percent is usually a good balance between initiator and invitee speaking). Your story may serve to explain your own involvement, to inspire the other person, or to give permission for openness. If you have a good sense of this person, you can choose the story you will tell ahead of time, but be open to using a different story if the moment calls for it. Your storytelling should sound natural, not rehearsed, but should also be efficient.

- If you find points of connection between this person's story and your own, you may point out these connections or tell another story of your own. Be sure, however, that you are devoting the majority of your time to learning about the other person, not talking about yourself.

- End the conversation at the agreed-upon ending time, or earlier if it feels over. Don't drag out the discussion unnecessarily. Remember that not every one-to-one meeting is successful, deep, and inspiring. Some one-to-ones are just duds, and some will just help you practice becoming more skillful at them.

- Upon concluding, explain again that this conversation is part of a community-wide social justice process. If you sense that this person could be a potential leader in your effort, ask whether he or she would like to become more involved in this process. If so, explain how the follow-up will happen.

- Remind the person that you will be sharing the contents of your conversation with the leadership committee, and ask whether there are any elements of the story that he or she does not want to share.

- Thank the person for his or her time.

- Ask the person whether there are other people in the community with whom you should talk. Take down these people's names and (if possible) phone numbers or e-mail addresses.

- Fill out your reporting form immediately, before you forget the conversation.

SAMPLE ONE-TO-ONE REPORTING FORM

Your name:

Name of interviewee:

Major themes of conversation (passions, fears, hopes):

In a few sentences, summarize the key story that this person told.

Does this person want to be more involved in the social justice process?

Do you think that this person would be good at and interested in conducting his or her own one-to-one conversations?

What talents, experiences, or relationships does this person bring to the table?

Any other comments about your conversation?

DISCOVERING NEW LEADERS

The one-to-one process not only uncovers the passions, fears, and hopes of members of your community, but also reveals potential new leaders. In each of your conversations, you should ask yourself whether your conversation partner has the interest and talent to play a leadership role in the project. Some of the questions you might ask yourself include:

- Does this person tell his or her story passionately and clearly?

- Does this person have a history of acting on his or her convictions?

- Is this person interested in the community's social justice project? Does he or she express excitement about getting involved?

- Does this person have relationships with other members of the community, especially with others whom the process has not yet involved?

Remember that the key qualities of leadership in community organizing are different from some other kinds of "committee work." You are not looking for people who just like to come to committee meetings or who reliably complete logistical tasks (although these are also valuable qualities). You are looking for people with passion, humor, interest, and a network of relationships that they can draw upon.

As you discover potential leaders, invite these people to join an expanded leadership team. New members of the leadership team should undergo the same training process in which initial members participated. They will then take responsibility for conducting their own one-to-one conversations. You may begin your process with ten leaders, each of whom agrees to conduct eight one-to-one meetings, for a total of eighty meetings. At the end of the process, you might have thirty leaders, who collectively conduct more than two hundred meetings. In the course of these meetings, each of these thirty members will also develop several new relationships, cultivate a new skill, and probably learn more about themselves in the process.

HOUSE MEETINGS

In addition to scheduling hundreds of coffee dates, your team may choose to conduct some or even many of the one-to-one meetings in community members' living rooms. House meetings have both advantages and disadvantages. On the plus side, these meetings build community by allowing some time for socializing. Attendees may feel more excited about the process when sitting in a room with ten or twenty others than when chatting with a single person over coffee. Stories can spark one another. Finally, house meetings can be efficient vehicles for doing a large number of one-to-one meetings in a short period of time.

But house meetings also present new challenges. Some people may feel uncomfortable showing up at a stranger's home. If all of the meetings are in the evenings, those who work at night or have small children may not be able to attend. You can mitigate this latter problem by scheduling some meetings early in the morning or on Sundays.

For each house meeting, you will need a host and a facilitator. The host opens up his or her living room to the group and may also provide coffee, dessert, drinks, and/or snacks. The facilitator will run the meeting. The host and the facilitator should *not* be the same person. During the meeting, the host will be preoccupied with opening the door for latecomers, hanging coats, refilling the coffee urn, and disciplining the family dog, and will not be able to focus on facilitating the meeting. A person who volunteers both to host and to facilitate may host in his or her own home but should facilitate a meeting in someone else's home. It may be helpful to have two cofacilitators (in addition to the host) who can support each other and compare notes afterward.

The house meeting aims to inform and excite attendees about your institution's social justice process, to elicit attendees' passions and stories, to build community among attendees, and to model a Judaism that integrates ritual, learning, and justice practice. As such, the meeting should include a *d'var Torah* (teaching based on the Torah portion of the week or on an upcoming holiday) or opportunity for Jewish learning, time for explanation and questions about the process, one-to-one conversations, and space to socialize. A typical agenda may look something like this:

7:00 PM	Guests arrive. Host greets guests at the door, takes coats, and invites guests into the living room. Time for coffee, cake, and shmoozing.
7:15	Facilitator introduces goals for evening and reviews agenda.
7:30	Community member offers a *d'var Torah* or facilitates a short text study.
7:40	Facilitator introduces the communal social justice process and takes a few questions. Facilitator explains the concept of one-to-one conversations and presents a question that will guide the conversations for the evening.
7:50	Group breaks up into pairs for short one-to-one conversations based on the question posed.
8:20	Group comes back together. Facilitator asks for a few volunteers to share themes or commonalities that emerged from their conversations, allowing for some organic cross-talk to develop.
8:30	Facilitator reviews the social justice process and takes questions.
8:45	A community member closes the meeting with an inspirational thought, a song, or a blessing.

SAMPLE TIME LINE FOR HOUSE MEETINGS

Three months before the first house meeting:

- Appoint lay chairs for the house meeting campaign.
- Formulate goals for the number of meetings you will hold and for the number of people who will attend each meeting.

- Solicit volunteers to host and facilitate house meetings.
- Schedule meetings and assign facilitators to each meeting.

Six weeks in advance:

- Develop agenda for meetings.
- Announce to community the times and dates of the meetings, and provide an easy way for community members to sign up for these meetings (online, or through calling or e-mailing the coordinator).

Four weeks in advance:

- Hold training for facilitators.
- Call hosts to make sure that they are ready, and answer any questions that they might have.
- E-mail community members reminding them to sign up for the meetings.
- Begin calling community members to remind them about the meetings and recruit participation.

Two weeks in advance:

- Compile final list of who is attending each meeting.
- Continue phone calls as necessary to ensure target attendance at each meeting.

Two days before each meeting:

- Call or e-mail each participant to remind them to attend.

One week after house meetings:

- Collect reports from each meeting.
- Hold meeting (required for facilitators and leadership committee, optional for hosts) to evaluate the process and interpret what was heard.

FROM INDIVIDUAL STORIES TO COMMUNAL NARRATIVE

As you hear more and more stories from your community, you will begin to notice some themes emerge. For example, you might learn that many members of your community struggle to afford their mortgages or worry about the impact of climate change on future generations. Perhaps some community members belong to the "sandwich generation"—those caring simultaneously for elderly parents and for children still at home. Some may speak about family members who have inspired them to take action or about difficult childhood experiences that have sensitized them to the pain of others.

Your leadership team should sort through all of these stories in order to identify the most prevalent concerns. Aim to narrow the list to two or three issues that are broad enough to allow for a variety of types of action, but not so broad as to be all-encompassing. You might, for example, break down a large category like "poverty" into contributing issues such as "access to health care," "children in need," and "good jobs."

Remember that you are not just counting how many times a particular issue arose—for that you could have taken a survey. You are paying attention to where the good energy and good stories lie. Nor are you just looking for a list of "issues." You are looking for insights that help you to weave together individual stories into a communal narrative that speaks to your community's identity and purpose—what it cares about and why.

Based on what you learn through this process, you will begin to develop a communal narrative that reflects the individual stories you have heard. For example: "Many members of our community originally lived in a neighborhood a few miles away and have fond memories of growing up there. We are worried about the poverty in this neighborhood, and would like to help make it a better place for the children living there now." "Our community includes many people who are simultaneously taking care of children and elderly parents. We are therefore interested in ensuring quality child care and elder care for everyone in our society."

You may craft your communal narrative in written form, to be published on your website, in your newsletter, and in other appropriate forums.

In addition, it is often helpful to hold an event to celebrate the completion of your one-to-one process. For this event, invite a few members with especially moving stories to share these with the entire community.

Now that you have crafted your communal narrative, you are ready to seek out partners interested in the issue and to determine ways to act on the issue. In the next few chapters, we will look at some practical issues related to finding partners and determining a course of action.

QUESTIONS FOR CONSIDERATION

1. What stories from your own life inspire you to pursue justice? Who are the people who have served as role models for you in this regard?

2. What places are most important to you? What are your most significant memories of these places?

3. What experiences have led to your becoming part of this Jewish community? What are your hopes for this community? What do you envision this community looking like in ten or twenty years?

4. What questions or concerns keep you up at night? What issues are so important that you would put aside a Sunday afternoon to work on them? Why are these issues so important to you?

5. Do other people in your community have stories and experiences similar to your own? Where are the similarities and differences in your stories?

6. What story can your community tell about how it came to be, about who belongs to this community, and about what impact this community might have on the world?

5
Creating an
Integrated Jewish Life

Mitzvah Day won't die. Every year, well-meaning lay leaders at synagogues, schools, Hillels, and JCCs beg, cajole, and guilt members into showing up on a Sunday. They make peanut butter and jelly sandwiches for the homeless, pack toiletry baskets for domestic violence shelters, pick up trash in a nearby park or beach, and draw greeting cards for hospital patients. Sometimes, representatives of local organizations are invited to host a table for a few hours in the hope of attracting volunteers or money for their programs. At the end of the day, everyone goes home feeling happy, accomplished, and grateful that the next Mitzvah Day phone call will not come for another year.

One could conceive of a Mitzvah Day that serves as a low-barrier point of entry and that gives participants a taste and an appetite for longer-term service and justice involvement. But more often, Mitzvah Day (which also goes by the name "a day of service") becomes both the beginning and the end of most community members' engagement with social action.

Designating a single day as "Mitzvah Day" communicates the message that social justice or social action stands apart from the regularly scheduled programming of the synagogue, school, or organization. By definition, if one day is "Mitzvah Day," the other 364 days are not. Furthermore, the enormous energy that generally goes into planning and executing a major

103

program burns out the volunteers and staff who might otherwise focus their energies on less dramatic but more sustained service and justice initiatives. For many institutions and individuals, a successful Mitzvah Day becomes an excuse for minimal involvement during the rest of the year. "Two hundred people came to Mitzvah Day," we tell ourselves. "I, personally, made a hundred sandwiches." Pride in our accomplishments quickly turns into a sense that our job is done.

The Mitzvah Day problem often extends to the social action committee as a whole. The social action committee generally consists of a small number of dedicated volunteers who have been plugging away for years at creating service projects or guest lectures, most of which are sparsely attended. Social action committee members rarely sit on the board of the institution and seldom have real power within the institution. In contrast, high-powered board members or top donors typically sit on the investment committee, the development committee, or the ritual committee. The presence of such individuals communicates that these functions are most important, and the professional staff are likely to distribute their attention accordingly. Social action budgets are generally minimal—only a small handful of synagogues, schools, JCCs, and youth groups have dedicated staff for social action and social justice, whereas most of these institutions do dedicate full-time staff to education and other programming.

Instead, let's imagine a community in which social justice is fully integrated into the institution. In this community, Mitzvah Day does not exist—or, if it does, it serves as a kickoff for a much broader social justice program. Every population within this community, from nursery school students to board members to seniors, takes part in social justice work. Social justice finds its way into the educational agenda of the institution, into ritual practice, and into decisions about budgets and contracts.

SOCIAL JUSTICE AS A SPIRITUAL PRACTICE

The Rabbis taught, "More than the wealthy person does for the poor, the poor person does for the wealthy" (*Vayikra Rabbah* 34:8). The simplest reading of this text assumes a quid pro quo theology in which those who give will be rewarded either in this world or in the world to come. The poor person benefits the wealthier person by granting the one who gives *tzedakah* (material support to the poor) a chance to fulfill a *mitzvah* and merit a divine reward.

In a less literal vein, we can read this statement as a description of a certain kind of giving or service relationship. Those who give time or money often describe the "warm fuzzy feeling" that such actions engender. Some social scientists have even produced research to demonstrate that altruistic people are happier and healthier.[1] It is difficult for volunteers or any but the largest donors to have a profound impact on the life of any individual or community. However, even a single service experience or a single meaningful encounter with communities in need can bestow on the giver a sense of purpose and possibility. The supposed giver often ends up receiving more than he or she gives.

Developing an ongoing commitment to justice, service, or *tzedakah* also can give us a sense of ourselves as powerful agents, able to change the world around us. Many of us look around at the problems in the world and feel ready to throw up our hands in defeat. But committing ourselves to ongoing justice work, together with a community of like-minded individuals, can restore hope in the possibility of change and in our own abilities to bring about this change.

These are lofty ideals. But it is much harder to maintain a sense of passion and purpose when the day-to-day work consists of making dozens of phone calls, collating mailings, and losing political battles. And this is where the real spiritual work begins.

I believe that Jewish practice offers a framework for transforming our social justice work from something we do for other people to a meaningful spiritual practice for ourselves. This type of spiritual practice begins with the traditional notion of *chiyyuv*, "obligation." In traditional Jewish practice, accepting the notion of *chiyyuv* means that I pray, observe Shabbat, and give *tzedakah* because I believe that I am obligated to do so, and not necessarily because I feel like it. Yet the idea of *chiyyuv* runs counter to the modern ethos of individual choice. In the United States, no one tells me what to believe, where I may live, or whom I may love. While social, economic, or political factors may influence my decisions, and while each choice comes with its own consequences, I am not legally forced into one course of action. In the realm of Judaism, no one can force me to show up at synagogue, to shun cheeseburgers, or to donate to my local Jewish Federation. Outside of the Orthodox community, most Jews who engage with Judaism do so out of a desire for spiritual connection, for community, or for a link to history and tradition.

The move toward individual choice is, on the whole, a positive development. There is no end to historical and contemporary examples of religion becoming an oppressive and abusive force. But we also lose something when we dispense with the notion of *chiyyuv*. Absent a sense of obligation, we are likely do only what we feel like in the moment. If I do not pray regularly, I may not know how to pray in moments when I seek comfort or closeness with the Divine. Observing kashrut forces me to be mindful of what I put into my body. Reciting blessings before eating allows me to experience gratitude every time I eat. Resting from work each Shabbat helps me to balance work with time for family, community, and myself.

Applying the notion of *chiyyuv* to service, *tzedakah*, and social justice helps us to turn these areas of work into a daily practice, rather than allow ourselves to think of this work as optional service, to be done when we are moved to do so.

Within this framework, we may decide to set aside a certain number of hours per week or a certain amount of money to devote to such causes or activities—and then hold ourselves to those commitments. Even when we don't have time, and even when we feel like doing something else, we force ourselves to maintain the practice and thereby deepen our sense of ongoing responsibility to the world. By taking on this approach, we may start to think about social justice and social action as spiritual practices, and not as volunteer activities.

Let's take the example of *tzedakah*. Jewish texts emphasize the requirement for *tzedakah* to be a consistent practice, rather than a one-time magnanimous act. In Deuteronomy 15:8, the Torah employs the phrase *patoach tiftach* in its demand that we give material support to the poor. Most translations render this phrase as "you shall surely open." This translation accurately captures the meaning of the phrase but loses the Hebrew construction, which consists of a doubling of the verb *p-t-ch* (open). The midrash picks up on this double verb and interprets the phrase to mean that one must open one's hand over and over—even giving to the same person one hundred times (*Sifrei D'varim* 117). Commenting on the statement in *Pirkei Avot* (a third-century compendium of ethical teachings) that "all depends on the quantity of good deeds [*rov ma'aseh*]" (3:19), Moses Maimonides writes:

> Desirable character traits are not achieved through the size of the deed, but rather according to the quantity of deeds. This means that the traits are reached through repeating good deeds many times ... for example: if a person gives one thousand dinars once to a single worthy person, this person does not achieve the trait of generosity through this one large deed; this is in contrast to one who gives one dinar one thousand times, with each dinar given generously, as this multiplies this person's acts of generosity one thousand times, and this person achieves the trait strongly. But in the case of this one-time act, this person's soul is awakened in a major way to do a good deed, and afterwards this feeling departs. Similarly, the reward for one who redeems one captive for one hundred dinars, or who gives one hundred dinars of *tzedakah* to a poor person, thereby filling this person's need, is not the same as one who redeems ten captives, or who fulfills the needs of ten poor people, even with ten dinars each.
>
> (Commentary on *Pirkei Avot* 3:19)[2]

Rabbi Isaac Caro, a sixteenth-century Spanish commentator on the Bible, even argues that this type of regular giving should bring joy:

> There are people who give *tzedakah* in order to fulfill the *mitzvah*, but who do so against their own desires. About this, the text says, "Give to him readily, and have no regrets when you do so" (Deuteronomy 15:10). It does not say, "You should have no regrets in order to give to him," as it says, "You are hostile to your needy brother and you do not give him" (Deuteronomy 15:7), but rather it says, "You should have no regrets when you give to him."... How do we know when a person has acquired the trait of generosity? When one acts with joy, this is a sure sign that one has already acquired the trait of generosity.... For this

reason, the text says, "Surely give [*naton titen*]" (Deuteronomy 15:10). When you accustom yourself to giving, you will not have regrets when you give. The meaning of "give" is "with joy," such that there will be no doubt that you have accustomed yourself to giving, and that you have no sorrow when giving, only joy."

(Commentary to Deuteronomy 15)

With these comments, Maimonides and Caro suggest that there is more to *tzedakah* than fulfilling the needs of the poor. In addition to that goal, the practice of *tzedakah* aims to create generous people who give regularly and who do so happily. As Caro points out, the practice of giving precedes the emotion; a person does not wait until he or she will have no regrets about giving, but instead gives and gives until the desire to give follows. At the same time, as Maimonides notes, the focus of *tzedakah* remains always on fulfilling the needs of the poor to the best of one's ability. *Tzedakah* can never become a purely spiritual practice, as the amount of money donated can have life or death implications.

In recent years, many Jews have rediscovered *mussar*—a type of ethical spiritual practice that originated in Eastern Europe in the nineteenth century. *Mussar* challenges individuals to examine and improve their own *middot*, or personal characteristics—including compassion, generosity, humility, patience, and other qualities. In *middah* practice, individuals study texts related to these qualities and practice exercising each, often one at a time. For example, a person might study about the *middah* of humility, reflect on his or her own practice of humility, and then focus on cultivating humility for the next week or month.[3]

Middah practice is a highly internal process that also aims to affect the ways in which individuals relate to the world. A person who successfully cultivates generosity will give more; a person who successfully cultivates humility will allow more space for others to take leadership (without falling into self-abnegation); a person who successfully cultivates patience will probably enjoy better relationships with children, partners, and colleagues.

In the context of social justice practice, the cultivation of these traits can lead to groups and institutions in which individuals model the ideal that they are trying to achieve. Such efforts can have a major positive effect on the social justice world. Social justice organizations and movements are notorious for breeding bad behavior. For some people, a single-minded focus on winning campaigns translates into impatience and even rudeness toward colleagues and partners. Many social justice initiatives fail to practice the egalitarian and anti-discriminatory ideals that these projects support in theory. *Mussar* practice can help individuals to, in Gandhi's words, "be the change you seek." This practice should not, however, become solely about changing oneself to the exclusion of needs exterior to ourselves. The challenge of social justice *middah* practice is to maintain a simultaneous focus on the improvement of one's own practices and on the transformation of the world—and to see that each process depends on the other.[4]

CONNECTING RITUAL WITH ACTION

Every morning, Jews traditionally recite a series of blessings that thank God for a series of everyday miracles, such as clothing the naked, freeing captives, fulfilling our needs, and making us free people. When we are feeling healthy and successful, these blessings remind us to give thanks that we can open our eyes each morning, get out of bed, and meet our basic physical needs. When we struggle with our health or our finances, we say these prayers in the hope that our fortunes will change.

These simple but powerful blessings force us to spend the first few minutes of our morning being mindful of our physical abilities and limitations, of our freedom or lack thereof, and of our abilities or inabilities to meet our own physical needs. But these blessings are not simply a means of giving thanks or petitioning God. Rather, these blessings set an intention for our own contributions to the world. We cannot simply thank God for opening the eyes of the blind without ourselves making the world more accessible to those with physical limitations. We cannot thank God for giving us freedom without working to end the enslavement of others. And we cannot thank God for fulfilling our own needs without also striving to fulfill the needs of others.

We often think of prayer as a one-way conversation between ourselves and God. We ask, plead, praise, call out, and hope for a response. For many of us, prayer serves as a means of connecting to divinity, feeling comforted, and expressing our deepest desires. But this picture captures only one aspect of prayer. Prayer also makes demands of us. We cannot simply leave it to God to perfect the world for us. We ourselves have to take on that challenge—but we also ask for help in a task that feels too big for any one person, even any one generation, to complete.

But is prayer really worthwhile? Just as those committed to ritual sometimes dismiss social justice work as "not religious," so too Jews committed to social justice sometimes have little time or patience for prayer and ritual. Who can stop to pray when there is so much work to be done in the world? Besides, ritual demands belief in God, knowledge of Hebrew, and familiarity with strange customs and rules!

Every Yom Kippur, social justice activists point to the haftarah (prophetic) reading for the day, in which Isaiah chastises the people of his time for observing empty rituals. In the words of the prophet:

> "Why have we fasted," they say, "and You have not seen it? Why have we humbled ourselves, and You have not noticed?" Yet on the day of your fasting, you do as you please and exploit all your workers. Your fasting ends in quarreling and strife, and in striking each other with wicked fists. You cannot fast as you do today and expect your voice to be heard on high. Is this the kind of fast I have chosen, only a day for a person to humble oneself? Is it only for bowing one's head like a reed and for lying on sackcloth and ashes? Is that what you call a fast, a day acceptable to Adonai? Is not this the kind of fasting I have chosen: to loose the chains of injustice and untie the cords of the yoke, to set the oppressed free and break every yoke? Is it not to share your food with the hungry and to provide the poor wanderer with shelter—when you see the naked, to clothe him, and not to turn away from your own flesh and blood?
>
> (Isaiah 58:3–7)

These words are often understood as a privileging of ethical commandments over ritual practices. But Isaiah does not condemn ritual for being ritual. He does not order an end to fast days, or to prayer. Instead, he condemns *empty* rituals, or ritual for ritual's sake. The point of fasting, he says, is to promote self-reflection and to generate empathy for those who are suffering. If fasting becomes only a means of showcasing our own piety, then it has no meaning at all.

But it is also not enough to focus on ethics in the absence of any ritual life. Such an approach can easily lead to a different kind of idol worship. For some people, involvement in justice sparks a sense of self-importance. The work begins to feel like the only thing that matters. As a result, some committed activists dismiss or even mistreat colleagues or partners in service of a single-minded focus on the work. Ritual functions as a corrective to this tendency for justice work to serve the ego. For example, stopping to pray—especially in community—reminds us that the achievement of a perfected world will require the collective efforts of millions of people, perhaps with some divine help. Reciting *kavvanot* (words that set an intention for our work) focuses our attention on *why* we are engaged in this work and helps us to avoid the temptation to get sucked into petty power struggles.

Ritual also helps to sustain us through a lifetime of justice work. Every year, thousands of idealistic twentysomethings sign up to become organizers or to work on election campaigns. After a year or two of fifteen-hour days, seven days a week, a large number of these young people burn out and move on to other careers. In synagogue social action committees, it is typical for new members to join in a burst of energy. After a few months of nonstop work, these volunteers begin to drift off. Or volunteers spend years seeing the same people eat at the same soup kitchen or tutoring kids in schools that continue to fail. After a while, it may not seem worthwhile to serve one more dinner or to run through the multiplication table one more time. Rituals can help us to maintain the strength to follow through for years on end. For instance, Shabbat grants us a day to breathe, to spend time with family and friends, and to regain the energy to continue our work. Jewish holidays, most of which celebrate miracles of the past, challenge us to believe that miracles are still possible in the present and future.

Finally, incorporating blessings, prayers, and *kavvanot* into our justice work marks this work as sacred. If, for example, I recite the blessing that thanks God for freeing captives before I write a letter in support of prison reform, I remind myself that creating a more humane criminal justice system is a way of doing God's work. If I say *Hamotzi*, the blessing over bread, before eating my lunch during a service project, I recommit myself to partnering with God to provide food for all people.

PRAYERS AND BLESSINGS FOR SOCIAL JUSTICE

The Hebrew word *avodah*, often defined as "service," refers to both worship and work. This concept, which the ancient Rabbis classified as one of the pillars of the world, reminds us that we serve God both through ritual actions such as prayer and through our work in the world (*Pirkei Avot* 1:2). If Hebrew collapses these two types of service into one word, it stands to reason that we should also see our worship and our social justice work as intrinsically linked.

Integrating prayers and blessings with social justice is a two-way proposition. Those of us already doing justice work can enrich this work by taking time out for prayers and blessings. Those of us who already have a prayer practice can use our prayers as an inspiration for engagement in justice practice. Ultimately, we can each achieve a personally meaningful balance between ritual and action.

Judaism mandates blessings for all kinds of occasions: eating and drinking, seeing a rainbow, surviving dangerous situations, going to the bathroom, and even meeting a friend we have not seen in some time. These blessings call our attention to miraculous moments that we might otherwise take for granted. Instead of simply gulping down our food, we stop to give thanks for the natural world and for the human labor that ensures we have enough to eat. Encountering natural beauty—whether mountain ranges and oceans or fragrant trees and unusual animals—calls for blessings. Even when going to the bathroom, we acknowledge the miracle of our bodies, which digest food and expel waste in order to keep us alive.

Given the wide range of blessings included in the Jewish liturgy, we might be surprised that there are no blessings for performing ethical commandments, such as giving *tzedakah*, freeing hostages, or feeding the hungry. There are a few traditional explanations for this absence. First, poverty is understood to involve degradation. Since blessings are meant to celebrate the positive, there is a disinclination to recite blessings over degradation. Second, we generally say blessings over actions that we intend to complete immediately. Once we have lit Shabbat candles and recited the appropriate blessing, we have completed the *mitzvah* of lighting candles. We say a blessing over eating matzah on Passover and immediately fulfill the *mitzvah* of eating matzah. But we almost never discharge our obligations in regard to ethical *mitzvot*. No matter how much *tzedakah* we give, we will probably never succeed in fulfilling the obligation to provide for all of the needs of the poor. Even if we feed the hungry this week, we have not solved the problem of hunger.

Rabbi David ben R. Yosef Aboudraham, a fourteenth-century Spanish liturgical scholar, offers one additional reason for not saying blessings before giving *tzedakah*. The poor person, he writes, has the option to accept or to reject the gift.[5] Reciting a blessing indicates an assumption that the action will be completed. Since the recipient may reject the offered assistance, a person who gives *tzedakah* can never be sure that he or she will, in fact, complete the deed. This explanation acknowledges the agency of the poor in the practice of *tzedakah*. It is easy for *tzedakah* to become a one-way process, in which those who have money give it, praise themselves for their generosity, and derive spiritual satisfaction from the act. This paradigm deprives the recipient of the chance to reject the gift, request a different gift, or challenge the giver to offer more. In Aboudraham's conception, the recipient always reserves the ability to deny the giver the spiritual satisfaction of having completed a *mitzvah*.

Nevertheless, some contemporary Jews do sanctify their giving and justice work through blessings. These liturgies generally take into account the traditional discomfort with reciting blessings over ethical *mitzvot* and avoid suggesting that the work is complete or soon to be complete. The Reform movement, for example, has written a blessing for the commandment to "pursue justice." By focusing on the pursuit of justice, rather than its attainment, this blessing acknowledges that the work of justice will not be achieved immediately after the recitation of the blessing. While pursuing justice per se is not traditionally counted among the 613 *mitzvot* of the Torah, it is possible to argue that other specific *mitzvot*—such as paying a worker on time and providing fair trials—fall into this more general category. Some liberal communities, then, may feel comfortable reciting the following blessing before setting out for a service project or demonstration, or even to start a meeting about an advocacy campaign:

> Blessed are You, Eternal our God, Sovereign of the universe; You hallow us with Your mitzvot and command us to pursue justice.[6]

Some years ago, students at the Reconstructionist Rabbinical College, under the guidance of Rabbis Toba Spitzer and Natan Fenner, composed the following blessing for giving *tzedakah*:

> Blessed are You, YHVH, Source of Abundance, for providing us with the financial and spiritual ability to give. All humanity participates in the flow of riches that come in and go out. May we use our resources well, and may this exchange be fair and equal. Blessed are You, Provider of Manna, who enriches us all.[7]

This blessing, too, avoids any overarching statements about the effectiveness of any gift. Instead, the text offers thanks for one's own resources and indicates an intention to use these resources for positive effect.

Another popular blessing in liberal communities classifies involvement in communal needs as a *mitzvah*: "Blessed are You, Adonai our God, Sovereign of the universe, who has sanctified us with Your commandments and commanded us to occupy ourselves with the needs of the community [*la'asok b'tzorkhei tzibbur*]." The phrase "to occupy ourselves with the needs of the community" appears in many traditional contexts, including a prayer for the welfare of communal servants and volunteers recited on Shabbat morning in many synagogues.

Communities less comfortable using the language "Blessed are You" for new blessings may employ the following formulation: *Y'hi ratzon mil'fanekha Adonai Eloheinu v'Elohei avoteinu (v'imoteinu)*, "May it be God's will, our God and the God of our forefathers (and foremothers)." This phrase traditionally begins personal or communal prayers, including the prayer recited by travelers setting off on their journey and the Shabbat morning prayer for the well-being of the community mentioned above.

After the traditional opening, you may insert your own words, in Hebrew or English. For example:

> *Y'hi ratzon mil'fanekha Adonai Eloheinu v'Elohei avoteinu (v'i-moteinu)* that we will see the end of hunger in our own time.

> *Y'hi ratzon mil'fanekha Adonai Eloheinu v'Elohei avoteinu (v'i-moteinu)* that our efforts to serve this community will be well received.

> *Y'hi ratzon mil'fanekha Adonai Eloheinu v'Elohei avoteinu (v'i-moteinu)* that we will make just decisions regarding the distribution of our *tzedakah.*

In addition to composing new blessings, we can also integrate traditional blessings into our justice, service, and *tzedakah* work. For example:

- Reciting *tefillat haderekh* (the travelers' prayer) before setting out on a bus ride to lobby in the state capitol.

- Saying the words *Barukh dayan ha'emet*, "Blessed is the righteous judge," the traditional response to news of a death, before volunteering for or donating to a disaster relief effort.

- Reciting blessings for aspects of the natural world, including fragrant trees, oceans, and beautiful vistas, that we encounter in the course of our work.

All of these prayers appear in a standard *siddur* (prayer book).

SHABBAT AS A SUSTAINABLE PRACTICE

As an old labor slogan would have it, the unions are "the folks who brought you the weekend." While it might be true that the unions fought for the five-day week in the United States, the idea of taking one day off each week goes back to the Torah. As we think about how to build an integrated life of spiritual activism, it's worth taking a look at Shabbat as a model for balancing work and spiritual practice.

In the biblical narrative, God creates the world in six days and then rests on the seventh. This divine retreat becomes the precedent for Shabbat, a twenty-five-hour period each week when Jews traditionally refrain from adding to or subtracting from creation. For traditionally Shabbat-observant Jews, this means taking a break from writing, cooking, gardening, or partaking in other activities that fundamentally alter the world around us.

In the past few years, many of us have had our eyes opened to the extraordinary amount of waste that human beings produce. Our lives are consumed with stuff: closets full of clothes that we never wear, fancy electronics that we will cast aside when the next model comes out, and mountains of take-out containers from the lunches we eat at our desks. When my family recently returned from a yearlong sabbatical abroad, I was shocked to see how many boxes emerged from the self-storage facility. I had been looking forward to being reunited with my own books, clothes, and dishes. Instead, I felt a strong urge to throw everything in the trash. All of our stuff suddenly felt oppressive.

Shabbat offers a break from accumulating stuff. On this one day a week, Jews traditionally do not spend money, browse the Internet, or otherwise produce or acquire more. For those who do not drive or use electricity on Shabbat, this day also serves as an interruption in the consumption of natural resources. For one day a week, in principle at least, we stop changing the world; we stop trying to impose our will upon creation.

The Torah also offers a second rationale for Shabbat. During the period of slavery in Egypt, the Israelites work nonstop. According to one midrash, the Egyptian taskmasters even force the men to sleep in the fields, so that they will be able to work from dawn until dusk, and to prevent them from sleeping with their wives (BT, *Sotah* 11b). Slaves have no control over their time, and no power to set aside time for their families. When the Israelites leave Egypt, they broadcast their new status as free people by setting aside one day a week on which not to work. Through this day off, they learn to put aside the workaholism that they developed during their years of slavery and instead take time for themselves. In our time, this day can be free from deadlines, cell phones, e-mails, memos, and other devices that enslave us during the week. No matter how intense the time pressures of the week, Shabbat reminds us that the mark of a free person is the ability to set limits on one's time.

The biblical verses recited during Friday evening *Kiddush* (blessing over wine) describe Shabbat both as a "reminder of creation" and as a "reminder of the Exodus from Egypt." On this day, human beings take a step back from doing and creating, and we revel in our freedom.

For those of us involved in social justice work, Shabbat forces us to come face-to-face with our limitations. Even if we work all day, every day, we will not save the world in this generation. That can be a difficult thing to admit. Worse, such work habits are bound to burn us out and turn us into unpleasant human beings with no time for family or friends and little patience for colleagues.

A couple of years ago, I oversaw Jewish Funds for Justice's service learning programs, in which Jewish teens and college students spent a week painting or repairing houses in the Gulf Coast. The organization had a policy that the group would not work on Shabbat, and the students knew about this policy before coming on the programs. Still, during almost every trip, when Friday afternoon came around, at least a few students would get upset about the prospect of stopping work. After a few days of painting or hammering, they felt accomplished and capable. They had seen how much work still needed to be done. And they worried about wasting any time. "We have only a week," they would argue. "In one more day, we can shingle another roof or paint another home. How can we take a day for ourselves?"

In conversations with the group, the leaders would talk about the limits of what could be done in a day, or even in a week. Yes, the group could shingle one more home on a Saturday. But shingling one more home would not make a dent in the massive reconstruction project. Even more importantly, we would stress, the students did not "have only a week." They had a lifetime. Taking Shabbat off during an intensive service experience forced them to stop thinking about the trip as their week of service and to think about it instead as an introduction to a lifetime of obligation.

In an integrated Jewish practice, Shabbat is not something that "religious people do," nor is it time off from justice work. Rather, Shabbat becomes an essential part of justice work. We can make these connections explicit by celebrating Shabbat with our social justice partners, speaking about Shabbat as a model for sustainable living, and using Shabbat as the inspiration to fight for freedom for all people.

EDUCATING FOR SOCIAL JUSTICE

In a famous Talmudic episode, the Rabbis debate whether study or action is more important. After a bit of back and forth, the text concludes, "Study is great, because study leads to action" (BT, *Kiddushin* 40b). In other words, the Rabbis want to have it both ways. With this statement, they maintain the primacy of Torah study, but only if the study generates a practical response. It is not enough simply to sit in the *beit midrash* (study hall) for hours on end; the texts studied there also must motivate action in the world. On the flip side, if we take action without ever stepping back to learn and to reflect, we are likely to take major missteps.

Despite the Rabbinic dictum that study should lead to action, we often fail to make the connection between learning and doing. It is uncommon in a synagogue setting for the adult education committee and the social justice committee to plan the year together. In a school setting, the service, social justice, and *tzedakah* projects generally constitute additions to the curriculum, rather than integral parts of the curriculum. In a JCC, "Jewish learning" appears on different pages of the catalogue from "social justice" or "community service," with no obvious connection between the two.

We can begin to bridge this divide by starting social justice and service activities with a *d'var Torah* or with a short text study. This practice helps to link this work with Jewish tradition and history. But it is not enough simply to bring in a text or two when we engage in social justice. Instead, we should be infusing social justice learning into ongoing adult education opportunities, school curricula, sermons and *divrei Torah*, and camp and youth group study sessions. Integrating social justice into the educational life of the institution emphasizes that social justice education is *part of* Jewish education, not something to be done on the side.

I do not mean to say that we should turn over our entire curricula to studying poverty, policy issues, and advocacy techniques at the expense of learning Hebrew, developing ritual expertise, or struggling with philosophical and spiritual questions. Rather, integrating social justice and education means finding ways to bring social justice methods into the classroom and to make what happens in the learning space relevant to the outside world.

At its heart, social justice aims to transform societal power structures so as to allow everyone a chance to succeed. In today's world, certain groups, including white people, residents of Western countries, men, the wealthy, and straight people, earn more money and enjoy greater access to opportunity than those not born into such luck. Some groups get to make more decisions, whether in the workplace or in society at large. Decision making, both in government and in the workplace, is also concentrated among some groups and held back from others. To make real change, these power structures will need to be altered on a global scale. On a smaller scale, we can begin to model a more equitable and shared power structure in interpersonal interactions—and even in the learning environment.

Social justice education begins with the assumption that everyone brings wisdom to the room, not only the official experts. The rabbi, cantor, teacher, youth director, or other professional or lay leader may possess a certain amount of expertise in a topic by virtue of years of study or practice. That said, everyone in the room has something important to contribute. Personally, I have found that the best insights come from people who have never before studied text. Every individual brings a diverse set of experiences, knowledge, and sensitivities to the table, and all of these diverse outlooks enhance our ability to understand the text. It has often happened that I am teaching a text I have taught dozens of times when a student new to Jewish learning timidly raises her hand and suggests a reading that entirely transforms my own understanding of the text.

Adopting social justice as a guiding principle in teaching means opening space for students to engage with the material, challenge the educator, and shape the curriculum to address their own concerns. While lectures may be appropriate at certain moments, such as when the educator needs to communicate a specific piece of information, the frontal mode of teaching should be the exception rather than the rule. This is not to say that the rabbi or educator should not share his or her own learning with the group. But this wisdom can be shared in such a way as to open up rather than shut down conversation.

This mode of teaching can begin simply by asking students to share their own experiences and knowledge. Theater games, such as those developed by Augusto Boal, founder of Theater of the Oppressed, can provide a safe venue for students to share their insights, to explore different modes of addressing a problem, and to expand their sense of what might be possible.[8] For example, an educator might use improvisation techniques to explore issues of power and privilege in the biblical story in which Moses intervenes to stop an Egyptian taskmaster from beating an Israelite slave.

After reading the text, three students might act out the scene with creative license to try out different possibilities for what could have happened. Did Moses have to kill the taskmaster? Did the taskmaster enjoy his role in society? Did the slave appreciate or resent Moses's intervention? What were Moses's motivations for getting involved? Other students can freeze the scene, "tap out" a player, and restart the scene in a new way. For example, a student might tap out Moses just at the point that he is about to kill the taskmaster, and instead pull the Egyptian aside for a conversation.

As a result, the scene might unfold quite differently from the written text. Through this method, students engage personally with the text and develop a stronger sense of the relationships among the characters. The debrief afterwards can connect this biblical episode with contemporary instances in which individuals use their power either for violence or for good. By reflecting critically on power dynamics in their own lives or in the world, students can begin to understand how to transform these dynamics in a positive way.

Social justice education also involves a constant effort to make connections between the curriculum and the world. In a school setting, a social studies lesson about Africa might send students to research poverty in Africa and to find organizations that address these issues. A math class on statistics might include word problems about the relationship between educational achievement and lifetime earnings. Students in a science class might measure pollution levels in a nearby river and publish their findings in a local newspaper. In Bible class, a lesson on the famines in the book of Genesis might lead to discussions of the causes of hunger in the contemporary world.

Within a synagogue, camp, or youth group setting, the curriculum may not be as fixed as the curriculum of a day school. Still, the institution can offer ongoing learning connected with the chosen social justice and service projects. For example, if a youth group has taken up homelessness as its issue for the year, then a yearlong program can include building a sukkah and discussing the definition of stable housing, studying texts about landlord-tenant relations, and comparing Jewish housing law with federal and state housing law. Even classes that do not directly connect to the institution's social justice campaign can reflect a commitment to connecting study with action. A synagogue adult education class studying Jews in medieval Europe might compare the models of community organization and community-based social service then with the models in the Jewish community today. Through this learning, the group may become more inspired to participate or to step up their participation in the social justice work of the community.

By integrating social justice with education, institutions break down the boundaries between the learners and the doers. Through this approach, we can live out the Talmudic dictum that learning should lead to action. This integration should take the form of classroom techniques that equalize power, specific courses and sessions tied to the institution's social justice campaigns, and efforts to connect Jewish sources and history with the concerns of real people in today's world.

MONEY MATTERS

A budget is a values document. I might say that I value ending poverty and building Jewish community. But if my credit card statements show that the majority of my discretionary money goes toward clothing and restaurant meals and that I give little to *tzedakah* or to my local community, then you might reasonably conclude that I actually place the highest value on my own appearance and physical pleasure. Of course, like any text, budgets can be interpreted in multiple ways. It is possible that I spend a lot of money on clothing because my job demands it or that I spend money on restaurant meals so that I can devote to my family the time that I would have spent cooking. Still, if I wish to live my values, my checkbook should bear more than a passing resemblance to what I claim to value.

Institutional budgets, too, should reflect the stated values of the institutions that live by them. No matter how much we talk about our values and our commitments, the true indicators of our priorities are the decisions about how to allocate our time and money.

Many of us are not accustomed to thinking about budgets as religious documents. After the Conservative movement's Committee on Jewish Law and Standards (known as "the Law Committee") passed a *teshuvah* (rabbinic legal opinion) I wrote, obligating Jewish institutions to pay a living wage, I was deluged with phone calls from rabbis who wanted their congregations to live up to this new standard. For the most part, the rabbis called for advice on dealing with their boards of directors. Often board members, many of whom were businesspeople, would tell the rabbi, "Rabbi, this isn't a religious issue. Let *us* deal with the finances." Fiscally conservative board members would argue that the synagogue could not afford to pay a living wage to its lowest-paid staff members.

But wages are very much a religious issue. As I have said, *halakhah* (Jewish law) does not distinguish between so-called ritual *mitzvot* and civil law. Both are obligatory, and both are encoded in the volumes of Jewish law. The same board members who argue that the synagogue cannot afford to pay a living wage would probably not tell the rabbi to allow nonkosher catering in the synagogue in order to save money (at least in a Conservative or Orthodox synagogue, and in some Reform and Reconstructionist ones as well). They would not suggest that the synagogue allow weddings on Shabbat in order to compete financially with the nearby botanical garden. Somehow, many of our communities have decided that Shabbat and kashrut fall under the rabbi's "religious" purview, but wages do not.

The most surprising calls I got in the months following the passage of the living-wage *teshuvah* came from early childhood teachers. While I had written the *teshuvah* with maintenance workers in mind, I learned that early childhood teachers are some of the worst-paid Jewish professionals. The job is designed with the assumption that the teachers are women who teach as a hobby while their husbands work "real" jobs to pay the bills. The reality, though, is that these women (and men) are talented professionals who may or may not have partners with better-paying jobs. I heard from single mothers, women whose husbands had lost their jobs, and others who depended on the wages from their preschool jobs to pay the rent.

The irony is that Jewish communities pay lip service to prioritizing early childhood education. And yet, we continue to pay these essential teachers with poverty wages. A values-based budget would ensure that these teachers do not have to scramble to find health care and that they would be able to support their families without relying on a spouse who earns significantly more.

Some synagogues, even ones without large budgets, are finding ways to ensure that their budgets reflect their values. When Adat Shalom, a small Reconstructionist synagogue outside of Washington, D.C., prepared to move into their new building, they went looking for a cleaning company to handle their janitorial services. They learned that most other area synagogues used the same cleaning contractor. This contractor, Adat Shalom learned, paid workers only seven dollars per hour. Furthermore, workers did not receive health care until they had been with the company for several years. Montgomery County, Maryland, where Adat Shalom is located, had passed a living-wage ordinance a few years earlier. While the county-wide living wage of eleven dollars per hour applied only to certain government contractors, Adat Shalom members decided that they wanted voluntarily to follow the county guidelines. The synagogue decided to hire the company that specialized in cleaning synagogues but negotiated a contract that would pay the workers a living wage. The increased costs of janitorial services—about thirty-five dollars per household a year—were significant, especially as the synagogue had just finished a capital campaign and had raised dues to pay for the new building. But, with the encouragement of the rabbi and key lay leaders, the congregation decided to take the financial risk in order to be true to the values of the community.

Because Adat Shalom paid higher wages, the most talented and dedicated employees of the cleaning contractor rushed to take jobs at the synagogue. In general, janitorial jobs turn over frequently, as workers find better-paying positions. But the Adat Shalom janitors stayed and got to know the synagogue and its members. After a few years, the synagogue decided to hire the workers directly, rather than go through the cleaning contractor. At this point, the synagogue learned that many of the workers had no health insurance. Even though the cleaning contractor offered insurance to longtime employees, many found the plan unaffordable. Adat Shalom began paying into the workers' health insurance.

Six months later, one of the workers became ill with appendicitis. After his surgery and recovery, he told community members that he would not have gone to a doctor if not for the health care that Adat Shalom made possible. To this day, he credits the congregation with saving his life.[9]

In addition to wages, other areas of the personnel policies can and should reflect Jewish values. One of the most significant of these areas is health care. The Adat Shalom story illustrates the need to ensure that every employee receives health-care coverage. In Judaism, human life is sacred. The biblical assertion that God created human beings in the divine image translates into legal obligations to save a life even when doing so involves breaking other laws. For this reason, Jewish law requires doctors to treat patients, prohibits charging excessively high prices for medicine, demands that individuals care for their own health to the extent possible, and even asks the community to set aside funds to provide for the needs of the sick.[10] In countries that have socialized medicine, the government takes on responsibility for ensuring that its citizens have access to quality health care, even if imperfectly delivered. In the United States, where most individuals do not qualify for government health-care programs, Jewish institutions must protect the health of their employees by providing health insurance coverage.

Similarly, the community should demonstrate its professed desire for more Jewish children by providing generous family leave, flextime options, and lactation rooms even when not required by law to do so. These policies may be expensive or logistically complicated, but they are no less important than paying for kosher food for events.

I recently did a consultation with a small synagogue in the process of renewing contracts for several senior employees. While board members did not anticipate problems with any of these contracts, they decided to take the opportunity of renewing several employees at once as a chance to think about how Jewish values might affect the terms of the contract. Together, we studied relevant Jewish texts and talked through some of the stickier issues. While I do not know what the contracts will eventually say, I do know that the board has taken a major step toward integrating the business side of the community with the spiritual side. This community offers a model of how to think about personnel decisions and contract negotiations in our own communities; instead of beginning with what we can and can't afford, let's start with our values, and only then move on to finances.

Instead of assuming an us-versus-them relationship between employer and employee, let's assume that what is good for the employee is good for the institution. Adat Shalom learned that janitors who earn more and receive health insurance stay longer, do better work, and remain healthy. The same can be said for employees who receive family leave and have the option of flextime or job sharing.[11]

The disconnect between the stated values of Jewish institutions and their budgets appears also in the budget allocated to social justice / social action committees and projects. Few synagogues operate without rabbis, cantors, and educators; few JCCs get by without someone heading the gym; and few schools would forego a math teacher. Yet only a handful of institutions pay full-time staff to work on social justice. Those who do have some of the most robust programs in their fields. When social justice work becomes the fifth thing on the plate of an assistant rabbi, a youth educator, or a social studies teacher in a day school, it is likely to fall off the agenda. Only someone who is truly *meshugah l'davar* (passionately committed to the endeavor) will find a way to do this work when it is not at the top of the community's list of priorities.

In examining the budget of your own institution, think first about your values. Is it important that every member of the staff be physically and emotionally healthy? Do you want your institution to make a positive contribution to slowing global warming? Do you believe that social justice should be at the center of what your community does? Are you committed to buying kosher food? To purchasing meat produced in the most humane way possible? If so, the budget should reflect these priorities.

SUMMARY: CHARACTERISTICS OF AN INTEGRATED SOCIAL JUSTICE INSTITUTION

In an integrated institution, social justice will be part of the everyday life of the community. In this chapter, I have identified the following essential principles for creating such an institution. These include:

1. Connect social justice to the ritual life of the community.

2. Make explicit connections between Shabbat and justice work.

3. Transform social justice into a daily or weekly practice, rather than a sporadic activity.

4. Involve members of all of the institution's subcommunities in social justice.

5. Integrate social justice into the educational life of the community, through both teaching methods and subject matter.

6. Create a budget and personnel policies that reflect the values of the institution.

QUESTIONS FOR CONSIDERATION

1. Does social justice feel central to our community? Why or why not?

2. Is social justice integrated into all areas of communal life? How could we bring a social justice lens to every part of our community's practice?

3. When we look at our institution's budget, what values do we see reflected? How might we make this budget more reflective of our community's values?

6

Partnerships and Power

We often speak of social action work as "helping" others. Those of us who enjoy relative privilege may wish to share what we have with those with less privilege. We may want to "give back" to society to express our gratitude for what we have received. There is much to admire about this altruistic posture. For the most part, the instinct to help stems from concern for others and a commitment to making the world better. The recipients of our money, food, clothing, and time often do benefit from this assistance.

However, this approach to social action and social justice—in which one party gives and the other receives—may ultimately hamper progress toward the ultimate goal of a more just world.

The beneficiary-recipient relationship often reinforces ingrained stereotypes that portray white and upper-middle-class people as experts and donors, and low-income people and people of color as needy and passive, lacking agency over their own destiny.

Let's imagine that a group of predominantly white and middle-class synagogue members decide that they want to help hungry people in their community. Most often, such a group will volunteer in a soup kitchen, sponsor a canned food drive, and donate leftovers from catered dinners to a shelter. As a result of this work, a few more people enjoy a hot meal, and the soup kitchen, food pantry, and shelter may save some money on food costs.

Beyond these material benefits, what impact do the volunteer projects have on the people on each side of the serving table? In the best-case scenario, the volunteers will learn about the day-to-day struggles of those who request emergency food aid, and they will understand better the difficulty that these individuals have in getting ahead. In the worst-case scenario, the volunteers will confirm racial or class stereotypes regarding the behavior, attitudes, and competencies of people who come to emergency food sites. The recipients may similarly find justification for their own stereotypes of white people or Jews. As for the recipient organization itself, it may be grateful for the volunteers and contributions, or it may discover that accepting these resources overtaxes the staff.

Of course, not every synagogue or school goes about its social action work as described above. But I have seen this mode of action so many times that I worry that much of the Jewish community's social action / social justice work will deepen, rather than mend, the divide between communities of different races, ethnicities, and classes.

When we think about starting a social action project, we often begin by thinking about others who might need our help. But we would be better served by looking for people and organizations with whom to form long-term partnerships that will benefit both parties.

In 1967, Rabbi Abraham Joshua Heschel wrote the following summons for his fellow Jews to involve themselves in interfaith justice efforts:

> The world we live in has become a single neighborhood, and the role of religious commitment, of reverence and compassion, in the thinking of our fellow men is becoming a domestic issue. What goes on in the Christian world affects us deeply. Unless we learn how to help one another, we may only hurt one another....
>
> The world is too small for anything but mutual care and deep respect; the world is too great for anything but responsibility for one another.[1]

With these words, Heschel recasts the standard call for altruism into a demand for shared responsibility. The well-being of each community, he says, depends on the health of every other community. In approaching our relationships with other religious, ethnic, or social communities, we would do better to begin not with the intention to *help* the other, but with an intention to work together for our common benefit.

In the Bible, covenants begin with a face-to-face encounter. In one relationship that begins with a miscommunication, Abraham assumes that Abimelekh, the king of Gerar, will kill him in order to take Abraham's wife, Sarah, as his own. As a protective measure, Abraham declares Sarah to be his sister and allows Abimelekh to take her into his harem. God appears to Abimelekh to warn him to return Sarah to her husband, and Abimelekh confronts Abraham about the lie. Once Abraham and Abimelekh sit down one-to-one, they succeed in reconciling with one another and in establishing an economic pact (Genesis 20–21). In another moment of misunderstanding, the priest Eli sees Hannah, a childless woman, praying out loud and assumes that she has come to the Temple drunk. When Eli actually stops to speak to Hannah, she tells him that she is not drunk, but is simply pouring out her heart asking for a son. Eli hears her pain and prays also on her behalf. In the end, Hannah gives birth to a son, and Eli becomes a partner in rearing him for divine service (1 Samuel 1).

When Moses faces his most difficult leadership challenge—the rebellion of the Israelites, expressed through the construction of a golden calf—he demands that God show him God's face (Exodus 33:11–23). It is as though Moses says to God at this point, "Until now, we have partnered on bringing this people into freedom without a face-to-face relationship. But now that the work has become much more difficult, I need to deepen my relationship with you. A relationship of the necessary depth requires that we speak face-to-face." While God declares that Moses may see only God's back, and not God's face (whatever these anthropomorphic descriptions might mean in the divine context), the Torah also describes God and Moses as speaking face-to-face at this point (Exodus 33:11).

As mentioned in chapter 3, the philosopher Emmanuel Levinas describes the face-to-face encounter with another person as a demand to accept total obligation for this other:

> The gaze that supplicates and demands, that can supplicate only because it demands, deprived of everything because entitled to everything, and which one recognizes in giving ... this face is precisely the

> epiphany of the face as a face. The nakedness of the face is destitute-
> ness. To recognize the Other is to recognize a hunger. To recognize the
> Other is to give. But it is to give to the master, to the lord, to him whom
> one approaches as You [*Vous*] in a dimension of height.[2]

When two people meet face-to-face, Levinas says, each becomes vulnerable
to the other, and each accepts infinite responsibility for the other. However,
this acceptance of responsibility constitutes not an altruistic "helping," of
the other, but rather an acknowledgment of obligation toward God.
Applying this to our own encounters within the context of social justice
and service work, we might approach every meeting with the other as an
opportunity to recognize our own deep responsibility toward this other as
a manifestation of our relationship to the Divine.

This is a lofty goal. But in practice, how do we enter into such an all-
encompassing partnership? The first step involves listening to the needs,
passions, and concerns of the other, while also sharing our own needs, passions, and concerns. In Levinas's terminology, this means simultaneously
responding to the vulnerability of the other and exposing our own vulner-
abilities. This also means responding to the other person as a manifestation
of the divine presence, and therefore as one who has agency for his or her
own life and who also has the power to impose obligations on others.

With this theoretical background in mind, we turn our attention to the
question of how to create communal partnerships. This conversation must
begin with an examination of the ways in which power affects intercom-
munal relationships.

POWER DIFFERENCES

American Jews hate talking about power. For most, the phrase "Jewish
power" stinks of anti-Semitism. These words call to mind conspiracy the-
ories about Jewish bankers, accusations that Israel exerts too much control
over U.S. foreign policy, and complaints about Jewish involvement in the
media and Hollywood. Yet for some, the term also brings to mind pride in
Israel's accomplishments, in Jewish contributions to the world, and in the
Jewish people's endurance over thousands of years.

Even for those who take pride in the influence that Jews have been able to achieve, uttering the term "Jewish power" remains taboo. As journalist J. J. Goldberg has written:

> To this day, American Jews remain largely oblivious to the sea change in the status of the Jewish community in the last half-century. Much of the world views American Jewry as a focused bloc of influential, determined believers, firmly entrenched in the American power structure. The average American Jew views his or her community as a scattered congregation of six million-odd individuals of similar origins and diverse beliefs, fortunate children and grandchildren of immigrant tailors and peddlers.
>
> Politicians and diplomats point to the Jewish community as a model of success and assurance. American Jews—by a large and growing majority—consider themselves to be members of an isolated, vulnerable minority.[3]

The tension that Goldberg identifies, between Jewish self-perception and the ways in which other communities view the Jewish community, can weaken and even destroy partnerships. In order to build true and lasting partnerships, it is crucial to understand the role that Jewish power and perceptions of Jewish power play in relations between the Jewish community and others.

Power differences color virtually every human interaction. Sometimes these power dynamics result from differences in position and authority; for example, in a business meeting, the opinion of the CEO carries more weight than the opinion of a lower-level employee, because the CEO is the official decision maker and also has the ability to fire the employee. Other times, power dynamics reflect more deep-seated differences of race, gender, sexuality, or age. Such disparities can affect even casual conversations between coworkers, neighbors, friends, and strangers. In these interactions, the person with more social power—in most circumstances, the person who is white, male, straight, and/or in a privileged age range—may be less receptive to what the other person says. In turn, the person with less power may show deference to the more powerful player.

We rarely give voice to this power. Even though power differentials based in race, gender, age, sexual orientation, and social class regularly determine the outcome of negotiations, decisions, and day-to-day interactions, people rarely draw attention to these differences. For those with more power, naming these differences would undermine their own authority. For those with less power, naming these differences would set up a confrontation likely to end badly.

But this collectively agreed-upon silence may make the power differences even more potent. The famous legend of the Golem of Prague illustrates this danger. In this story, the Jews of Prague are under attack. In a desperate attempt to defend the community, Rabbi Judah Loew creates a golem—a clay man whom Rabbi Loew brings to life through the utterance of a secret name of God. The golem goes on a rampage, brutally murdering the attackers. Finally, when the danger has passed, the rabbi puts the golem to sleep. According to one version of the story:

> To this day the golem lies hidden in the attic of the Prague synagogue, covered with cobwebs that extend from wall to wall. No living creature may look at it, particularly women in pregnancy. No one may touch the cobwebs, for whoever touches them dies....
>
> The golem, you see, has not been forgotten. It is still here! But the Name by which it could be called to life in a day of need, the Name has disappeared. And the cobwebs grow and grow, and no one may touch them. What are we to do?[4]

As long as the golem is alive, its power has limits. The golem is frightening—when activated, it can murder, destroy property, and wreak havoc on an entire city. At the same time, everyone knows that Rabbi Loew can put the golem back to sleep in an instant. But once the golem goes silent, its power becomes limitless. Now the golem no longer has to touch anyone in order to cause harm. The mere sight of this creature or even the brush of the cobwebs around it suffices to endanger life. The direct power of the golem pales in comparison to the exaggerated power conferred by the legends and superstitions that sprout up around the silenced monster.

The story also speaks to the Jewish fear of owning and accessing power. On the one hand, the story represents a Jewish fantasy of overpowering the non-Jewish oppressors. On the other hand, as soon as the Jewish community realizes the power they have unleashed, they try to contain it and hide it, rather than naming and controlling it. They won't destroy the golem altogether because they are unwilling to give up on the possibility of power. But they also will not fully accept the power in their hands, as doing so would mean surrendering some of their claim to being an oppressed and vulnerable group. This legend reflects the situation of Jews in America today, who are simultaneously proud and afraid of the power we have attained, and who try both to own and to deny this power.

A midrash on Song of Songs reflects the typical attitude of American Jews toward power:

> "Before I was aware, she set me in the most lavish of chariots" (Song of Songs 6:12). Rabbi Chiyya taught: This may be compared to a king's daughter who was gathering stray sheaves [of wheat, because she was living as a poor peasant]. The king passed by and recognized that she was his daughter, so he sent his friend to take her and to seat her with him in his carriage. Her friends looked at her in astonishment, saying, "Yesterday you were gathering sheaves and today you sit in a carriage with the king!" She said to them, "Just as you are astonished at me, so am I astonished at myself"; and she applied to herself the verse, "Before I was aware, she set me in the most lavish of chariots."
>
> Similarly, when the Israelites were in Egypt, they had to work with bricks and mortar, and they were repulsive and contemptible in the eyes of the Egyptians. When they became free and were delivered and placed in authority over the whole world, the nations were astonished and said: "Yesterday you were working with bricks and mortar, and today you have become free and rule over the whole world." And Israel said to them: "Just as you are astonished at us, so we are astonished at ourselves"; and they applied to themselves the verse, "Before I was aware, she set me in the most lavish of chariots."
>
> (*Shir HaShirim Rabbah* 6:12)

We do not know whether the king's daughter in this story has been banished from the palace, has run away, has been kidnapped, or has wandered away in an amnesiac fog. Regardless, she has so internalized her identity as a poor sheaf gatherer that she no longer thinks of herself as a princess.

When returned to her former position, the princess does not immediately embrace her change in status. Instead, she expresses surprise that she, a poor girl, should suddenly be elevated to the status of princess.

Similarly, the midrash continues, the Jews in Egypt become so accustomed to slavery that they forget that they were once free. Suddenly, God whisks them out of slavery and places them in an exalted position, about to conquer the nations of Canaan and establish a sovereign society. Even from this new vantage point, the Jews fail to embrace their new status, but instead continue to view the world from the perspective of impotent slaves. (The description of the Jews in biblical times ruling over the entire world seems more like wishful thinking on the part of Rabbi Chiyya, who lived under Roman occupation in late-second- to early-third-century Palestine. Of course, in a less literalist reading, the text refers not to the Jews' actual power, but to their access to God by means of divine chosenness.)

As Goldberg points out, Jews tend to feel more comfortable seeing themselves not as a powerful force in politics and society but as a power-less minority—or at least one whose limited power can be taken away at any time. This self-portrait leads to much hand-wringing about anti-Semitism, assimilation, and intermarriage. Beyond causing fear of survival, the sense of powerlessness also mitigates against acknowledging one's own privilege or taking responsibility for the oppression of others. In the context of social justice work, this posture often manifests in the Jewish community's unwillingness to identify as white people or as members of the owning class who have disproportionate access to power and opportunity.

To illustrate this dynamic, Paul Kivel, a longtime Jewish activist and antiracism trainer tells the following story:

> A colleague and I were doing a workshop on racism and we wanted to divide the group into a caucus of people of color and a caucus of white people, so that each group could have more in-depth discussion. Immediately some of the white people said, "But I'm not white."
>
> I was somewhat taken aback. Although these people looked white they were clearly distressed about being labeled white. A white, Christian woman stood up and said, "I'm not really white because I'm not part of the white male power structure that perpetuates racism." Next a white

gay man stood up and said, "You have to be straight to have the privileges of being white." A white, straight, working-class man from a poor family then said, "I've got it just as hard as any person of color." Finally a straight, white, middle-class man said, "I'm not white, I'm Italian."

My African-American co-worker turned to me and asked, "Where are all the white people who were here just a minute ago?" Of course I replied, "Don't ask me. I'm not white, I'm Jewish!"[5]

Of course, not all Jews look white. While the majority of the American Jewish community descends from Eastern European immigrants, many Jews also trace their ancestry to North Africa, India, Ethiopia, the Middle East, and other parts of the Diaspora. To this list of nonwhite Jews, we can add those adopted domestically or internationally, products of mixed marriages, converts, and others.

But even as the American Jewish community has become increasingly multiracial, most American Jews still look white. White Jews enjoy most of the same privileges as other white people. Police officers do not racially profile white Jews for random stop-and-frisks. Store owners do not hover over white Jewish teenagers out of suspicion that these teens plan to shoplift. Employers do not hesitate to interview applicants with noticeably Jewish names. There may be exceptional cases, but the situation of Jews who look white does not compare to that of African Americans and other minorities.[6]

Jews did not always enjoy such privilege. For much of the nineteenth and early twentieth century, the American populace generally did not regard them as white at all. Take, for example, the following scene from Betty Smith's classic novel *A Tree Grows in Brooklyn*. In this episode, a group of gentile boys bullies a Jewish boy on his way to synagogue. Ten-year-old Neeley, whose parents are Irish and Austrian, objects to his friends' behavior:

"I know that kid. He's a white Jew." Neeley had heard papa speak so of a Jewish bartender that he liked.

"They ain't no such thing as a white Jew," said the big boy.

"Well, if there was such a thing as a white Jew," said Neeley with that combination of agreeing with others, and still sticking to his own opinions, which made him so amiable, "he would be it."

"There could never be a white Jew," said the big boy, "even in supposing."[7]

A variety of factors helped to turn Jews—as well as Italians, Irish, and other ethnic minorities—into white people. During World War II, the U.S. Army mixed Jewish and other immigrant soldiers into "white" units in the armed forces, while maintaining segregated units for African Americans and Asians. The weakening of the quota system in higher education, combined with the Jewish pursuit of advanced degrees, has resulted in disproportionate representation of Jews in elite universities. Postwar housing policies encouraged and enabled white people (including Jews and other immigrant populations) to take out mortgages and move to the suburbs.[8]

The African American writer James Baldwin comments:

No one was white before he/she came to America. It took generations, and a vast amount of coercion, before this became a white country.

It is probable that it is the Jewish community ... that in America has paid the highest and most extraordinary price for becoming white. For the Jews came here from countries where they were not white, and they came here in part because they were not white; and incontestably—in the eyes of the Black American (and not only in those eyes)—American Jews have opted to become white.[9]

If (most) Jews have, as Baldwin says, "opted to become white" or accepted the whiteness thrust upon them by the ruling establishment, most have not accepted this identity as absolute. Even while enjoying the advantages of whiteness, Jews have clung to a sense of themselves as a distinct ethnic group, whose membership transcends race. American Jews thus end up navigating a mismatch between internal identity and outward perception. Jews who look white may *feel* different from other white people but end up benefiting from being perceived as white by other people.

In the history of anti-Semitism, there is a well-known cycle in which the ruling classes allow Jews a certain amount of privilege while also making the community vulnerable. Jews classically have accepted positions such as merchants, tax collectors, and members of the royal court, all of which afforded Jews some access to power while also exposing the community to anger from below. Those with less power blame the Jews for the oppressive system of rule, and the Jews then discover that the ruling class will not protect them from this anger.

In America, some Jews, especially those who represent major national organizations, have accepted the risks of identifying with and depending on the ruling classes. This approach brings some protections, such as the overwhelming governmental support for Israel. At the same time, over-identification with government, bankers, and other members of the ruling class, combined with the weakening of relationships with other minority communities, exposes Jews to anti-Semitism from members of the less powerful and less wealthy majority.

Some Jews take the opposite approach and ally themselves primarily with non-majority communities, often to the point of excusing these communities for anti-Semitic behavior. A heightened consciousness of one's own whiteness and access to power may result in a reluctance to stand up for Jewish needs. But recognizing our own whiteness does not mean ignoring anti-Semitism. In the context of partnership with other communities, Jews also need to expose and decry anti-Semitism and to stand up for specifically Jewish needs.

A number of years ago, I worked for the Jewish Council on Urban Affairs, a Jewish organization that invested money in affordable housing in low-income neighborhoods in the Chicago area. One day, a group of staff and board members traveled to a predominantly African American suburb to talk with the mayor and her staff about investing in housing there. After half a day of positive conversations, we agreed on a tentative plan for an investment "partnership." As the Jewish group was getting ready to leave, the mayor turned to us and said, "This works well—we need the housing, and you Jews have the money." We were stunned; how dare this woman ruin our "partnership" by bringing up the anti-Semitic stereotype about Jews and money?

But instead of ignoring the comment, we sat back down and talked about how her statement affected us. We acknowledged the heretofore unmentioned power differential and talked about the complicated feelings that Jews have about money.

The mayor could easily have avoided bringing up this power difference. The all-white Jewish group would have left feeling pleased at the new partnership we had formed, and the all–African American mayoral team would still have felt themselves to be the beneficiaries of gifts by rich Jews. Even silenced, this power difference would have colored every interaction between the groups. By voicing the dynamic, even in a clumsy way, the mayor facilitated the creation of a real partnership, in which the roles and expectations of each party were clear to both.

Rather than choose between an alignment with the ruling classes and an identification only with minority communities, American Jews should claim and integrate both identities. This means acknowledging that many of us have access to privilege as a result of (some of our) light skin, wealth, and education. At the same time, we need to recognize that we remain vulnerable to anti-Semitism, in part as a result of this access to privilege. When we partner with others, we must balance this complex mix of power and vulnerability. In joining forces with other minorities or with low-income communities, we should speak about our own experiences as an oppressed minority community. At the same time, we cannot pretend that our experience is the same as that of communities who currently enjoy less access to power. In our interactions with these communities, we must remember that they may see many of us primarily as wealthy white people, even if we do not feel comfortable with this characterization. We should hold our partners accountable for anti-Semitism through forthright conversations but cannot chalk up every moment of tension to anti-Semitism. In addressing anti-Semitism when it arises, we should be aware that our criticisms may be perceived as attacks by rich white people. Focusing our energies on developing honest partnerships first, rather than lashing out at communities with whom we do not have partnerships, will go a long way toward developing mutually beneficial relationships with minority and low-income communities.

Our understanding of the cycle of anti-Semitism should push us to pursue deep and lasting relationships with other oppressed communities. Because overdependence on the ruling classes has historically led to scapegoating, Jews should realize that the false and temporary safety of whiteness, access to power, and locking ourselves in gated communities will backfire in the end. Instead, we best keep ourselves safe by building long-term partnerships, built on trust and accountability, with other communities working to make America a more equitable, just, and economically stable society. The history of anti-Semitism has taught us that Jews are safest when everyone feels safe.

Having considered the ways in which our multiple and complex identities affect our attempts to build partnerships with others, I turn now to the more nitty-gritty matter of the different types of organizations with which we might partner and the advantages and challenges of working with each.

POTENTIAL PARTNER ORGANIZATIONS

Jewish institutions may partner with a range of interfaith and community groups. These may include social service agencies, interfaith organizing networks, and community organizing or advocacy groups. Each presents varying advantages and challenges. In choosing which types of groups you will partner with, you should carefully consider your own goals, the types of work you want to do, and the expectations and norms of your community. Different groups pursue social change through different strategies and according to different cultural norms (for more on different strategies for social change, see chapters 8–11). Successful partnership does not require finding groups identical in values and style to your own community, but does require looking for opportunities that will mesh with your own hopes and expected outcomes. Of course you may partner with more than one type of organization or community and may develop new partnerships as your own social justice program evolves.

In developing a partnership, be honest with yourselves about what you want out of this relationship. Do you want a learning experience for your members? Allies for an issue of your own? A chance to make a positive contribution to your community? The opportunity to work on a particular issue? Once you become clear about your goals, you should also be clear with potential partners about what you hope to gain. Addressing each group's needs and expectations up front will limit the possibility of misunderstandings later.

Social Service Agencies

Social service agencies may include food pantries, shelters, soup kitchens, tutoring programs, and other organizations that offer direct material, psychological, or educational support to those in need. These agencies are often, though not always, equipped to handle short-term volunteers and groups of volunteers. Your institution may already have relationships with one or more agencies of this kind. If not, or if you are looking to develop additional relationships, groups like this are not hard to find. You can identify the social service agencies in your area by talking to members of your community who work in the social service field, by asking other religious leaders in your area, or by browsing one of the many websites devoted to connecting agencies with volunteers. At this writing, the most developed of these websites are www.idealist.org, www.volunteermatch.org, and www.serve.gov. You may also find organizations by paying close attention to groups mentioned in your local newspaper or on local websites or TV stations.

Social service agencies can be important partners in developing service opportunities for your members and students. Most of these organizations do not engage in organizing or advocacy and therefore will be less likely to work with you on addressing broader social and economic issues. However, your members' experiences in these organizations can lead to increased interest in pursuing systemic change. If, for example, your volunteers spend several years tutoring in a local public school, they will start to ask bigger questions about the educational system in your town and state, and in the country as a whole. These conversations can be openings for pursuing larger-scale partnerships with education reform projects.

In approaching social service agencies, it is crucial to be clear about what you want out of the partnership and to listen carefully to what the organization hopes to gain from working with you. As we will discuss further in chapter 8, volunteers often start from what they can give—a few hours on a Sunday, knitted blankets, food, or a group of fifteen—and then seek out a recipient. Agencies may feel pressured to accept this help, out of a desire to attract new funding or to maintain a relationship with the organization offering its volunteers and resources. This mismatch of goals and expected outcomes easily leads to frustration on both ends.

Instead, start with an internal conversation about what you hope to gain from partnering with a social service agency. Do you want to learn about an issue or community? To contribute a specific skill set? To connect your members or students with the organization or community? Clarifying your own goals will help you to be clear with the organization about what you hope to gain and to contribute through the relationship.

In establishing a partnership, listen also to what the agency says, either explicitly or implicitly, about the relationship they would like to have. Sometimes, the agency representatives may be clear about what volunteer efforts will be helpful and may tell you outright if your services will be more of a burden on staff, who may expend more time supervising volunteers than they would have spent doing the work that the volunteers are contributing. Other times, the agency representatives may respond lukewarmly to your advances. Such lukewarm responses may be signs that the group feels pressured to accept your help, whether out of an expectation that money will follow or out of a general desire for a relationship with your institution or with the Jewish community as a whole. With an awareness of the ways in which race, class, gender, and other power dynamics affect your conversations, you might pick up on subtle signs that your desires and those of the agency may not match. Sometimes, you will be able to find a common ground that works for both of you; other times, you may conclude that the partnership will not work.

Once you have agreed upon a service partnership, you will need to prepare your volunteers for what to expect. One of the most common tensions in service programs arises from volunteers complaining about disorganization within the host agency. Volunteers who have too little to do often feel that their time is being wasted and that the beneficiaries do not sufficiently appreciate the assistance. For their part, social service agencies too small to employ a full-time volunteer coordinator (and even some who are) can be overwhelmed by the project of handling large numbers of unskilled volunteers.

The problem of volunteers feeling underused can easily become an opportunity for learning. When I oversaw Jewish Funds for Justice's service learning program, in which several hundred young people a year spent a week building homes or planting gardens in the Gulf Coast region and elsewhere, one of the most common complaints we heard from participants involved situations in which volunteers stood around for long periods of time waiting for equipment or for a site supervisor. We trained the leaders of these programs to seize these waiting periods for conversations about the competing demands on the staff of the organization hosting us and about the role of volunteers in nonprofit organizations. Through these conversations, volunteers developed a better understanding of the extent and limits of their own contributions. At the same time, we constantly checked in with host organizations to ensure that they still wanted our help, to get feedback about our group, and to offer feedback about our expectations. This honesty sometimes resulted in deciding not to continue the relationship, but it also resulted in stronger partnerships as each party learned more and more about the abilities, talents, and expectations of the other.

Community Organizing Groups

Community organizing groups are generally small, member-led organizations that mobilize groups of people to take action on issues that affect them. I will talk more in depth about community organizing strategies in chapter 11. In the meantime, I will say just a word about how to find these groups and when it may make sense for Jewish communities to partner with them.

With some exceptions, community organizing groups tend to be small and focused on mobilizing people in low-income communities. Most of these groups are not set up to accept volunteers, and most do not have dedicated staff people devoted to engaging religious communities. Some faith-based groups, though, such as Rabbis for Human Rights–North America, American Jewish World Service, or the affiliates of Interfaith Worker Justice, will be excited and ready to help religious communities get involved.

Congregation-Based Community Organizing

Congregation-based community organizing (CBCO) networks involve churches, synagogues, mosques, and other community and faith institutions in organizing efforts that primarily address local issues of mutual concern. These groups include the Industrial Areas Foundation (IAF), PICO National Network, Gamaliel, and Direct Action Research and Training (DART), each of which has affiliates in multiple states and cities.

In most cases, these organizations will offer your institution a powerful means of pursuing big-picture change in partnership with other faith communities. Because these networks are grounded in faith institutions, they are readily prepared to accept new institutions and to provide clear means for your members to become involved. These networks offer opportunities to get to know members of other faith communities; training in campaign planning, one-to-one meetings, and other organizing skills; "actions" and "accountability sessions" (described in chapter 11) that build momentum and seek commitments from public officials; and involvement with a well thought-out and winnable campaign guided by a professional community organizer.

These networks have been operating for three-quarters of a century. Until the past decade, however, the networks primarily involved churches and often felt inhospitable for Jewish groups. Over the past decade, however, largely through the efforts of Jewish Funds for Justice and Just Congregations (a project of the Union for Reform Judaism), interfaith organizing networks have become significantly more adept at involving Jewish communities in their work, and more than one hundred synagogues have joined. Some networks have even hired rabbis or organizers tasked with working primarily with the Jewish community, and some communities—including Boston, Manhattan, and the Bay Area—have created synagogue organizing projects in partnership with the broader interfaith network.

In general, I recommend joining an interfaith network if one exists in your area. I also offer a few thoughts to guide your work with these networks:

- Joining can be expensive. The cost of membership is usually calculated as a percentage of the institution's budget (typically about 1 percent, with a cap of thirty thousand dollars or more). You will need to set aside money or seek out grant money to help with these dues. Some networks may also be flexible about rates, especially in the first year or two of membership. It is important to have honest conversations about money with the organizers, rather than simply dismiss membership as unaffordable. Even so, consider how your budget reflects your values and priorities, and remember that committing money gives you an ownership stake in the organization.

- The interfaith nature of the endeavor limits the issues that these net-works will tackle. Most significantly, these networks will virtually never touch reproductive choice or lesbian, gay, bisexual, trans-gender, and queer (LGBTQ) rights, for fear of losing the participa-tion of Catholic or conservative Protestant churches. Some Jewish institutions have chosen to work with interfaith networks on eco-nomic issues, but to partner with other organizations around repro-ductive choice and LGBTQ rights. In addition, some LGBTQ Jews and their families report having positive one-to-one conversations with conservative Christians in their networks, who become more sympathetic to LGBTQ issues as a result of these interactions.

- The culture of interfaith networks can feel strange for some Jewish communities, largely because Christianity is generally the norm in these groups (though this is changing as more synagogues and mosques join, and networks hire organizers specifically to work with the Jewish community). Meetings and rallies may take place in churches, where some but not all Jews will feel uncomfortable. The name of Jesus may be invoked, and there will likely be an assumption that people will bow their heads when a benediction is recited. In fact, once when I gave an opening invocation for such an interfaith group, the person who introduced me instructed those gathered to kneel for the prayer! I, of course, then began by explaining that kneeling is not generally part of Jewish prayer practice. Partnering with a CBCO group, particularly one that does not currently engage many Jewish communities, may involve explaining such matters as Shabbat obser-vance, kashrut, and why Jews do not pray to Jesus.

- The pace of movement can be slow, and decisions are often made behind closed doors by the most senior leaders. Involving a community in CBCO requires significant training about what to expect from this engagement. The relationship will be most productive if one or more members of the Jewish community commit to significant involvement in the leadership of the network and report back about progress.

- Interfaith networks tend to work on local issues with short-term goals. This choice helps to ensure periodic wins on issues like health-care spending, bike lanes, and predatory lending, which build the power of the organization and the skills and enthusiasm of its member leaders. However, the networks often shy away from longer-term national efforts, although some networks have recently begun to tackle such campaigns. For your own community, you may choose to join the networks on a shorter-term campaign while also maintaining your own involvement in longer-term work if you have identified a broader social issue that you wish to tackle.

- Interfaith networks address issues that trickle up from the grass roots. This is an essential means of ensuring that the network achieves goals important to its membership. However, certain issues—such as global poverty, genocide, torture, human trafficking, or AIDS in Africa—are unlikely to trickle up from the bottom, as these issues do not generally affect the daily lives of individuals in the community. Some Jewish institutions choose to work on these issues separately, through advocacy organizations devoted to these causes.

Advocacy Groups

Advocacy groups generally work on legislative or policy solutions to local, state, or national issues. Whereas community organizing groups harness the power of individuals affected by an issue to pressure decision makers to change policies, advocacy organizations are more likely to marshal experts, lawyers, and research reports to focus on high-level political negotiations and court cases. Advocacy is therefore an elite strategy, while community organizing is a more democratic strategy. Organizing groups tend to promote leadership and training of members from the grass roots, while advocacy groups are led almost exclusively by staff and boards of directors. Of course, there can be overlap between these two types of groups. Organizing groups may also negotiate behind the scenes with political players, and advocacy groups also call on their members or supporters to help lobby elected officials and other powerful figures.

Some advocacy groups are well equipped to partner with faith-based institutions. These groups have made faith-based work an integrated part of their strategy for a long time. They have dedicated staff for this work, and these staff are well connected to faith communities (and ideally personally involved in a faith community themselves). They have ways to involve large numbers of congregants, and not only clergy and one or two lay leaders. In many cases, though, these advocacy groups struggle to find meaningful ways to involve faith-based groups in their work. They are typically accustomed to working with staff from other organizations or the offices of public officials. These people tend to share similar educational and sociocultural backgrounds and professional expertise that leads to talking in jargon, holding coalition meetings downtown during the daytime when volunteer leaders are working and can't be there, or in other ways being inaccessible. Another common problem arises when faith engagement is a hasty add-on to their core work. Warning signs of an advocacy group not prepared to engage faith communities include the absence of dedicated staff, or dedicated staff who are very junior and have no real power in the organization; a tendency to request a rent-a-rabbi at the last minute rather than involve clergy in an ongoing way; and an excessive focus on clergy sign-on letters above all.

PUTTING IT INTO PRACTICE: QUESTIONS TO ASK ABOUT POTENTIAL PARTNERSHIPS

1. What do we want from this partnership? What do we want our members/students to learn, experience, or contribute? How do we want this partnership to affect our institution?

2. What expectations do our partners have of us? Do their needs match the goals, skills, and time commitment we can offer? What are this partner's hopes for a long-term partnership?

3. How might race, class, gender, and other power dynamics affect this partnership? How might these dynamics manifest in our work together? How can we talk about these dynamics in such a way as to advance our partnership?

4. How might this partnership advance the contribution that our institution and the partner institution want to make in the world?

7
Sacred Words
Engaging with Text and Tradition

Rabbi Chanina son of Tradyon used to say: If two sit and do not exchange words of Torah, it is a gathering of scorners ... but if two sit and exchange words of Torah, the divine presence rests between them.... Rabbi Shimon used to say: If three eat at one table and do not speak words of Torah, it is as if they have eaten of idolatrous sacrifices ... but if three eat at one table and speak words of Torah, it is as if they have eaten at God's table.

(Pirkei Avot 3:3–4)

These words sound harsh. If I grab coffee to catch up with a friend and we don't talk about Judaism, do we suddenly become scorners? If my family sits down to dinner and we just share stories of our day, does our tofu stir-fry turn into a pagan sacrifice?

Perhaps. But I find it hard to believe that even the Rabbis of the Talmud talked about Torah all day long. After all, we find stories of them working menial jobs, falling in love, sharing folk medicine, and telling tall tales.

Instead, I understand this text as hyperbole meant to drive home the necessity of basing human interaction around Torah. Ignoring Torah altogether, this text warns us, will likely end with our taking food and other blessings for granted.

In his commentary on this passage, Rabbenu Yonah (Jonah Gerondi, Spain, d. 1263) defines the word "scorners" (*letzim*) in two ways: first, as people who speak evil of others, and second, as people who purposefully organize gatherings to talk about nonsense. He writes, "There is no pride greater than [speaking evil about another person] for those who do so want the entire world to hate this person—their own hatred for this person is not enough." As for those who get together for the purpose of discussing nonsense, he comments that such people "throw off the yoke of Torah."[1]

In the end, Rabbenu Yonah interprets the text in accordance with this second definition of "scorners" as those who get together for the purpose of speaking nonsense. But both definitions help to answer the question of why and how to use Jewish source texts in social justice work.

In political contexts, it is very easy to fall into a pattern of denigrating the other side. We decide that anyone who doesn't agree with us is stupid, fascist, naïve, insane, soft-hearted, and so on. Political "conversation" quickly devolves into name-calling sessions that end with each side deciding only to speak to those already in their own camp. Within these camps, the vitriol can become even more extreme, as individuals on each side egg each other on to lobby more and more harsh words against the other side. In Rabbi Yonah's words, the goal often seems to be to make "the whole world hate" those on the other side. Rhetoric that vilifies the other makes seeing other sides of an issue increasingly difficult.

In my experience, text can cut through this stalemate. When I sit down to teach a new group, I often ask people to introduce themselves and say a word about why they have come. Sometimes, when the subject is controversial, such as employer-worker relations, each member of the group feels compelled to state his or her position from the beginning: "I'm here because I'm a small business owner and I believe that unions are nothing but trouble." "I'm a labor organizer and I have no sympathy for the bosses." I ask the students to put aside these initial commitments and to jump into the text. Together, we examine sources that present the perspective of workers trying to earn enough to feed themselves and their families, along with that of employers worried about getting their crops harvested, and that of communities interested in preserving sustainable wages and food prices. By the end of the discussion, the labor organizer and the business owner probably still disagree on most points. But through the text, each has become more sympathetic to the other side and better able to see the nuances of the debate. Instead of vilifying the other, the two now can have a conversation about their differences.

Rabbenu Yonah's second definition of "scorners" criticizes those who get together explicitly for the purpose of discussing nonsense. The invitation for such a gathering would read, "Nonsense Party: No Torah allowed!" A person who puts out such an invitation effectively declares that Torah has no place in certain areas of life. In contrast, a person who talks about Torah all the time perpetually looks to Jewish wisdom for guidance on every aspect of life, whether that be child rearing, employment practices, or financial decisions.

Classical and modern Jewish texts emerge from real-life debates about subjects ranging from home life to business practices to ritual behaviors to criminal law. These texts do not answer every challenge of the contemporary world. But they result from generations and generations of thoughtful people studying, talking, writing, and trying things out in practice. So these texts do contain significant wisdom about human nature, strategies for human relations, and descriptions of how a more ideal world might function. It is a common hubris of contemporary life to assume that the past has nothing to teach us. As the old saying goes, this attitude dooms us to repeat the mistakes of the past. Instead, we might begin with an openness to learning from Jewish texts. When we open ourselves to the texts, we may be surprised at the new perspectives and insights that emerge from these ancient words.

"JUSTICE, JUSTICE SHALL YOU PURSUE"

The most common criticism of Jewish social justice contends that this term describes slapping a Jewish text onto modern liberal values. Very often, this critique has merit. I refer to this strategy as the *"Tzedek tzedek tirdof syndrome"* ("Justice, justice shall you pursue" [Deuteronomy 16:20]). That is, organizations or individuals will typically quote a very short text, generally from the Bible and very often this same verse, as a means of legitimizing a preestablished position. An Internet search of "Justice, justice shall you pursue" turns up more than five hundred thousand instances of this phrase, used to justify everything under the sun, including opposition to the war in Iraq, support for Israel's actions in the Palestinian territories, opposition to Israel's actions in the Palestinian territories, reproductive choice, universal health care, and hundreds of other issues. In some cases, the author quotes a commentary on the verse or otherwise develops a working definition of "justice" for the purpose of explaining his or her position. In other cases, the author simply cites the verse without explanation, and with the implicit assumption that the verse automatically justifies his or her position. This well-known verse has become shorthand for defining any given issue as inherently Jewish. Since each reader can interpret "justice" as he or she wishes, the verse can be read as support for anything that a given author or teacher deems "just."

While *Tzedek tzedek tirdof* may be the most commonly used verse in Jewish social justice circles, other verses play a similar role in legitimating particular positions without inviting in-depth analysis of the issue in question. For example, the numerous biblical verses mandating protection of strangers, widows, and orphans often serve as justification for certain positions on poverty or immigration issues; the verses mandating the timely payment of day laborers appear as support for all types of workers' rights issues; and the description of humanity as having been created *b'tzelem Elohim* (in the image of God) helps to cast myriad policies as attempts to protect human dignity. Certain well-known quotes from the Talmud or other Jewish sources play similar roles in defining a particular position as Jewish.

I am not dismissing this use of individual biblical verses or short quotations in the Jewish discourse around social justice. Quoting a short text offers a means of instantly locating one's work within a Jewish context, casting social justice in a religious light, and connecting with others who share this Jewish language. I would argue only that this approach is limited in its ability to meet two crucial goals. First, this approach does not help us to gain new insight into the issue at hand. The absence of real discussion of the verse at hand essentially eliminates the possibility that the citation will add a new perspective to the target issue. Second, this method of quoting a single verse cannot engage sectors of the Jewish community who are not already convinced of the stated position. This method also alienates those who take Jewish learning seriously and who therefore resent seeing texts used for purely political purposes.

THE PEDAGOGIC APPROACH

A second approach to using classical text sees this text primarily as a peda-gogic tool. Those who employ this method begin with the assumption that text can be a valuable means both of bringing committed Jews to social jus-tice and of helping committed social justice activists to connect to their Judaism. Many Jewish social justice organizations sponsor periodic text studies that challenge participants to explore texts in depth and to apply these texts to contemporary situations. These text studies serve the purpose of creating a learning community among activists and potential activists; combating burnout among activists, who can derive energy from casting their work in a religious light; and offering a nonthreatening and compelling means for Jews to enter social justice work.

Most Jewish social justice curricula similarly seek both to engage students in explorations of Jewish text and to instill in students a commit-ment to social justice work. As such, these curricula employ the solid educational methodology of meeting students where they are, drawing on existing knowledge, and then helping students to reach new insights. Within a Jewish context in which students are accustomed to studying text, social justice texts offer an accessible and meaningful way of entering the world of activism. Students already committed to Jewish life will be more likely to remember and relate to social justice issues when these appear in the context of a familiar mode of engagement. For those already committed to activism but less involved in Jewish life, studying social jus-tice texts may offer a welcome way to reconnect with Judaism and the broader Jewish community. Social justice texts may also provide a means of spiritual replenishment for those who devote themselves long-term to the high-burnout fields of organizing, social service, and related work. Ultimately, text study can facilitate the creation of a Jewish community committed both to learning and to activism.

The pedagogic approach differs from the "*Tzedek tzedek tirdof* syndrome" by virtue of its genuine desire to understand the texts in question, rather than simply to jump to a justification of the speaker's position on the target issue.

Much of the time, this pedagogic approach to text still allows for only one view of an issue. Educators often present only text that will make participants feel good or that will lead to a predetermined conclusion. Texts that present alternative viewpoints rarely enter the discussion.

TAKING TEXT SERIOUSLY

I propose a third approach to text study, which I classify as "taking text seriously." Taking our texts and our history seriously means engaging in a dialogue between Jewish texts and contemporary issues in which we bring each to bear on our understanding of the other. This demands diving deeply into Jewish civil law and bringing these texts into conversation with real-life experiences and with social science. In some cases, real life may challenge initial readings of text; in other cases, the texts will give new insight into how we understand what happens in our world. In all cases, participants who are open to letting the texts have an impact on them will emerge with a more nuanced outlook on the issue at hand.

Let's take just one example. Conversations about workers' rights in Jewish law generally focus on the halakhic obligations of employers to pay workers on time. These conversations may also include the right of a worker to quit a job in the middle of the day, and the permission—even encouragement—for workers to form unions. It is true that the vast majority of Jewish sources in this area emphasize the need to protect the worker, who risks abuse at the hand of the more powerful employer. However, some texts do take the perspective of the employer. For example, a passage in the *Talmud Yerushalmi* appears to sanction the practice of setting up sweatshops in faraway places. In this text, the Rabbis consider a situation in which two nearby cities, Tiberius and Beit Maon, have two different sets of customs regarding working hours:

> The people of Tiberius did not start work early and did not work late; the people of Beit Maon started work early and worked late. The people of Tiberius who went up to Beit Maon to hire themselves as workers would hire themselves according to the custom of Beit Maon. The people of Beit Maon who came down to Tiberius to hire themselves out would hire themselves according to the custom of Tiberius. However, when one went from Tiberius to hire workers in Beit Maon,

he could say to them, "Do not think that I couldn't find workers to hire in Tiberius. Rather, I came here to hire workers because I heard that you will start work early and work late."

(JT, *Bava Metzia* 7:1)

On its face, this text permits an employer to say, "Why did I bother to set up a factory in China, if not to pay lower wages?" or "Why did I trouble myself to bring nurses from the Philippines, if not so that they would work for less than American nurses?" The owner of a business that outsources to India might hold up this text as Jewish justification for his practices. On the other hand, a committed anti-sweatshop activist might point to this text angrily as evidence that Judaism has nothing worthwhile to say about contemporary labor struggles.

Yet bringing this text into conversation with other Jewish texts and with real-life experiences complicates the picture. Lest one use this source to justify paying poverty wages to residents of other countries, other laws forbid the mistreatment of workers and stipulate that full-time workers should earn enough to support themselves and their families.[2] But before we throw this text out completely in favor of others, we might take a moment to listen to its challenge to those who label outsourcing as an unmitigated evil.

Today's world presents us with no shortage of stories about workers who earn a dollar a day laboring under unsafe conditions to make clothing for the Western market. Some of these workers are children; some get fired for trying to organize a union. Some pay smugglers tens of thousands of dollars only to end up as indentured servants in a foreign country. These abominable practices clearly run afoul of Rabbinic dictates on human dignity and prohibitions against abusing low-wage workers.

However, the contemporary world yields other stories as well. Some families manage to eke out a living on wages paid by American companies. Some village economies depend on the presence of a Western factory. When such a factory departs for a country with even lower labor standards, the newly unemployed workers and their families may find themselves thrust into even more dire poverty.

The response to these latter stories should not be to relax labor standards altogether, nor to ease pressure on companies that operate sweatshops. But neither can the answer be to end outsourcing or to focus on closing individual factories. Instead, we might recognize that different countries do have different standards of living, and so lower salaries might be justified—and even desperately needed—in certain places.

Including the story of Tiberius and Beit Maon in a text study about employers and workers opens space for anti-sweatshop activists, pro-business conservatives, opponents of outsourcing, low-wage workers, and employers of low-wage workers to engage in a collective conversation about the complexities of the global labor market. Presenting a range of texts about any issue allows us to learn from a variety of viewpoints, to clarify our own outlook, and to hear the opinions of people with whom we are accustomed to disagreeing.

TEXTS AND HISTORY

The "history guy" shows up at almost every class I teach. This character, always a different person of course, is usually a man in his sixties or seventies. He has read some amount of ancient and medieval history and is eager to place the texts we are reading in historical context. In the course of our discussion, he raises his hand several times to point out that "back then" the world was different, and so the texts we are reading may not have relevance for our contemporary reality.

As irritating as he can be, the history guy has a point. Placing texts in their original context does help us to understand these texts better. In fact, one of the major contributions of the early Conservative movement in Judaism was the introduction of a mode of study that takes into account the history of text and law.

Looking at the historical context of laws and traditions represents an important step in taking texts seriously. In the next few pages, I will consider how we can bring history to bear on our textual-based discussions of social justice issues.

The first element of this approach involves noticing the ways in which textual variations might reflect the differing concerns of the editors and copiers of sacred texts. For example, a well-known Rabbinic passage (*Mishnah Sanhedrin* 4:5) compares saving a single human being to saving the entire world. There are actually two versions of this text, distinguished by a single word. But this single word makes all the difference. Standard printed editions of the Talmud have the Rabbis declaring, "Anyone who saves a single soul of Israel—it is as though this person has saved an entire world." This statement suggests that Jews have more value than other people and that the Jewish responsibility to preserve life applies only to saving fellow Jews. But the history of this text tells a different story. Most earlier manuscripts render the statement simply, "Anyone who saves a single soul—it is as though this person has saved an entire world." The word *me'yisrael* ("of Israel") appears to be a later addition, inserted by a scribe with more particularistic leanings.

Indeed, within the context of the surrounding text, the universalist version makes more sense. The famous quote regarding saving a single person appears within a discussion about the story of Cain and Abel, the first fratricide in the Torah (Genesis 4:1–8). Through a clever reading of the biblical text, the Rabbis suggest that God holds Cain responsible not only for killing his brother, but also for preventing the birth of the thousands of generations that would have come from Abel's line. Since Cain and Abel were not Jewish, we must conclude that this interpretation assumes the infinite value of *every* life. Thus, in this context, the reading "one who saves a single life" makes the most sense.

Those with universalist leanings might say, "Aha—the Talmud believes that all human beings are created equal." These readers might write off the insertion of the phrase "of Israel" as a mistake. But those with more particularistic leanings might respond, "All lives are important, but the addition of the phrase 'of Israel' was made for a reason: to tell us that Jews have a primary responsibility to care for other Jews." Which reader is right? Perhaps both and neither. The two versions of the text point to an ongoing internal debate about the relative responsibilities of Jews to one another and to the world as a whole. Conversations about this text might consider what circumstances might compel Jews to prioritize service to other Jews and what circumstances might mitigate against the prioritization of Jewish needs.

A historical look at Jewish text also takes into account the real-world issues that provoke changes in *halakhah*. For example, in the medieval period, some European rabbis became lenient about permitting *Ma'ariv*, the evening prayer service, to be recited during daylight hours instead of after sundown, in response to the reality of northern Europe, where the sun does not go down until nine or ten o'clock at night during the summer.[3]

Another example concerns a breast-feeding woman who, on Shabbat, produces more milk than her baby can drink. She may not express her remaining milk, because doing so is considered a form of work prohibited on Shabbat. Instead, the legal authority Mordechai ben Hillel (Germany, 1250–1298, known as the Mordechai) ruled, "If the Jewish woman has too much milk and she is in pain, she is allowed to nurse the child of a non-Jewish woman."[4] Even though Jews are generally forbidden from becoming wet nurses to non-Jewish children (though the reverse is permitted), this woman may feed a neighbor's child in order to relieve her own pain. Anyone who has ever breast-fed can sympathize with this woman's dilemma. Concern for the health and comfort of the woman, presumably combined with a reality in which Jews and non-Jews had fairly close relationships, prompted the Mordechai to change the law (perhaps goaded on by his wife).

These historical insights help us to understand our received texts better. First, a historical perspective humanizes the law. Instead of seeing *halakhah* simply as an intellectual pursuit, we can imagine men obligated to stay at the synagogue until late at night instead of helping to put their children to bed, or women tormented by breast pain on Shabbat. Second, acknowledging that texts have history reminds us that legal texts come out of debates and discussions among human beings. This process of legal inquiry does not end in the medieval period but continues even today. Modern Jews, too, have license to read and interpret received texts within the context of our own cultural milieu. This latter point also grants permission to reinterpret or sometimes to set aside laws and interpretations that clash with our own ethics. For example, traditional laws regarding the position of women assume a world in which women primarily work as caretakers for children and for the home. Laws regarding same-sex relationships fail to understand homosexuality as a biological category. Recognizing that these laws emerged from a specific historical context allows contemporary Jews to change some laws when the historical context changes dramatically, just as ancient and medieval Jews adapted to their own contexts.

Reading texts with a historical lens can be liberating, but it can also be limiting. The history guy who shows up at my teaching sessions most often argues that *nothing* in the texts can be understood outside of its historical context. That is, laws regarding the relations between employers and workers, the distribution of *tzedakah,* or the provision of health care, he says, respond to a specific economic situation and cannot be extrapolated to modern-day affairs.

This approach would essentially shut down Jewish text study as anything but a scholarly, archival endeavor. Rather than searching for personal meaning and relevant wisdom in the sources, we would read these texts only as clues to understanding the issues of the past. But Judaism, like every other legal system, has always looked to the past in order to respond to the present and to plan for the future. We don't act as though we are the first Jews to have had a question about how to behave ethically and religiously in the world. Instead, we look to the deliberations of past generations for guidance in addressing current issues. In studying text, then, we should ask about the historical motivations for the material, but we should also assume that the text has something to teach us now.

When we do encounter text that reflects a different historical reality than our own, we may ask ourselves what value the text is trying to express. For example, few women today would nurse a baby other than her own (though I do know a few who have done so). A woman who feels engorged is more likely to apply hot compresses and take a pain killer. Still, we can read this text not only as a historical artifact, but rather as a glimpse of the possibility for Jewish/non-Jewish relations based on closeness and total trust. In the case of more difficult texts, such as those permitting a father to marry off his underage daughter, reading becomes more difficult. Looking for the value that drives this text may lead to a discussion about the evolving vision of marriage, about ensuring economic protections for women, and about the relationships among parents, children, and in-laws. Even while rejecting the possibility of betrothing a three-year-old, we can learn from the process of discussing these texts the complexities of creating a marital system that meets everyone's needs.

GUIDELINES FOR STUDYING TEXT

When we use text in social justice work, we should seek to respect the wisdom of the texts, find inspiration for our work in the texts, and use the texts as a means of understanding the issue and ourselves better. The following guidelines can help in this endeavor:

1. **Don't use texts to justify preexisting positions.** Approach each text with an openness to discovering what this text might teach us.

2. **Embrace difficult texts.** If we open ourselves to learning something from even the most problematic texts, we may develop more nuanced perspectives even on issues we thought we knew well. In the spirit of the Rabbinic principle *D'rosh v'kabel s'khar*, "Study and receive reward" (BT, *Sanhedrin* 71a), some texts may be studied as a means of sharpening our minds and clarifying our thinking, rather than as practical laws to be applied today.

3. **Bring texts into conversation with one another.** A single text never *proves* what Judaism "says" about one issue or another. Historically, for example, the citation of a single verse or Talmudic quote has served to justify the exclusion of women, gays and lesbians, and others from Jewish life. But examining a broader selection of texts yields a much more complicated picture of gender and of sexual relations. The modern rereading and reinterpretation of these texts has opened space for formerly excluded groups to find a place in Jewish life and communal leadership.

4. **Take stories seriously.** Rabbinic material is generally divided into two categories: *halakhah* (law) and *aggadah* (stories). The Talmud contains both. Amid legal discussion, the Rabbis sometimes launch into a story that confirms, illustrates, or challenges a particular legal position or that brings a note of humanity or humor into the discourse. In traditional yeshivot, students often learn to skip the stories and to focus on the "serious" legal material. But the stories remind us that law is not a theoretical concept, but rather an attempt to create a functional society made up of complex people whose lives make a mess of our neat abstractions. Rabbinic stories

also often allow a glimpse of the experience of women, servants, non-Jews, and others whose voices play less prominent roles in legal discussions but without whom we cannot understand the full implications of the *halakhah*.

Taking stories seriously also means listening to the real-life experiences of people in our own world and bringing these stories into conversation with the texts. In doing so, we should ask how our own experiences or the stories of others confirm, challenge, or shed light on the textual discussions. We should also consider how the texts might help us to make sense of these contemporary narratives. (See chapter 4 for an extensive discussion of using stories for social justice.)

5. **Put politics aside for the moment.** As I mentioned in discussing my experience teaching about labor issues, individuals are often eager to stake out their position on the right, left, or center. Instead, invite participants to put aside these assumptions and engage with the texts on their own terms. Allow room for everyone to share his or her perspectives on these texts. Sometimes the most important points come from the participants who are most difficult to hear.

6. **Let the texts motivate action.** It is easy to get so caught up in the complexities and contradictions of text that we become unable to act. Per the Rabbinic dictum "Study is great, for study leads to action" (BT, *Kiddushin* 30b), our texts should ultimately inspire us to take positions and to act. These positions will by nature not be perfect and will not satisfy everyone. But to be effective, law must operate in the world and not just sit on paper. After communal deliberations about the texts, engagement with real-life stories, and study about proposed solutions to the issue at hand, your community will ultimately need to make a decision about how to act.

Some key questions to elicit thoughtful discussion about texts and current issues include the following:

- What are your emotional reactions to this text? What in the text excites or inspires you? What in the text upsets or offends you?

- What in this text affirms your beliefs? What in this text do you find challenging or perplexing?

- How does this text confirm or challenge the realities that you have seen in the world?

- What concerns or values do you think motivate the authors of this text? What kind of system are they trying to create?

- What new perspectives does this text offer us? Does this text challenge any of our own assumptions?

- Do any of the stories we have heard or observations we have made in our own world challenge the text? How might the text and our experiences speak to or argue with one another?

QUESTIONS FOR CONSIDERATION

1. Have you experienced text study in the context of social justice or service work? How were these texts presented? What effect did this study have on your work? What effect did the work have on your approach to these texts?

2. In what contexts can you imagine bringing text into your community's social justice and service work? What purpose would such text study serve? What would you hope the effect of this study would be?

3. Have you ever experienced text study that connected with your life in a powerful way? In what context? What made this study so successful?

PART THREE

Taking Action

Wₕen I teach teenagers, I often pose the following scenario to them: Imagine that your next-door neighbor loses his or her job. How do you help him or her? The students quickly brainstorm a long list of ideas: they can invite the neighbor over for a meal, lend him or her money, offer to babysit, or even help him or her to find a job.

Then I pose a more difficult question: Imagine that a factory has closed down in your town, and five hundred people are out of work. What do you do now? After a few minutes, the students come up with more suggestions: open a food pantry, start a job training facility, create a microfinance program that will lend money to people for starting small businesses.

Now, the problem gets harder: There is a national or a worldwide economic crisis, and millions of people are out of work and struggling to get by. What do you do? Students have to think longer about this one, but still they come up with answers. At this point, they propose passing legislation that stimulates job creation, making food more affordable, or guaranteeing health care for everyone.

And what about your neighbor? I ask. Has this individual gotten lost in our new drive for long-term economic sustainability? And if we go back to focusing on our single neighbor's needs, will we have time and energy to achieve the bigger changes?

The most important biblical passage on poverty and *tzedakah* attempts to balance immediate needs and long-term solutions. Within the space of a few verses, God both promises to end poverty and predicts that the poor will always be present in society:

> There shall be no needy among you—for Adonai will surely bless you in the land which Adonai your God gives you for an inheritance to possess it if you diligently listen to the voice of Adonai your God and observe and do the commandment that I command you this day.... If there is among you a needy person, one of your brethren, within any of your gates, in your land which Adonai your God gives you, you shall not harden your heart, nor shut your hand from your needy brother; but you shall surely open your hand unto him, and shall surely lend him sufficient for his need in that which he wants.... For the poor will never cease from the land. For this reason, God commands you saying, "You shall surely open your hand to your brother, to the poor and the needy in your land."
>
> (Deuteronomy 15:4–12)

Biblical commentators most often read the apparent contradiction between "there shall be no needy" and "the poor will never cease" as a divine admission of human failure. According to this interpretation, God pledges to eradicate poverty if and only if the Jewish people follow the entire Torah to the letter. However, based on the people's inability to obey divine commands even during the forty years in the wilderness, God assumes that the Jews will never merit the promised end to poverty. Therefore, God pessimistically predicts that "the poor will never cease."

I find this explanation problematic. We assume that God gave the Jews the Torah with the expectation that we would follow its laws, albeit with a few bumps along the road. It hardly seems fair that God would assume from the start that we will never be able to meet these expectations.

Instead, we can read the passage as simultaneously offering two prescriptions for addressing poverty. The text dares us to believe in the possibility of eradicating poverty and to work toward long-term solutions. At the same time, this text demands that we give our attention to the hungry person standing in front of us, right here and now. We cannot provide immediate services with no intention of addressing the big problems that cause the need for those services. And we cannot pursue those big idealistic changes while ignoring the suffering that exists today.

People who choose to engage in social action sometimes begin to see the type of action they are doing as inherently better than the other kinds. This debate can even lead to snobbery among those invested in one mode or another. For example, those devoted to advocacy and organizing for long-term change sometimes dismiss the provision of services as band-aids that only divert attention from systemic issues. Those who work day in and day out to serve meals and staff shelters sometimes regard advocates and organizers as out of touch with the urgent work on the ground.

Instead of falling into the trap of arguing that one response to poverty is always best, I will suggest that a comprehensive approach to ending poverty includes a number of different strategies. In chapters 8–11, I will offer basic definitions of five of these strategies: direct service, advocacy, *tzedakah*, community investment, and organizing. I will discuss the advantages and disadvantages of each and will suggest some approaches to doing each in the most effective way possible. I will also point to how each can be most effective when complemented by other strategies in an integrated way.

8

Direct Service

Direct service aims to meet a person's immediate, short-term needs. Examples of direct service include providing food, shelter, clothing, medical care, or other necessities; cleaning up a disaster zone; helping an individual with a résumé or interviewing skills; or tutoring a child. Most volunteer efforts fall into the category of direct service.

A cursory glance at Jewish texts and historical precedents finds much support for direct service as a means of poverty relief. In interpreting the biblical command to give a poor person "what he or she lacks" (*dei machsoro* [Deuteronomy 15:8]), most legal authorities focus on the provision of immediate needs. For example, Moses Maimonides summarizes the obligation for *tzedakah* as follows:

> The command, without a doubt, is that we should feed the hungry, clothe the naked, and give a bed to those who have no bed, and coverings to those who have no coverings, and marry off the single who are not able to get married, and give a horse to ride to those who are accustomed to ride, as it is explained in the Talmud, that all of this is included in the phrase *dei machsoro*.[1]

Along with a nod to the long-term stability that he expects marriage to bring and the maintenance of dignity for those "accustomed to ride," Maimonides here focuses on the day-to-day survival of those in the most dire straits. Similarly, Rabbi Moshe Sofer (Germany, 1762–1839) ruled that a person is obligated first to give *tzedakah* to those who are starving, and only secondarily to support those with less life-threatening needs.[2]

The Talmudic system of poverty relief also tends to emphasize the alleviation of immediate needs rather than the pursuit of long-term solutions. The Rabbis describe community-appointed *tzedakah* agents traveling door-to-door collecting food and money to be distributed on a daily or weekly basis to those in need of emergency food relief. Agricultural laws mandate that farmers leave for the poor the corners of their fields, as well as any sheaves that are forgotten or dropped along the way. Talmudic stories describe rabbis and their wives inviting the poor home for meals or being reprimanded for failing to do so.[3] Beyond emergency food relief, the category of *g'milut chasadim* (acts of loving-kindness) includes virtually any type of service, whether provided to the wealthy or the poor. Famously, the Rabbis even describe God as undertaking acts of *g'milut chasadim*:

> Rabbi Chama son of Rabbi Chanina said: What does this text mean: "You shall walk after Adonai your God" (Deuteronomy 13:5)? Is it, then, possible for a human being to walk after the divine presence? For has it not been said: "For Adonai your God is a devouring fire" (Deuteronomy 4:24)? Rather, [the meaning is] to walk after the attributes of the Holy One, blessed be God. As God clothes the naked—for it is written: "And Adonai made for Adam and for his wife coats of skin, and clothed them" (Genesis 3:21)—so too you should clothe the naked. The Holy One, blessed be God, visited the sick, for it is written: "And Adonai appeared unto [Abraham] by the oaks of Mamre" [when he was recovering from circumcision] (Genesis 18:1)—so too you should visit the sick. The Holy One, blessed be God, comforted mourners, for it is written: "And it came to pass after the death of Abraham, that God blessed Isaac his son" (Genesis 25:11)—so too you should comfort mourners. The Holy One, blessed be God, buried the dead, for it is written: "And God buried [Moses] in the valley" (Deuteronomy 34:6)—so too you should bury the dead.... Rabbi Simlai expounded: Torah begins with an act of loving-kindness and ends with an act of loving-kindness. It begins with an act of

loving-kindness, for it is written: "And Adonai made for Adam and for his wife coats of skin, and clothed them." And it ends with an act of loving-kindness, for it is written: "And God buried [Moses] in the valley."

(BT, Sotah 14a)

This text describes God engaging in one-time service efforts by providing clothes to the naked first couple, visiting the newly circumcised Abraham, comforting Isaac after the death of his father, and burying Moses. God's actions all correspond to *mitzvot* incumbent on Jews, who are also expected to give *tzedakah*, visit the sick, comfort mourners, and bury the dead in a dignified manner.

Throughout history, Jews have taken seriously the obligation to do direct service of these sorts. Each community has traditionally sponsored a *g'mach* (an acronym for *g'milut chasadim*), which collects and distributes everything from food to clothing to medical supplies. Individuals and groups engage in *bikkur cholim* (visiting the sick). Communities sponsor *chevra kadisha* groups, which tend to the needs of the dead and their families. Today, large Jewish organizations such as Jewish Federations of North America and their associated local Federations support social service agencies that provide food, job counseling, health care, and other services—to both Jews and non-Jews. And most synagogues and schools organize volunteers to serve at soup kitchens, to staff homeless shelters, and to collect food or clothing for distribution to those in need.

STRENGTHS OF DIRECT SERVICE

Direct service has many advantages. First and foremost, the results of this type of work are immediate and concrete. If I serve food at a soup kitchen or tutor a child, I know that someone ate a hot dinner or learned a bit more math as a direct result of my actions. And for some people, this type of direct help will be enough to get them through a difficult period. In some cases, as with visiting homebound seniors or hospital patients, direct service fills a need that even the best legislation could not. No matter how well we fund senior services and health care, there will always be a need for caring individuals to carry out the *mitzvah* of *bikkur cholim* (visiting the sick).

Second, the work ideally lets people from different communities interact in a way that benefits both. The seventh graders at Temple Aliyah in Needham, Massachusetts, volunteer every other week at a local soup kitchen. After each visit, the group spends time reflecting on their experiences. During one of these reflection sessions, one boy commented, "When I was first coming here, I was really nervous and anxious about coming here because it brought me out of my comfort zone, but now it seems so normal to do this."[4] With this comment, the student indicated that his stereotypes about who comes to a soup kitchen have been challenged. Instead of seeing soup kitchen clients as dangerous or scary, he now views them as part of his world. On the flip side, the clients of social service programs may gain a new understanding of Judaism and of the Jewish community. After Hurricane Katrina, I spent significant time organizing programs that brought teens, college students, and adults to volunteer in the Gulf Coast. Over and over, leaders of community organizations there told me, "I used to think that Jews only cared about your own people, but now I see that you care about us too."

From a practical angle, direct service projects are often set up to take volunteers, even ones with only a few hours or a few days to give. It is relatively easy, in the best-run direct service opportunities, for new volunteers to show up, be assigned a task, and contribute a needed service with only minimal guidance. These volunteers feel fulfilled and inspired by the experience. Some projects, such as soup kitchens and home construction projects, readily absorb large numbers of unskilled volunteers for short amounts of time.

In many cases, service projects allow children and teens to participate. Involving children in service can be a powerful way of beginning family conversations about money, privilege, and responsibility. My own daughter is not quite two, but already I worry about her growing up with a sense of entitlement. She has more toys than she needs, full-time daycare, and as much cottage cheese as she can eat. In the future, we will have to negotiate how much allowance she receives, whether she can have the next hot electronic device, and—more seriously—whether to use our knowledge and privilege to get her into a charter school or gifted and talented program. Like many parents, I worry that she will grow up believing that she deserves everything she has. Taking her with me to volunteer will be one means of ingraining a sense of gratitude paired with responsibility toward the world.

Finally, many Jewish institutions also view direct service as "nonpolitical." While it may be difficult to garner support for a piece of legislation or an advocacy campaign, few community members object to direct service projects. I would argue, though, that direct service is deeply political—and, in fact, that this is one of its strongest features. If we spend months and years delivering food, tutoring children, and building houses, we will eventually ask, "Why are wages so low that working people rely on food pantries?" "Why are public school students in low-income areas not learning?" "Why is there such a lack of affordable housing in this country?" Direct contact with the people most affected by this issue can inspire us toward expanding our involvement in the issue.

CHALLENGES TO OVERCOME

Creating powerful and effective direct service programs requires overcoming a few common challenges:

1. Direct service does not necessarily lead to long-term solutions.

2. Service projects can create more work than benefit for the hosts.

3. Volunteer service can be inefficient.

4. Service projects can reinforce rather than break down stereotypes.

5. Volunteers come to believe that service is the entire answer.

1. Direct service does not necessarily lead to long-term solutions.

Every day of the year, thousands of volunteers ladle up bowls of chili, help children with homework, and sort donated clothing. All of this work must then be repeated the next day, and the next day, and the day after that. But these efforts do little to bring an end to poverty. As a result, volunteers may become disillusioned, and beneficiaries of direct service may start to see themselves as stuck in a rut of always relying on outside help.

2. Service projects can create more work than benefit for the hosts.

I often receive phone calls that go something like this: "Our synagogue is looking for a place where fifteen people can volunteer for three hours on a Sunday afternoon." "For my son's bar mitzvah, we made toiletry baskets to use as centerpieces. Do you know of a place where we can donate these?" "Our school would like to take the eighth graders on a weekend trip to rebuild homes in the Gulf Coast. Can you help?"

These questions all stem from good intentions and from the realities of our busy lives. We want to help out when we can. We want to expose our children to people of different backgrounds and financial means. We want to link the bar or bat mitzvah and religious education to a responsibility to the world. Demanding work and school schedules leave us with limited time to volunteer. Sundays are the day when religious school meets and when large groups of synagogue members can get together.

However, our desire to volunteer at specific times and in specific ways often imposes an undue burden on organizations that host us, especially if their capacity is limited by small staffs and rudimentary facilities. In his study of the effect of service learning on small community organizations, researcher Randy Stoeker comments, "I have talked to a group of organizations in another small city who look with dread upon the annual spring ritual when the high schools empty and force all of their students to do community service."[5]

Most service organizations are, unfortunately, ill prepared to accept groups of ten or fifteen volunteers at all, and many are closed on Sundays. Training unskilled volunteers who can only devote a few hours to the cause can result in a net loss of time for the staff of these small organizations. The organizations often feel pressured to please the volunteers, whom they see as potential sources of funding or political support, and therefore create projects such as painting walls or sorting supplies. Volunteers identify these as make-work projects and leave feeling frustrated that they did not contribute more significantly, or even resentful that the host site did not make effective use of their energies and skills. At the same time, organizations begin to view volunteers as a burden rather than a help. As a result, both volunteers and the host organization lose the opportunity for a meaningful and productive encounter. The fault for this situation lies both with the organization and with the volunteers: an organization that wishes to engage volunteers should identify projects suitable for volunteers and then clearly articulate to potential volunteers what will and will not be possible. As discussed in chapter 6, volunteers should begin by asking what would serve the organization well and should also be clear about their own abilities and time constraints.

Sometimes even volunteers who are willing to commit to long-term service begin by thinking about what they can give, rather than what the community needs. A few years ago, I sat down with a rabbi who hoped to open a soup kitchen in her synagogue. She explained to me that synagogue members had identified hunger as the issue most important to them and decided to act on this concern by providing emergency food in their local area. There was only one problem: In the neighborhood where this synagogue stood, there was already a consortium of churches that ran soup kitchens every night of the week. Those in need knew which church to visit each night of the week, and the churches were already able to cover the demand for food. Telling me about this situation, the rabbi concluded, "We don't know when we can do our soup kitchen; every night is already taken!" I suggested that the community might not need a new soup kitchen. Perhaps instead, the synagogue should meet with community groups to learn what needs were going unfulfilled. Or synagogue members could commit to volunteering regularly in one or more of the existing church soup kitchens.

But the rabbi was determined. Her members had decided that they wanted to address hunger by opening a soup kitchen. They had visited a soup kitchen run by a synagogue in another town, and they had been impressed with its impact. They were convinced that their own commitments and good intentions would suffice to guarantee that their work would benefit the community.

In contrast, when students at Columbia University Hillel decided that they wanted to use their new building to serve the neighborhood, they launched a three-month needs assessment process. During this time, students talked with local nonprofits, soup kitchens, the police, and homeless and low-income residents. They learned that the two biggest needs in the neighborhood were for a day care center and a clothing pantry. Because of the cost, time commitment, and licensing issues, a day care center wouldn't be possible.

The students decided to pursue the clothing pantry idea and embarked on another three-month process, during which they toured clothing pantries around the city, interviewed the directors of these pantries, and identified a set of best practices to incorporate into the planning of the Columbia Hillel clothing pantry, which has now operated for more than eight years.[6]

The Torah mandates giving the poor person *dei machsoro asher yechsar lo*, "sufficient for this person's needs, for what the person lacks" (Deuteronomy 15:8). Many of the commentaries on this verse emphasize that it is the poor person, not the giver, who defines what is lacking. Even if this person asks for something that seems unnecessary, the giver must respond to the best of his or her abilities. In one Talmudic story, a formerly wealthy person finds himself down on his luck. In his better-off days, this person had been accustomed to riding on a horse with a servant leading the way. Hillel, one of the most important rabbis of the Talmud, provides this person with a horse—and he himself takes on the role of the servant, even running three miles before the horse (BT, *Ketubot* 67b).

The same page of Talmud reports two more instances in which a poor person seems to demand too much:

> A certain man once came before Rabbi Nechemiah [looking for *tzedakah*].
> "Of what do your meals consist?" [Nechemiah] asked him.
> "Of fatted meat and aged wine," the other replied.
> [Nechemiah asked,] "Will you consent to live with me on lentils?" [The man] lived with him on lentils and died.
> "Alas," said Nechemiah, "for this man whom Nechemiah has killed!"
> On the contrary, he should have said, "Alas for Nechemiah, who has killed this man!"
> However, [the man] should not have gotten used to stuffing himself to such an extent.

> A man once came before Rabba [looking for *tzedakah*].
> "Of what do your meals consist?" he asked him.
> "Of fatted chicken and aged wine," the other replied.
> "Are you not concerned about the burden on the community?" [Rabba] asked him.

He said to him, "Am I eating what is theirs? I am eating [the food] of the All Merciful, for we have learned, 'The eyes of all wait for you, and you give them their food in his time' (Psalm 145:15). Since it does not say 'in *their* time,' but 'in *his* time,' this teaches that the Holy One, Blessed Be God, provides food for each individual in accordance with that person's habits."

Just then, Rabba's sister, who had not seen him for thirteen years, arrived and brought him a fatted chicken and aged wine.

"What chance!" Rabba exclaimed. He said to him, "I apologize to you. Come and eat."

(BT, *Ketubot* 67b)

In each of these situations, a poor person has cultivated expensive habits and asks a benefactor to support him in the manner to which he is accustomed. While the Talmud does criticize these individuals for accustoming themselves to rich food, the text simultaneously reprimands the rabbis who believe themselves to know what the recipient of their *tzedakah* needs.

Similarly, in the discussions of what constitutes a "poverty line" in Jewish law, Rabbinic authorities acknowledge that different people should receive different levels of support. Rabbi Joseph Caro, the author of the *Shulchan Arukh*, the most authoritative code of Jewish law, comments:

Not all places or all people are the same. There are some places where one who does business with a small amount of money can live off of the profit, and there are places where even four times this much would not be enough. Similarly, there are people who are talented at business and succeed in it, and there are people who are not. Also, there are people who have few needs and are happy with very little, and people who need more.

These Rabbinic conversations caution against making assumptions about what any individual needs. While the Rabbis do not encourage the poor (or the wealthy, for that matter) to cultivate wasteful habits, Jewish law allows recipients of *tzedakah* a great deal of latitude in determining their own individual needs and wants. Rather than cast the poor in the role of passive recipients who gratefully accept the handouts of the wealthy, Judaism insists on the dignity of even the poorest person. This demand to honor the agency of the poor reminds us to begin by asking what the potential recipient needs and wants, rather than by asking what we would like to give.

3. Volunteer service can be inefficient.

When a massive earthquake devastated Haiti in 2010, people around the world responded by sending millions of dollars, as well as medical personnel, search and rescue teams, and skilled construction workers. These resources were crucial in saving lives and preventing further catastrophe.

The organizations working in Haiti put out a plea for those without specialized skills to send money and stay home. But some people wanted to get more directly involved. The *New York Times* described one Brooklyn store that collected canned goods, ramen noodles, and bottled water, and sent a delegation of twenty-five New Yorkers to fly these items to the Dominican Republic for ground transport into Haiti.[7] In an op-ed for the Jewish Telegraphic Agency, one young Jewish man with no discernible disaster-relief skills bragged of hitchhiking across the border into Haiti and then begging the Israeli medical delegation there to take him on as a volunteer.[8] On the one hand, I understand his desire to be there, to see what was happening, and to have a direct effect on people's lives. Sending money can sometimes feel too impersonal. Yet, in a major natural disaster, what was most needed was money and trained experts, not well-meaning but unskilled volunteers or bulky consumer goods. These are extreme examples. But on a regular basis, churches, synagogues, and schools collect cans and dry goods to donate to shelters and soup kitchens. We collect school supplies for children in Israel, Africa, and elsewhere and then recruit travelers to schlep these notebooks and pencils halfway across the world.

In an interview with the *New York Times*, Pastor Ann Kansfield, who runs a food pantry in Brooklyn, described the frustrations of dealing with well-meaning food donations:

> "While the good deeds people want to do are heavenly, the inadvertent waste and the wasted money—they're of the devil," she said. Instead of

collecting food, she urges those who ask: please collect money, and then give it to her food pantry for things she really needs (like garbage bags and a new sink) or to the Food Bank.[9]

In the worst-case scenario, the recipient organizations end up with cast-off cans of mandarin oranges, packages of stale matzah, and drink mixers. At best, members intentionally buy cans of beans, tuna, baby cereal, and other more useful items. Still, for the same dollar amount, social service agencies could purchase far more of the same items in bulk. Instead of sending school supplies across the world, we could buy the same supplies for less in the target country and support the local economy to boot.

A few years ago, I brought a group of seventh and eighth graders on a service learning trip to New Iberia, Louisiana. Working as hard as middle school students can, the twenty of them spent a full day priming a house that had been rebuilt after Hurricane Rita. After a day of painting, the students met with the director of the community organization hosting us. She asked the students what they had learned so far. One twelve-year-old boy raised his hand and said, "I've learned how much can be done without money. We just painted a house for free." The director questioned his assumption. "Without money?" she asked. "Do you think that the staff with you is getting paid? Am I getting paid to be here? Are our volunteer coordinators getting paid? Were your airplane tickets free? Is your food free?" After some discussion, we worked out that the cost of the twenty preteens' labor had been roughly thirty thousand dollars, which was enough to have hired a professional crew for the same amount of time to do much faster work.

The students got it. They understood that we had not taken them to Louisiana because we thought that the most efficient way to paint a house would be to import Jewish preteens from New York. Instead, the goal of the program was to educate and empower them to become responsible citizens. Back home at their synagogue, the students raised money for the community we had visited, spoke about their trip to the congregation during Shabbat services, and set up a meeting with their congressperson to voice support for increased federal funding for the Gulf Coast.

In some cases, service *can* be the most efficient means of providing services. When volunteers offer professional-level skills, meet an expressed need of the organization, and make a long-term commitment, volunteers can save organizations time and money. But when volunteers take up more of the organization's time than they save, and when volunteers focus more on what they want to give than on what the organization needs, the best-intentioned plans can lead to waste and can sap small organizations of time and other resources.

To be sure, there are still good educational reasons to do service in less than efficient ways. For children, dropping off a can may lead to a more concrete understanding of hunger than watching their parents write a check. Taking groups of students to do service work on the Gulf Coast or at sites in the developing world represents an investment in creating a generation of young people who have seen injustice firsthand, and who therefore commit themselves to advocacy, *tzedakah*, and ongoing service. For their part, community organizations often understand their mission to include educating others. According to one representative of a community organization involved with service learning:

> Just because a service learner comes here today and doesn't set the world on fire doesn't mean that the information they gained, the education they gain here, doesn't change them dramatically ten years from now or fifteen years from now. So, in some sense, we have to take a longer view of our role. Frankly, if we were going to look at what a service learner gives us, or gives our clients, we would never do this. There's more to it than that ... because someone's got to be doing this work twenty years from now.[10]

In each case, the groups bringing volunteers and those accepting volunteers must clarify whether the primary goal of the experience will be service or education. If both parties are most interested in having an impact on the issue at hand, then the two should identify a project that meets a real need and that volunteers can do efficiently, with the recipient organization devoting as little time as possible to managing and supervising volunteers or sorting donations. If the parties agree to prioritize education over more concrete contributions, then the two groups should agree on the expected outcomes of the program (including whether the volunteers will be expected to donate or collect money, or assume an advocacy role), and on the amount of time that each side will devote to the volunteer effort.

IS YOUR PROGRAM MORE ABOUT SERVICE OR EDUCATION?

Some service programs meet a real need for the community. Others primarily teach volunteers about an issue. Either goal can be an acceptable one, as long as both you and the service partner are clear about what you are doing and why. Here are a few questions to ask yourselves when figuring out what category your own programs fall into:

- Does this program meet an articulated need of the service partner?
- Could this work be done more efficiently in some other way?
- What do we hope that our members/students will learn from this experience? What do we hope they will do afterwards?

If your program aims first to educate and only second to offer needed service, be clear about this aim with both volunteers and the service partner. You should also make sure to structure in time for learning about the issue, reflecting on the experience, and discussing how to follow up on the issue at hand. Service learning of this kind should inspire volunteers to do even more.

4. Service projects can reinforce rather than break down stereotypes.

Picture this situation: A group of seventh graders spends an evening volunteering at the local soup kitchen. Most of the students are white, and most of the soup kitchen clients are African American. In the course of the evening, not a single person—neither from the school nor from the soup kitchen—mentions race. On the way home, one of the students comments, "It felt really good to help people who can't help themselves."

Another situation, true-life story: In the course of a service learning program in the Gulf Coast, a college student commented to me, "It's amazing— two days ago, I had never shingled a roof before, and now I'm an expert!" He continued, "We should come back and start a job-training program to teach people who live here to shingle roofs." I was thrilled that this student felt so empowered by his experience. And I appreciated his thinking about long-term solutions to joblessness and rebuilding. But his comments, like those of the student who wants to "help people who can't help themselves," are typical of the way that many upper-middle-class people think of service. Many people in this income bracket assume that their own education, privilege, and wealth automatically confer on them the ability and expertise to help communities with less formal education, privilege, or wealth. These eager volunteers perceive the communities being "helped" as pure recipients, with little of their own to contribute or teach. The student who boasted to me about his shingling skills had a week available to volunteer and the money to fly to Biloxi, but his Ivy League pedigree added nothing to his roofing abilities. The suggestion that he and his friends would be well suited to start a job-training program in the Gulf ignored the reality that thousands of Gulf residents were more qualified builders than he and would be happy to work if jobs were available. Instead, the rebuilding process has been plagued by insufficient government funding; battles among state, local, and federal government agencies; corruption on the part of contractors; and the import of low-wage migrant workers, who often have received illegal wages or even no wages at all.

Our service work often reinforces the stereotype that low-income people of color must be the recipients of service and that better-off and predominantly white communities should be the providers of such service. In fact, people with less money demonstrate extraordinary levels of volunteerism.[11] Much of this volunteering happens through church ministries or in less formally structured ways, often through quiet assistance to neighbors and friends. The unidirectional model of service contributes to racism, classism, and other forms of prejudice by reinforcing the idea that people with less money and people of color cannot care for themselves or make decisions for themselves. Sometimes, this model of service even prevents communities from receiving the aid they actually need. As discussed above, people from upper-middle-class backgrounds easily assume that they know what lower-income people need, and they often plunge into giving without first taking the time to learn about the resources and needs of the target community.

Yet a Rabbinic maxim teaches: "More than the wealthy person does for the poor, the poor person does for the wealthy" (*Vayikra Rabbah* 34:9). In one Rabbinic story, a poor person asks two rabbis for *tzedakah* by saying, "Acquire merit through me" (JT, *Pe'ah* 8:9). In other words, the poor man does not ask the rabbis to feel bad for him, or to act altruistically; instead, he effectively says, "I'm prepared to do you the favor of getting credit for a *mitzvah*. All you have to do is give me a few coins."

This Rabbinic teaching challenges us to view service as a two-way relationship, rather than a one-way gift from above. When those who do service take time to listen to the experiences and wisdom of their partners, to meet low-income people who are working to transform their own communities, and to support efforts initiated by and led by these communities, these encounters create the opportunity for learning and long-term change. But when upper-middle-class communities simply drop in to "help," such service may meet a short-term material need but lead to even more deeply entrenched misunderstandings or prejudices—on both sides—in the long run.

Some of the service projects we undertake reinforce stereotypes in another way—by communicating that it would be too dangerous or complicated to actually meet the people we are trying to help. When we make sandwiches without seeing where these sandwiches are going, or collect food and other items without learning about the recipients, we inadvertently reinforce the separation between our own community and others.

Even when we do pursue collections that meet a defined need, we can also turn these collections into opportunities for learning. At Temple Isaiah in Los Angeles, bar and bat mitzvah students used to regularly fulfill their required ten hours of service by setting up bins to collect various materials for local social service providers. Rabbi Dara Frimmer, the associate rabbi, worried that students were neither learning nor contributing meaningfully through these collections. She instituted a new policy: Any student who wanted to do a collection for his or her bar/bat mitzvah project must meet with her to discuss the issue that the student hoped to address and to talk about whether and how the collection would address this issue. Then, the student must spend his or her service hours sitting in front of the bin during a time when many people come in and out of the synagogue, and talk with passersby about why he or she cares about the issue and about the organization that will receive the donations. The synagogue also limited collections to three at a time.

Through this approach, the collections (which have dropped in frequency since the implementation of the new policy) become an opportunity for learning. Instead of simply collecting cans of food for a shelter, the student enters into a conversation about why he or she cares about the issue, what factors have led to the issue, and about how to bring about change. Rabbi Frimmer and her community hope that students will become even more passionate about the issue they have chosen, will ultimately engage directly with people facing this issue, and will continue to work on the issue long after their ten hours of service have been completed.

5. Volunteers come to believe that service is the entire answer.

Think back to the twelve-year-old service participant who was so delighted to learn how much can be accomplished "without money." If this student had not come to terms with the real financial costs of his service trip, he might have concluded that the way to repair the Gulf Coast would be to send even more short-term volunteers there. But no matter how many volunteers devote weeks, or even years, to service, this hodgepodge effort can never fully address the issues of low-income communities.

Ideally, service alerts us to the need for large-scale change in our society. Youth volunteers returning home from working on the Gulf Coast, for example, may be moved to lobby for increased government funding for rebuilding efforts. But when participants report simply that they feel good about having helped or that they have learned the importance of service, the wrong message may have gotten across. To think back to Deuteronomy 15: while service may serve as a temporary fix for the "needy person ... within your gates," direct service will never lead to a world in which "there shall be no needy."

MAKING OUR SERVICE WORK COUNT

In this chapter, I have identified some of service's wonderful strengths and advantages as a mode of addressing injustice and suffering. I have also discussed several challenges and pitfalls that can prevent service work from reaching its potential. Here are a few principles that can help us to ensure that our service is meaningful both to the volunteers and to the partner organization and that this service moves us a bit closer to the vision of a world without poverty:

1. **Listen to communal needs.** The institution supplying the volunteers should begin by forging partnerships with community organizations and asking about the needs of these organizations and the communities of which they are a part. If the volunteers can meet these needs, you have a good match; if not, it's better to be honest about what you can or cannot do, rather than risk disappointing one side or the other.

2. **Respond to the passions of the volunteers.** Once you have gone through a process of storytelling and of identifying the passions of your community (as described in chapter 4), look for service opportunities that respond to these passions. Even if you have not undergone a storytelling process, ask volunteers to articulate why they are interested in the issue, what they hope to gain from the service experience, and how they expect this experience to affect their own lives.

3. **Have clear expectations.** The volunteers and the partner organization should agree at the beginning of the relationship about the time commitment, skills needed, and training required for the project.

4. **Be honest with volunteers.** The institution and the volunteers should have clear shared expectations about what will happen during the program. If the volunteers expect to build houses but end up doing clean-up work, they may be upset unless they are prepared for the possibility that the work will change.

5. **Look at the bigger picture.** The service work should be an opportunity for education about the causes of the issue at hand, about

Jewish perspectives on the issue, and about the ways that race, class, and other power relations affect social problems.[12]

6. **Use service as a step toward systemic change.** The service work should inspire a longer-term commitment to the issue. In the context of the service work, talk about what else you can do to make change in this area, and craft a plan for making this change. In the next few chapters, I will talk about making change through money, advocacy, and organizing.

7. **Make service commitments for the long run.** The model of synagogue and school volunteer projects is often "mitzvah days" or one-time programs. Instead, make a long-term commitment to provide volunteers every week or every month. If the same people can't volunteer every week, create a rotation system. Remember also that some volunteer efforts—such as sorting food at a food pantry or collating mailings—may work well for one-time or periodic volunteers. Projects that build relationships, such as tutoring, may demand a yearlong commitment on the part of each participant—but the rewards are great. Volunteers and service clients get to know each other; volunteers have the opportunity to learn and to reflect on their work; and volunteers can develop new skills, make mistakes, and try again.

9

Giving and Investing Money

Few of us enjoy talking about money. We may be embarrassed about how much or little we earn; we may struggle to make ends meet; we may worry about who has more or less than we do.

But money is not inherently evil. Money enables us to feed our families, to enjoy art and music, to study, and to travel to interesting places. And money can even transform the world.

In this chapter, I will consider how we can use money to advance our social justice goals. I will offer some strategies for giving and investing money, either as individuals or as institutions.

First, let's talk about our ambivalence about money. This ambivalence is not particular to the modern world. Even the ancient Rabbis wondered whether money should exist at all. An ancient Rabbinic story teaches that God originally considered not creating gold.[1] After all, thought God, gold would only drive human beings to greed, theft, and conflict. But in the end, God decided to create gold for use in building the Temple in Jerusalem and of the *mishkan*—the sacred tabernacle that the Israelites built to serve God during their forty-year journey through the wilderness.

As this midrash points out, money used inappropriately can lead to conflict, corruption, and oppression. But used ethically, money has the potential to heal, to lift individuals and societies out of poverty, and even to create a more holy world.

Recalibrating our society's attitudes toward money starts with a countercultural assumption: the money does not belong to us; we are only its stewards. This is a hard concept to swallow. The American culture of overconsumption begins with the assumption that if we work hard and succeed, we have every right to spend every penny we earn. "I deserve this," we tell ourselves, as we buy a fancier car, a bigger house, or an elaborate vacation. "After all, it's my money."

In the *Arukh HaShulchan*, a nineteenth-century legal code, Rabbi Yechiel Epstein (Russia, 1829–1908) comments, "One should not say, 'How can I take away from my own money to give to the poor?' For this person should know that the money is not his own, but rather is a *pikadon* [a deposit left for safekeeping] in his hand in order that he may do the will of the one who left it. And [God's] will is that the person should give *tzedakah*."[2] With this statement, Epstein challenges us to rethink our relationship with our bank account. Instead of asking ourselves, "How should I use my money?" he demands that we ask, "How can I best steward the money that God has entrusted to my care?"

I should say from the outset that Judaism is not an ascetic tradition. Religious people—even rabbis—do not take vows of poverty or celibacy. Judaism responds to physical pleasure—whether food, sex, or money—by sanctifying, not forbidding. Rather than ban such pleasures, Jewish law prescribes blessings for enjoying food, nature, and even sex in holy and sometimes restricted ways. These blessings remind us to be grateful for such pleasures and help us to elevate such pleasures from the realm of the physical to the realm of the sacred.

But this appreciation for the pleasures of the world stops short of giving in completely to physical desires. If I live a traditional Jewish life, I can enjoy good food as long as it is kosher. I may have sex but only within the context of a monogamous and committed relationship (which, in my interpretation of Jewish law, includes both heterosexual and homosexual relationships). Such restrictions remind me that these pleasures come from God, who generously shares the divine world with humanity.

Similarly, Jewish text and tradition remind us again and again that money and property ultimately belong to God. Most strikingly, in chapter 25 of Leviticus, God repeats over and over that "the land is Mine." The Israelites, to whom God has promised the Land of Israel, will never be more than sojourners there. God retains the right to expel the people if they misbehave. As a reminder of God's ultimate ownership, the people must allow the land to lie fallow for one year out of seven.

As with land, so with money: Jews are expected to set aside between one-tenth and one-fifth of their earnings for support of the poor. This practice finds biblical precedent in the patriarch Jacob's declaration to God, "All that you give me, I will set aside a tenth for you" (Genesis 28:22).

Consistently putting aside at least a tenth of our salary acknowledges that the money belongs to God, who has endowed human beings with the responsibility of distributing this money appropriately. By distributing our money in this way, we also recognize that our success results in part from the efforts and sacrifices of others, including the people who make and serve our food, sew our clothing, clean our offices, and perform other often unnoticed jobs. In the next few pages, we will consider tzedakah and community investment loans—two means of enacting social change through money.

TZEDAKAH

Jewish institutions honor philanthropy with plaques, dinners, and awards. In speeches and written tributes, we praise these donors for their generosity. But traditional Jewish texts rarely relate to *tzedakah* as an expression of "generosity"—that is, as a voluntary act reflecting one's extraordinary personal character. Instead, Judaism constructs *tzedakah* as more like a tax than a gift. The Talmud even describes pairs of community-appointed collectors visiting each household to assess its wealth and thus its *tzedakah* obligation. According to traditional Jewish law, individuals may be forced to give *tzedakah* according to their financial abilities, just as people have long been forced to pay taxes according to their yearly income.[3]

The Talmud mandates that *tzedakah* collection be done by two people, as no single person may exercise such authority over the populace. Decisions about how to distribute *tzedakah*, however, should be made by three people, as three constitutes a court eligible to decide financial cases (BT, *Bava Batra* 8b).[4] But why does the Talmud not require a civil court also to collect *tzedakah*? Ordinarily, only such a court has the authority to force one person to pay another. Rabbenu Tam, a medieval legal authority, explains that "the amount that each person should give is known."[5] In this system, *tzedakah* obligations are a matter of public record and are not left to the whim or the generosity of the individual or the persuasiveness of the fundraiser. Those who give the requisite amount are no more praised for being generous than I am praised for my generous donations to the federal government each April.

So what does the word *tzedakah* actually mean? This term comes from the word *tzedek*, meaning "justice." In the Bible, *tzedakah* refers to an individual act of justice or righteousness. That is, *tzedek* is the broad vision of justice, whereas *tzedakah* refers to any act that manifests a commitment to this vision. In later Jewish texts, *tzedakah* begins to refer more specifically to money or other material goods given to alleviate poverty. Still, built into Jewish law is the understanding that giving money to the poor should be a means of restoring the justice of the world.

Whereas the English word "philanthropy" can refer to money donated to any organization, *tzedakah* refers specifically to money or other material goods used to help the poor. Thus, money given to an organization not at all involved with poverty relief—such as a museum or an animal rights organization—may be philanthropy, but it does not constitute *tzedakah*. To be sure, there's plenty of gray area within this definition. For example, some museums, orchestras, and dance troupes bring art education into low-income neighborhoods. Large, wealthy universities use most of their money for facilities and salaries, but they also provide financial aid and do research that may result in an end to certain kinds of suffering. Synagogues primarily devote their budgets to salaries, programs, and building maintenance, but they may also offer quiet support to members in distress.

Jewish law includes numerous lively debates about whether donations to synagogues, books purchased for public and private use, and money devoted to other *mitzvot* constitute *tzedakah*. Most authorities conclude that *tzedakah* money must benefit the poor in some way, though this benefit may come through books intended for public use or through the sponsorship of weddings or *brit milah* celebrations for those who could not otherwise afford such events.[6] Reasonable people can disagree on whether any particular contribution addresses poverty. However, we should begin with the intention that the money we set aside for *tzedakah* will help to alleviate poverty and the suffering of poor people. The details of how best to do that can then be up for debate.

APPROACHES TO *TZEDAKAH*

A community can integrate *tzedakah* into its social justice plan in a number of profound and engaging ways. Individuals may discuss their *tzedakah* decisions in community or organize a collective fund to be distributed by the community as a whole. It is rare for individuals to talk with one another about where and how much they give or even how they make those decisions. Sometimes, even the people closest to one another have not had these conversations. I once taught a class on *tzedakah* choices at a large synagogue. At the beginning of the session, I asked the group to divide into pairs and to share with one another the major factors that influence their *tzedakah* decisions. I suggested that participants work with someone other than their spouses in order to hear a new perspective on these issues. A few members of the group protested: "I want to hear what my husband/wife thinks," they exclaimed. "We've never talked about this!"

Bear Stearns, the now-defunct investment bank, used to mandate that the top thousand earners donate 4 percent of their salaries to charity. Some of these executives reported that this forced giving encouraged them to talk more about their contributions among their peers at the company. According to a *New York Times* story about this policy, "[One employee] said the rule created an open dialogue about giving. Before she came to the bank, she worked at another financial company, and she said she never discussed giving with her fellow workers. It would have been awkward, she said, because she would not have known for sure if people gave."[7] The bank's policy lifted the taboo against talking about giving and allowed employees to talk out their questions and to learn from one another's experience.

In a synagogue or JCC setting, members might gather to study Jewish texts about *tzedakah* and have frank conversations about how to make decisions about giving. In a school or youth group, students might discuss how to allocate money that they receive as bar/bat mitzvah presents or as allowances. These conversations will enable participants to explore their own questions about giving, learn how others think about giving, and potentially even challenge one another to give more or to revise their list of recipients.

Some communities also form giving circles, in which each member commits to donate a certain amount of money to the collective pot. Members then propose potential recipients of these collective funds and debate how best to distribute the money.

Such a *tzedakah* collective should begin by building trust among members. Money tends to inflame passions. Even among a close group of friends, the challenge of sharing and distributing money can easily lead to fighting. Members can establish this trust by sharing stories and speaking openly about their feelings toward and history with money and giving. Other options are to study texts about money together and to begin and end meetings with a *kavvanah* (intention) or prayer.

QUESTIONS TO ASK IN ESTABLISHING A GIVING COLLECTIVE

Before collecting even a penny, your giving collective should grapple with the following questions, which will determine your collection and donation processes:

- How much is everyone expected to give? Should each member give a fixed amount (either a set dollar figure or a certain percentage of income), or should each member give whatever he or she chooses to give?
- How much are members expected to divulge about their finances and giving patterns? Should each member's gift be public information (within the group), or will members give anonymously? Do members have the same voting privileges regardless of the size of their gifts, or will those who give more have a greater say?

- Where will the money live? Will you place the money in a donor-advised fund or in a bank account that is cosigned by two or more members of the group?
- Will you have a specific area of focus, or can your money go to any cause? How many organizations will you support? Will all of the money go to one place, or will it be divided among several groups? What characteristics will you look for in the groups that you support? What standards will you set?
- How will you research and choose organizations? Will each person be responsible for researching and presenting organizations, or will you assign teams of people to issue areas?
- What about members' "pet" organizations? Will you consider gifts to organizations for which members of the group work or serve as board members?
- Should the giving tie into the service, advocacy, or learning projects in which the institution is engaged?
- How often will you give? Once a quarter? Twice a year? Once a year?
- Are members who are unhappy with one of the organizations that the group selects allowed to divert their money away from the gift to that organization?

Once you have arrived at shared responses to these questions, you will be ready to discuss potential grantees.

COMMUNITY INVESTMENT

Community investment refers to the practice of lending money to individuals or organizations who are working to develop a sustainable local economy. Examples include loans to affordable housing developers, microloans to individuals who are starting small businesses, and investments in community banks that lend in turn to underserved communities for similar purposes. Jewish law views loans as an essential component of *tzedakah*. Famously, Moses Maimonides (known as the Rambam) classifies loans among the highest forms of *tzedakah*. Many Jewish legal scholars even consider loans to be obligatory. This obligation stems from the Torah, which instructs, "If you lend money to my people, to the poor among you, do not act toward them as a creditor; exact no interest from them" (Exodus 22:24). A simple reading of this biblical verse suggests that the decision whether to lend money is left to each individual. The Rabbis, though, refuse to leave the decision about whether to lend money to the whims of the individual: "Rabbi Yishmael said: Every 'if' in Torah is optional, other than this one" (*Midrash Mekhilta Masekhta D'Kaspa* 19). In the sixteenth century, Joseph Caro codified this principle in the *Shulchan Arukh*, which became widely considered the most authoritative volume on Jewish law. There, he unequivocally declares that "it is a positive commandment to lend to a poor Jew, and this is a greater *mitzvah* than *tzedakah*" (*Choshen Mishpat* 97:1). The move to shift (interest-free) lending from the apparently optional act described in the Torah to a compulsory commandment responds to two dynamics: the unwillingness of many wealthy people to part with their money, even temporarily, and the necessity of loans to help the poor accumulate capital and survive difficult periods.

The Rabbis considered loans to be so crucial that they even dared to undermine biblical law in order to keep the system of lending and borrowing constant. The primary biblical text about poverty threatens divine punishment for those who refuse to lend money in the time leading up to the *sh'mittah* year (the sabbatical year occurring once every seven years), when all loans would have to be forgiven. Yet by the first century CE, Hillel, one of the most important rabbis of the time, noticed that individuals were ignoring the biblical caution and holding back on loans in the year before *sh'mittah*. In response, Hillel instituted *prosbul*, a roundabout means of allowing loans to be repaid, even after the *sh'mittah* year. Through *prosbul*, a court takes possession of the loan prior to *sh'mittah*. Since debt forgiveness applies only to private loans, the court can maintain and collect on the loan and then transfer the money to the original lender.

In the short term, *prosbul* undermines the biblical demand that loans be forgiven every seven years. By canceling this biblical obligation, Hillel risked condemning the poor to lifelong debt. In the long run, this arrangement benefits both lender and borrower: the lender can rest assured that the money will be repaid, and the borrower has access to credit even in the year before *sh'mittah*. Was Hillel right to institute this legal work-around? Or should he have found some way to force the wealthy to comply with the biblical expectation of debt relief? Either way, the possibility remains that the poor would have ended up unable to borrow the capital they need to get back on their feet. Hillel's caution about preserving a functional lending system reverberated during the recession that started in 2007, when banks stopped trusting one another, withheld loans, and caused an international crisis because credit was no longer available.

Jewish law assumes that loans are lent by the wealthy to the poor. A person who has experienced crop failure or who simply needs a bit of help getting through a tough period might prefer the dignity of taking out a loan over the potential embarrassment of accepting *tzedakah*.

But in the modern world, the wealthy most often lend to the wealthy. Most loans take place at the level of bank-to-bank transactions. Even at the level of loans to individuals for a mortgage or a small business, borrowers must already have some degree of wealth. They must demonstrate both a credit history and some means of paying back the loan. There is wisdom in this approach: the housing crisis that set off the global financial collapse of 2008 resulted, in part, from individuals taking out loans larger than they could repay and from lenders ignoring evidence of borrowers' inability to pay.

But if banks will not lend to people without a significant credit history, then it becomes difficult for low-income individuals who dream of starting small businesses or investing in their first home to get the credit they need to do so. Rather than pulling themselves out of poverty by accumulating capital and a means of income, these people may remain reliant on charity, government programs, and low-wage jobs for the rest of their lives.

Often the only loans available to low-income people are predatory and exploitative. People who function without bank accounts pay high prices for services that bank customers get for free. For example, these individuals may use check-cashing services that generally charge fees of 2 to 4 percent for a service that comes free to bank customers. One study has found that these fees may add up to forty thousand dollars in fees over a customer's working life.[8] They may also fall into the traps of high-interest payday loans or "instant refunds." Payday loans allow individuals to take out small loans, with the expectation of paying these back when they receive their paychecks. These loans can carry interest fees of 400 percent or more.[9] As of 2010, fifteen states had instituted laws banning payday loans or capping fees at rates intended to cut off payday loans altogether. In 2006, Congress instituted a law that capped payday loans to military personnel at 36 percent.[10]

Such predatory loans are a living example of what the Torah terms *neshekh*, "usury." One Rabbinic text notices that this biblical term comes from the root meaning "to bite":

> To what is *neshekh* compared? To a person who is bitten by a snake, but does not feel the bite until the swelling begins. Similarly, in the case of *neshekh*, a person doesn't feel it until the swelling begins.
>
> (*Sh'mot Rabbah* 31:5–6)

Like a snakebite, a high interest rate may not be immediately noticeable. A person desperate for a few extra dollars to pay the rent or to buy groceries for the rest of the month may neglect to read the small print or simply hope that he or she will somehow manage to repay the loan. But a few weeks or years later, the small print comes back to "bite," as the borrower struggles to pay hundreds or thousands of dollars in interest on what started as a small loan.

Community development financial institutions (CDFIs) provide an antidote to this untenable situation. As a general term, CDFIs include community banks, credit unions, and other financial institutions that operate in neighborhoods or with constituencies traditionally underserved by larger financial institutions. While these banks make a profit, their primary mission is the economic development of the neighborhood or the group. Therefore, these banks charge low interest fees and work with clients to create payback plans that minimize rates of foreclosure or default. Many CDFIs offer financial literacy classes, and some even offer financial incentives to first-time account owners, such as matching every dollar saved. In addition, these institutions may provide home and car mortgages and small business loans. Some larger CDFIs also invest in bigger projects such as the development of affordable housing, social service facilities, or other community infrastructure.

Surprisingly, CDFIs boast a lower default rate on loans than do traditional banks, even though these community-based institutions work with a higher percentage of low-income borrowers. This low default rate stems, in part, from regulatory differences that prevent CDFIs from engaging in some of the high-risk behavior that led to the 2008 housing collapse. Beyond this safeguard, the staff of CDFIs develop relationships with borrowers, prevent clients from taking out excessive loans, and work with borrowers to create repayment plans that will avert foreclosure.

APPROACHES TO COMMUNITY INVESTMENT

Jewish Funds for Justice (through a program initiated by the Shefa Fund prior to its merger with Jewish Fund for Justice), offers a major program that helps individuals and institutions to invest in these ways. There are many ways for individuals and institutions to support community investment. Some synagogues, such as the Society for the Advancement of Judaism in Manhattan, have pooled funds for community investment. Some Jewish organizations, including the Union for Reform Judaism, place a percentage of their investments in CDFIs. In the Christian world, a number of denominations invest large portions of their endowments and pension funds in community development funds or community banks, often through participation in the Interfaith Center for Corporate Responsibility. Individuals may choose also to put their personal money in a community bank or to invest in community investment through Jewish Funds for Justice, Calvert, or a local CDFI.

Investing in this way involves little risk, but the rewards may be greater than we imagine. Rabbi Israel Meir Kahan, better known as the Chofetz Chaim (Poland, 1838–1933), offered the following reflection in his treatise on loans and *tzedakah*:

> When someone comes to you with a request for assistance, as far as the borrower is concerned, the transaction is a minor one. Through this

transaction, the borrower will gain a few pieces of silver. But for you, the lender, the one who performs the kindness, behold: what has been presented to you is something major—a chance to perform a positive commandment of the Torah, for which there is no end to the reward. You should have rejoiced. You should have received this person with excitement. You should have run after this *mitzvah* if God has helped you such that you have the power to do such kindnesses. As it says, "One who runs after righteousness and mercy finds life, prosperity, and honor" (Proverbs 21:21).[11]

The boards and budget committees of Jewish institutions are charged with taking good care of the fiscal resources of these institutions. This responsibility entails creating balanced budgets, living within the organization's means, and planning for the future. As I suggested in chapter 5, the budget should also reflect the values of the institution. Devoting some of the institution's resources to community investment is one way to serve two purposes at once: to take good care of investments, while also marshaling these investments toward relieving poverty.

10
Advocacy

Advocacy refers to an effort to create long-term change by influencing the policy makers. Examples of advocacy include lobbying an elected official to vote yes or no on a bill, bringing a class action lawsuit that will result in a change of law, holding a city agency accountable for enforcing existing statutes, or even persuading the synagogue board to institute a policy requiring providing health care for all employees.

Are there parallels to advocacy in traditional Jewish sources? On the surface, Jewish texts about poverty and inequity generally speak explicitly about providing direct services to those in need. But implicitly, these texts often recognize that only a policy change will have a major impact on society as a whole. In fact, much of the change in *halakhah* (Jewish law) takes place when an ordinary person persuades a rabbi—the authority figure in this context—to change a law that has negative consequences.

In our discussion of storytelling in chapter 4, we looked at the case of the daughters of Tzelophechad, who ask Moses to change the laws of inheritance in order to enable women to inherit their fathers' property. These five women, who have little official power, harness the power of their story and their skill for argument. Moses decides to approach God—the ultimate power—with their dilemma. God hears the women's story and mandates a change in the law.

Since the early medieval period, rabbis have interpreted, applied, and even transformed Jewish law through *teshuvot* (rabbinic opinions, known in English as responsa). *Teshuvot* can touch on any area of human activity, ranging from end-of-life decisions to Shabbat observance to criminal justice. An individual or a community struggling with a particular question might turn to a trusted rabbi to write a *teshuvah* on the matter. In some cases, the question concerns an issue not addressed by earlier legal literature, such as acceptable use of a new technology. In other cases, the person or group seeks a reinterpretation of the law in response to a contemporary situation. The rabbi writing the *teshuvah* examines earlier literature and responds based on his or her understanding of the legal issues involved.

Theoretically, the rabbi bases the ruling on an "objective" reading of precedent. In reality, however, just as there is no one "objective" reading of the Constitution, there are no objective readings of halakhic sources. The story of the person or group presenting the question can sway the rabbi in one direction or another.

For example, in the fourteenth century, a Jewish community asked a prominent rabbi, Isaac ben Sheshet (known as the Rivash) whether they might use imprisonment as a form of punishment for crimes for which other forms of punishment were not available. Even though there is almost no precedent for prisons in Jewish sources, the Rivash permitted this institution because of what he called "the needs of the moment" (*l'tzorech sha'ah*).[1] In other words, the rabbi made his decision based not only on a close reading of Jewish sources, but also on a close reading of the needs of the community in question. While traditional Jews do not generally speak of the *teshuvah* process as one involving advocacy, the person or group presenting the case has the power to sway the authority figure in one direction or another. In some cases, an individual hopes for a legal response that will ease a difficulty in his or her life. In other cases, the community asks for a ruling that responds to a public concern. In either case, the resulting *teshuvah* sets a precedent that can have a lasting effect on the law. That is not to say that any one *teshuvah* represents the final word on an issue; the strength of the argument, the authority of the writer, and the relevance of this *teshuvah* at later moments in history all affect the ability of a given *teshuvah* to influence law in the long term.

STRENGTHS OF ADVOCACY

The strength of advocacy lies primarily in its ability to make long-term change. Legal decisions and policy enactments can transform the systems that contribute to suffering and oppression. For communities that have spent years feeding the hungry, tutoring students in low-performing schools, and collecting toiletries for domestic violence shelters, advocacy provides a means of tackling the big issues that create this constant, overwhelming need. Advocacy focuses on concrete policy changes, rather than vague dreams of "ending hunger," "bringing peace," or "alleviating poverty." As such, advocacy offers a clear and compelling focus for your community's work.

Through advocacy campaigns, communities can learn about current issues and ways to address these issues. Since it's actually possible to win an advocacy campaign—whereas small donations and volunteer service must be sustained indefinitely—advocacy may inspire and galvanize a community to work together on a common cause in a measurable time frame. If you do win your campaign, you will have an opportunity for a community celebration! And if you don't win, you can take the opportunity of the loss for learning and reflection about how to create the next campaign.

Advocacy offers the opportunity to partner with other religious communities, as well as other communal organizations. Through this process, your institution may develop new relationships that can lead to mutually beneficial work in the future. In addition, advocacy may allow you to draw on the specialized skills of community members, including lawyers, public policy professionals, and experts in the subject area. These members may not previously have engaged in social justice or social action work within the context of your community. Nevertheless, these professionals may appreciate the chance to share their expertise with their own community and may engage more deeply in the campaign as a result of this opportunity.

Through advocacy, members develop new skills and experiences, including public speaking, letter writing, and making constituent visits to elected officials. These experiences empower community members and recast the Jewish organizational space as a locus of learning and personal development. Community members who do not feel comfortable leading prayers or rituals or who do not have significant financial resources may find their place in the leadership of advocacy campaigns.

KINDS OF ADVOCACY

Your campaign may consist of engaging public officials, participating in public demonstrations or leafleting, educating your community about the issue, and taking part in legal advocacy. These undertakings vary in terms of the amount of effort you will need to invest, the risk and cost to the organization, and the chance of bringing about change.

The engagement of elected officials may include making phone calls, sending letters, and visiting your local, state, and federal representatives to talk about an issue of concern to your community and to ask for a particular action.

Public demonstrations and leafleting may include taking part in marches or rallies, staffing tables at events or on the street, walking in picket lines, or passing out leaflets to people who have the power to affect the issue. For example, leaflets might ask shoppers not to shop at a store that has fired workers engaged in organizing a union.

Education campaigns teach your community and the public about the issue. Such campaigns may include the publication of op-eds, blog posts, and other media pieces aimed at influencing public opinion about an issue. Creating research reports can serve both as a means for your community to learn together and as a valuable tool for changing public opinion. Sermons and *divrei Torah* (talks about the Torah reading of the week) may draw on Jewish sacred narratives and spiritual wisdom to provoke complex thinking and inspiring perspectives on the issue. Every advocacy effort should include these kinds of public education, but education cannot be the sole content of a campaign. In order to make change, you must also place direct pressure on decision makers.

Legal advocacy may include filing amicus briefs, or "friend of the court" petitions, in support of one side in a legal case. If, for example, your community is involved with a statewide effort to legalize same-sex marriage, your community may file an amicus brief to support the plaintiffs in a case that charges the state with discrimination. A lawyer or policy expert in your community can draft this statement, with input from those involved in the issue.

If appropriate, members of your community (or your community as a whole) may even join a class action lawsuit on an issue. For example, if an advocacy organization brings a suit regarding the distribution of public school funds, members who live in underfunded school districts may be eligible to join the plaintiffs.

Within a denominational context, legal advocacy may involve pushing policy-making bodies in the Reform, Conservative, Orthodox, or Reconstructionist movements to take on particular positions. You might advocate for the rabbinic or congregational arms to pass a statement or policy position that takes sides on the issue of concern. Within the Conservative movement, this may involve asking a rabbi to bring a *teshuvah* (legal position) on your issue to the Committee on Jewish Law and Standards (also known as the Law Committee), which sets halakhic guidelines for movement institutions. In the Orthodox world, you might also encourage a prominent rabbi to write a *teshuvah* on the issue. In all of the movements, you may push the umbrella organizations to pass resolutions that support your position. All of these types of statements can serve as encouragement for other communities to adopt the issue. In some cases, these statements will even put pressure on individual institutions to act in a certain way. For example, in 2010, Boston-area rabbis pushed the Central Conference of American Rabbis (the Reform rabbinic group) to issue a statement supporting the boycott of a Boston hotel that had replaced its housekeeping staff with underpaid temporary workers with no health benefits. As a result, many synagogues, organizations, and individuals stopped holding events at this hotel.

THE CHALLENGES OF ADVOCACY

Like other forms of social change, advocacy has its limits. In the next few pages, I will focus on three challenges of advocacy: the slow pace of change, the possibility for elitism, and the fear of controversy. I will devote the most space to this last challenge, as the fear of controversy is what most often gets in the way of Jewish institutions engaging in advocacy.

The Pace of Change

Individuals and organizations can pour years into advocating for a specific policy change, only to be crushed when Congress votes against a bill or decides not even to bring it to the floor, a judge rules against the plaintiffs in a class action suit, or the synagogue board rejects a proposal for change.

Direct service can be frustrating too, especially when we see the same people return for help again and again. But, in the case of direct service, we can console ourselves by remembering that we have at least provided hot meals or a shelter. Because advocacy can easily devolve into seemingly theoretical and wonkish conversations about the minor points of legislation, it can be hard to keep in mind the people whose lives will be changed by the details.

Advocacy efforts sometimes encourage the mistaken perception that if the decision makers just had the right information, then they would make the right decision. This belief leads to frustration if you present all of the best information and logical arguments, and your campaign fails anyway. Decision makers base their choices on many factors, including research, stories of people affected by the issue, ideological commitments, ego and ambition, relationships with other decision makers, and tit-for-tat agreements with other powerful actors. When you understand all of the factors that may influence a decision, you can use this knowledge to your advantage by finding ways to help decision makers realize that support for your position will be in their best interest. This may mean demonstrating that people who vote, donate money, invest in the local community, or have other significant power care enough to act on the issue.

Advocacy changes the world slowly because most successful advocacy campaigns result in adjustments to individual bills or policies but do not usually dramatically alter societal relations. In the biblical story, the daughters of Tzelophechad win the right to inherit their father's property, but they do not achieve any major change in the place of women in society. The women themselves argue their case not on the basis of gender equity, but on the grounds that their father's property stands to be transferred out of their tribe.

Later, this argument comes back to haunt the women when the other members of their tribe argue successfully that these women should be forced to marry within the tribe, so that their father's property will not be absorbed into the holdings of another tribe. The women comply and marry their cousins. Despite the partial liberalization of property rights, men still acquire ownership of their wives' property (Numbers 36:1–12).

Similarly, even the rabbis who write the most radical *teshuvot* maintain power over the supplicants. The authority of rabbis to determine law and to affect the lives of their communities through esoteric knowledge and logical systems remains unchanged. We can respond to this pitfall of advocacy first by remaining focused on the end goal. This means maintaining relationships with individuals and communities who will benefit from the change we seek. If, for example, we are working on a child nutrition bill, we can maintain a direct-service relationship with a school or other provider of free lunches for children. We can stay in touch with community and religious groups involved in the issue, always sharing information and receiving feedback. We can also identify small achievements along the way, celebrate those victories, and challenge ourselves never to be satisfied. Each accomplishment along the way should propel us to keep working toward the far-reaching changes we seek.

The Elitism of Advocacy

Advocacy is typically an elite activity, in which expert advocates and policy makers from similar socioeconomic backgrounds make decisions and compromises or face one another in court. Within your community, you may find that the "experts"—that is, the lawyers, the political science PhDs, and those with experience in government may automatically volunteer to lead the advocacy efforts. Those with high-level connections may volunteer to call the mayor's office, to arrange a meeting with an important businessperson, or to write the op-eds and the legal papers.

You should take advantage of this expertise, which is one of the resources that your community may bring to the table of a coalition. But ideally, the advocacy process will also be an opportunity for community members to develop new skills and areas of leadership. Achieving this aim will mean helping community members to educate themselves about the issue, holding workshops on effective letter and op-ed writing, and encouraging a range of members to take the lead in meetings and to speak in public.

Throughout the process, it will be important to remember the lessons about power discussed in chapter 6. This awareness will be especially important when working in partnership with communities whom decision makers perceive as having less privilege and status.

From 2002 through 2009, Jews for Racial and Economic Justice (JFREJ), a New York City–based group worked with Domestic Workers United, a local organization consisting mainly of immigrant women of color, to pass the statewide Domestic Workers Bill of Rights. This bill guarantees labor protections to nannies, home health aides, and others who had previously been excluded from labor laws. As of 2011, New York State remained the only state to have passed such legislation. Alex Weissman, a male member of JFREJ, recalls visiting a state legislator together with a group of Spanish-speaking domestic workers and a translator. After members of the group had finished introducing themselves, with the assistance of the translator, the legislator turned to this young man, the only native English speaker in the group. "So, I guess I'll be speaking with you," she said. "Actually," he replied, "you'll be talking with all of us." From there, the domestic workers shared their stories in Spanish and the interpreter translated. Alex also participated, sharing his own story of growing up in a household that employed domestic workers. Instead of accepting the privilege foisted on him by this elected official, Alex challenged her to listen to the voices of the domestic workers. At the same time, he did not discount the power of his own story; instead, he told this story as a means of explaining his own personal connection to the issue.[2]

Fear of Controversy

Many synagogues and other Jewish institutions shy away from advocacy. "It's too political," they say. "Religion has no business mixing with politics." "People come to the synagogue to get away from the problems of the world." Or: "We can't risk upsetting board members." "Not everyone in our community agrees about this issue."

These arguments stem from a series of myths:

MYTH 1: U.S. tax law does not permit synagogues and other nonprofit organizations to get involved with politics. Political advocacy may jeopardize a religious organization's tax-free status.

It is crucial here to distinguish between what is political and what is partisan. For our purposes, political work includes any involvement in public life, from attending rallies, to writing letters for or against legislation, to giving sermons about current events. Partisan work refers to supporting specific candidates or parties for public office. Political work focuses on issues, while partisan work focuses on elections.

U.S. nonprofits registered with the IRS as 501(c)3 organizations may devote up to 20 percent of their budget to political advocacy that does not cross over into partisan work.[3] For example, a school may take students to a Darfur rally, but it may not invite a candidate for public office to speak about his or her commitment to remedy the situation in Sudan. The school may, however, host a debate to which *all* of the candidates are invited, and it may host elected officials alone as long as they are not campaigning for reelection. A rabbi may give a sermon in support of campaign finance reform, but she may not exhort the congregation to vote for a particular candidate who supports such reform.

In the recent past, some churches and other religious groups have gotten into trouble for publishing voters' guides that purport to be neutral but that in fact steer readers to one candidate or another. Such guides, for example, might rate candidates according to their views on abortion or their support for Israel. A synagogue or other nonprofit organization can publish a voters' guide but only if candidates are allowed to speak for themselves. The nonprofit may ask the campaign staff to respond to specific questions about issues of concern. Those answers should be printed as received, without any additional commentary.

MYTH 2: Religion and politics don't mix.

The Bible is a political document. The core narrative of the Torah is the story of a slave revolt that results in the creation of a liberated nation. The experience of slavery and liberation becomes a template for later laws prohibiting the oppression of vulnerable populations, including widows, orphans, low-wage workers, and those simply down on their luck. The Bible and later Jewish law address issues as political as the appointment of kings, when and how to go to war, and what social support programs a community must provide to its members. The Hebrew word for "law," *halakhah*, actually comes from the verb *lalekhet*, meaning "to walk." Judaism conceives of *halakhah* not simply as a collection of religious rules, but as a way of walking in the world. Following *halakhah* means subscribing both to a set of ritual practices and to a social and political order. Only since the eighteenth-century Enlightenment have Jews in the West begun to imagine a sharp distinction between private religious belief and public political commitments. The shift to viewing Judaism as a religion rather than an ethnic identity allowed Jews to become assimilated citizens of their home countries, but it also had the effect of relegating Jewish practice to the synagogue and home.

If we define politics as engagement with the world, demonstrated through efforts to improve this world for the long run, then Jewish practice *must* be political.

But political does not mean partisan. Judaism is not Democratic or Republican. It is not Tory or Liberal. Despite the claims of some rabbinic voices in Israel, it is not even Labor or Likud, Kadima or Shas. In many cases, a thoughtful analysis of Jewish perspectives on a particular issue will produce a position more in line with one party or another. It is crucial, though, to maintain a focus on the issues, rather than try to make the case that Judaism demands loyalty to a single party.

MYTH 3: Service programs are "not political."

When I ask synagogues and schools what attracts them to collecting cans or volunteering at a soup kitchen, they often respond that such programs are "not political." But service is always political. We cannot blame hunger in America on crop failure or drought. If people are hungry in America, it is not because there is a lack of food. Rather, hunger stems from an array of explicitly political issues, including low wages and unemployment, expensive health care, and the power of agricultural lobbies to keep unhealthy food cheap. When disaster strikes in the United States or abroad, such as in the case of Hurricane Katrina, the Haiti earthquake, or the floods in Pakistan, relief work may feel nonpolitical. But the scope of the disaster most often stems from political factors such as the location of poor neighborhoods, whether rescue and evacuation plans exist, and the allocation of public money. And post-disaster rebuilding is always political. Elected officials, special interest groups, community organizations, and individual citizens always view the rebuilding effort as an opportunity to put into place their own vision for the affected locale.

In some cases, service makes an explicit political statement. For example, during the 1980s and early 1990s, even delivering food to AIDS patients could be understood as a direct challenge to governmental attempts to ignore the epidemic, stigmatize gay men, or blame sick people for their own suffering.

When we do service in response to hunger or any other issue, we implicitly accept one of the following propositions: either we believe in a small-government system in which charitable organizations take significant responsibility for social welfare, or we believe that volunteer programs represent a woefully inadequate means of making up for government lapses and corporate abuses. Either position is, by nature, political. The former will lead to efforts to recruit more and more volunteers and to develop and fund more private social service programs. The latter will lead to supporting legislation or corporate practices that address systemic issues or that increase public funding for social service. Either position may be defensible, but neither is politically neutral.

MYTH 4: Supporting Israel is "not political."

There is one type of political action in which most Jewish communities routinely engage: support for the State of Israel—specifically, the policies and actions of whatever Israeli government currently holds office, typically with respect to Israel's conflicts with the Palestinians and neighboring countries. These activities may include attending rallies, lobbying Congress for foreign aid to Israel, or even criticizing politicians who criticize Israel. Synagogues, schools, and Jewish organizations engage in such activities without fear of appearing to take sides on a political issue.

For example, during the second Intifada, Jewish schools up and down the East Coast closed their doors for a day, so that their students could pack the National Mall for an Israel rally. Organizers promoted the demonstration as an apolitical event to "support" Israel. But when Paul Wolfowitz, then the deputy secretary of defense for the George W. Bush administration, mentioned the suffering of Palestinians, the crowd booed him. I myself, then a rabbinical student at The Jewish Theological Seminary, attended the rally with a group of students calling ourselves "Rabbinical Students for a Just Peace." This ad hoc group, which a few friends and I had organized, held signs saying such things as "Pro-Israel, Pro-Peace." Other attendees screamed at us, called us self-hating Jews, and tried to rip away our signs.

On a more regular basis, synagogues annually sponsor delegations to AIPAC (American Israel Public Affairs Committee) conferences. Synagogue leaders generally present these delegations as a neutral means of "supporting Israel," rather than as a political activity that should stem from reflection about the community's values. But AIPAC is not a neutral body; rather, it is a political organization that pushes the U.S. government to direct foreign aid toward Israel, refrain from pressuring Israel to freeze settlement activity, and otherwise support the policies of the Israeli government. While AIPAC claims to support every Israeli government, regardless of which party is in charge, the organization has been charged with offering only lukewarm support to Yitzchak Rabin's Labor government and even with trying to undermine the Oslo peace process.[4]

On the other hand, synagogue leaders often view participation in organizations that publicly criticize some Israeli policies, such as J Street, Rabbis for Human Rights–North America, or the New Israel Fund, as provocatively political. But these groups are no more or less political than AIPAC, Conference of Presidents, or other more established organizations. All of these groups frame their involvement within the context of support for Israel, and all take political positions that reflect what they believe to be in the best interests of the Jewish state.

Reasonable people can differ on how the Israeli government should address the conflict with the Palestinians, the threat from Iran, or internal economic and social issues. But no matter what choices we or our institutions make in this regard, we must keep in mind that *every* choice is political. If you believe that the United States should intervene in the peace negotiations—that is a political position. If you believe that the United States should stay out of these negotiations—that is a political position. If you oppose the expansion of settlements—that is a political position. If you believe that Israel has the right to expand the settlements—that is a political position too.

Different individuals and institutions might make different decisions about whether to participate in advocacy efforts on the left, right, or center; whether to send delegations to the AIPAC conference, the J Street conference, neither, or both; and whether to put up posters in support of Israel, and if so, what these posters should say. But decisions in this area should be treated as political decisions, and not as neutral "support for Israel."

These discussions can be healthy ones for our communities. We can ask ourselves what support for Israel means to us. Does "support" mean sending money? Visiting Israel? Calling friends, relatives, or strangers who live there? Supporting the political position that we believe to be the best guarantee of a safe and secure Israel for the future? And, if the last, what is this position? How do we arrive at these conclusions? If we have some community consensus (or even if we don't), how do we act on our convictions?

A FORCE FOR CHANGE

Advocacy can be a powerful force for change. Through advocacy, members of your community can tackle an issue that corresponds with their passions, develop new skills and knowledge, form strong partnerships with other communities, and bring about real change in people's lives. You can take the next step on an issue that emerges from your service work, and you can take public leadership on this issue.

Taking on an advocacy campaign may also lead your community to have frank conversations about your values and commitments. You may find that you are already advocating for certain positions without having gone through a communal process of choosing these issues. Or, you may find that significant consensus exists around issues that your community has avoided for fear of provoking controversy. I have already hinted that taking on an advocacy campaign ought to involve organizing within your community. In the next chapter, we will explore what community organizing means and how to use this mode of action to build our capacity to work for social justice.

11
Community Organizing

In the last three chapters, we looked at direct service, *tzedakah* and invest-ment, and policy advocacy. Done well, these modes of social change work can all be effective, necessary, and sacred, each in different ways. Yet none of these suffices in itself. Direct service treats immediate needs but usually does not lead to more lasting change. *Tzedakah* and community invest-ment tends to keep givers at a distance from the reality of suffering and injustice. The same can be true of advocacy, which often takes the form of elite activity by experts. In all these methods, it is challenging (though not impossible) to ensure that (a) participants build relationships of partner-ship with other people and communities, and (b) participants grow in their skills and leadership abilities in order to build a solid organization that can take on more and more ambitious projects over time.

Community organizing is a process in which a group of people identifies shared goals and builds the power to effect change. It is ideally suited to cre-ating systemic change to laws or policies. Over the past ten years, hundreds of synagogues have become involved in a style of community organizing pio-neered by Saul Alinsky in the 1930s and known as congregation-based com-munity organizing (CBCO). This work has happened largely through the efforts of Jewish Funds for Justice and Just Congregations (a project of the Union for Reform Judaism).

Imagine that a community group wishes to create affordable low-income housing in an affluent town or neighborhood whose mayor and council oppose any changes to the area's "character." The organization may proceed in a few different ways. A direct service approach might lead them to volunteer at shelters to highlight the need for permanent housing. Through community investment, they can raise money from investors to build affordable housing in the community. As advocates, they can invite housing experts to present detailed arguments and plans to members of the city council and lobby the council to permit the construction of affordable housing. They can run a public education campaign through op-eds in local media and lectures at the public library about the benefits of affordable housing. If there are legal issues involved, such as a requirement to comply with a state affordable housing law, they can hire lawyers to take the town to court. Some or all of these strategies will probably be necessary, and any of these conceivably could succeed. But the group will be stronger and even more successful in the long run if it organizes a broad base of supporters and grassroots leaders to put pressure on the decision makers in the town and to hold them accountable once a decision is made.

Let's say that the community group mounts a successful legal challenge in court, and the judge forces the town to construct affordable housing. By some accounts, this constitutes a victory. The housing will be built, and a number of people who formerly could not afford to live in the town will move into the new units. But there may be lingering public resentment about the new housing and about the community group. Popular rumors may allege that the new buildings will house drug addicts and parolees. Town residents may worry that the value of their own homes will drop. And even for the community group, the victory may be fleeting. If, in a few months, the group decides to lobby for more frequent bus service to less affluent parts of town, the organization will need to start anew to garner support for this campaign among elected officials and town residents. The fact that the organization won a legal challenge around affordable housing will not necessarily make local officials any more or less inclined to support the new transportation campaign.

Imagine now that the group starts by bringing together a group of residents with a personal connection to the affordable housing issue. These may include people hoping to move into the new units, members of churches and synagogues who feel religiously obligated to ensure safe housing, and business owners who wish to attract new workers to the area. This disparate collection of individuals spend time getting to know one another and building trust within the group. They study affordable housing laws together, discuss religious and personal motivations for supporting affordable housing, and research the best ways to make political change in their community. Through interfaith text study and discussion of each other's faith traditions, they learn about home, homelessness, and housing in each other's traditions. They then strategize together about how to secure affordable housing in the town. These strategies might include legal action but may also involve members of the group meeting with elected officials, showing up to speak at city council or town hall meetings, or otherwise encouraging decision makers to support affordable housing. Group members might spend time talking to other stakeholders, including neighbors, business owners, and developers, to build community support for the new construction. Some of this action may be confrontational, especially if public officials resist meeting with the group or responding to their requests. In many cases, however, the group can avoid confrontation by helping decision makers to see why providing affordable housing will be in their own interest. Perhaps this housing will allow the elderly parents of town residents to live nearby. Perhaps the housing will bring new jobs, new workers, or new business to the town. Perhaps the housing will be part of a mixed-income construction project that will bring people of all income levels to the area. Perhaps the mayor or key city council members would enjoy being honored by community groups for their role in creating affordable housing. Perhaps some elected officials want to support affordable housing but are afraid of the reaction of wealthier residents; in this case, bringing wealthier residents to the table can provide the necessary political cover. By building relationships across religious, ethnic, and economic lines, individuals can start to move away from a win/lose mind-set and to think instead about how everyone can win.

The second approach will certainly take longer than moving straight to a legal battle. Both strategies may end with the same result: the construction of new affordable housing units. But the second strategy, which begins with organizing a group of interested residents, may have longer-lasting effects. There will be more public support for the new housing units, and perhaps even sufficient support to create additional units in the future. Individuals who were not previously involved in political action now have the training, experience, and sense of empowerment to make change in their own communities. Just as important, the people who came together to fight for affordable housing now have the motivation and the commitment to one another to take on additional campaigns. Elected officials feel accountable to churches, synagogues, business owners, and other key constituencies. And the classic barriers between people of different religions, ethnicities, ages, and economic abilities may have begun to weaken. There is an element of divinity in this group formation. Rather than see others as fundamentally different, each individual in the group now sees the commonalities between themselves and members of other communities.

The community organization itself now has a reputation for being a powerful player in local politics. Elected officials may begin turning to the community organization for support in passing legislation. Candidates for public office may seek the endorsement of the community group, which can lay out expectations for policies that will earn its support. Through patient organizing, what began as a small community group has achieved real power. The balance of power in that town has shifted, at least slightly, in favor of ordinary citizens. And these ordinary citizens have chosen to use their power to make the world a more just place. That, in itself, is divine.

SHIFTING POWER?
A NEW LOOK AT THE EXODUS

In the world of Jewish social justice, Moses is often described as the first community organizer.[1] In the biblical account, this unlikely leader persuades Pharaoh to free the slaves, intimidates the Egyptians with a series of plagues, and keeps an unruly collection of former slaves focused on the mission of reaching the Promised Land.

But a closer look at the biblical story yields a more complicated picture. Through a look at the Exodus story, we can learn more about how to organize a community and about what pitfalls to avoid along the way.

Moses does lead the Israelites out of slavery, but it is not at all clear that he does so by organizing. Rather, he relies on divine intervention to transport the people out of Egypt and to intimidate and ultimately eliminate Pharaoh and his army. At the beginning of the story in Exodus, a newly minted Pharaoh expresses fear that the Israelites will rebel against their Egyptian hosts. To prevent any such uprising, Pharaoh enslaves the Israelite immigrants, who had previously been living in Egypt as tolerated foreigners. As time goes on, Pharaoh imposes harsher and harsher restrictions on the Israelites and ultimately decrees that all baby boys be thrown into the Nile. Moses's mother saves the life of her newborn son by placing him in a basket at the edge of the river. Pharaoh's daughter discovers him there and takes him to be her own child.

Moses grows up as a prince, albeit one who also sympathizes with his family of origin. In his first recorded venture outside of the palace, Moses spots an Egyptian taskmaster beating an Israelite slave and kills the former. Later, Moses intervenes in a dispute between two Israelites, only to be reprimanded by them for his bravado. These two encounters reveal the leadership flaw that will continue to plague Moses throughout his life: perhaps as a result of the privilege of his upbringing, Moses feels comfortable making unilateral decisions and telling others what to do. He succeeds far less, however, in engaging others in taking responsibility for their own destiny.

Once appointed by God to lead the Israelites out of Egypt, Moses charges into Pharaoh's palace and demands the release of the slaves. He goes head-to-head with Pharaoh's magicians, as each tries to prove the power of his own god. Finally, God begins to shower plagues on the Egyptians. Pharaoh, in what will become the time-honored tradition of dictators, responds to this challenge to his authority by punishing the people even more harshly. Now, the slaves must gather their own straw while still producing the same quantity of bricks as before. The Israelites start complaining to Moses. They have been coping just fine in Egypt, they tell him. There is no need for a privileged outsider to meddle with the fragile status quo.

When he first returns to Egypt, Moses does make some attempt to rally support from the elders of the Israelite community. Following God's command, he appears before them, tells them that he has come to liberate the people from slavery, and performs a few signs and wonders as proof of God's involvement in the process. Persuaded by this impressive display, the elders agree to speak to the people on Moses's behalf. Does this meeting ever happen? How do the masses react? The Torah offers no clear answers.

I imagine, though, that the elders responded to Moses the way that most congregations respond to a stirring sermon. The rabbi masterfully weaves together Torah text with a lesson about the issue of the moment. She exhorts the congregation to take action. At *Kiddush*, several congregants approach her to congratulate her on the moving sermon. A few promise to "do something" about the problem. By the time Shabbat ends, these promises have been forgotten, and synagogue life returns to normal. Like Moses, the rabbi has offered a powerful argument for change without also doing the work to bring her congregation along and to train lay leaders to participate in moving the work forward.

The motif of the separation between Moses and the people continues, even after ten plagues have wreaked havoc on Egypt, God has parted the sea, and Moses has led the people into freedom. Throughout the forty years of wandering in the wilderness, the Israelites continue grumbling. They demand meat. They miss the leeks, cucumbers, and garlic that they ate in Egypt. They construct an idol to worship in lieu of their new, invisible God. Moses responds to these complaints and rebellions with a combination of anger, irritation, and surprise. He loses his temper, cajoles the people to behave, and bemoans his fate to God.

In one revealing moment, Moses declares, "How can I alone bear the trouble of you, your burden and your bickering!" (Deuteronomy 1:12). The word that begins this exclamation, *eikha* (how), appears only a handful of times in the Bible and usually begins an anguished lament. Most famously, this word begins the book of Lamentations, known as *Eikha* in Hebrew. There, the prophet Jeremiah looks at the ruins of Jerusalem and cries out "How does the city sit solitary, the city that once was filled with people!" (Lamentations 1:1). The word *eikha* points to utter loneliness and desolation. Like the city whose residents have been slaughtered or exiled, Moses feels utterly isolated. But Moses announces his loneliness among at least six hundred thousand followers.

Moses is not unusual in finding leadership to be a lonely task. Like many leaders, he has a vision of a Promised Land that his followers do not yet see. He charges out ahead of his people, effectively saying, "Trust me, trust God." But they do not trust him, they do not know God, and they do not understand where Moses is taking them. In their fear, they act out in ways that make the realization of Moses's dream even harder to achieve.

Immediately after giving voice to his loneliness, Moses notes that he previously responded to this burden by appointing tribal heads responsible for mediating among the people. The Torah does, in fact, report a few instances in which Moses appoints judges, consults with elders, and invites a small group to share in prophecy. More often, though, Moses seems unable to develop relationships with the very people he presumes to lead. When the Israelites whine or rebel, Moses most often turns immediately to God, rather than try to negotiate a solution with the people. It is no wonder that this group of former slaves never seems excited about the Promised Land. No one has engaged them in a process of envisioning this place and strategizing about how to reach it.

What if, instead of heading straight to Pharaoh, Moses had first spent time getting to know the Israelites? What if he had listened to their concerns, explained his vision, and involved them in planning how and when to leave Egypt? What if he had engaged a few key community leaders in making decisions along the way? Perhaps the people would have been more willing to suffer through a few weeks of hard labor and to forego meat on the way to the Promised Land. Perhaps the people would have challenged Moses's authority less often if they had felt that he truly understood their interests and included them in decision-making processes.

I mentioned earlier that organizing seeks to change the balance of power. In a successful organizing campaign, ordinary citizens develop a sense of themselves as powerful people who are capable of shifting their own reality. People overwhelmed by the difficulty of caring for elderly parents work together to create better senior services in the area. Public transportation riders persuade the city to provide as much bus service to low-income neighborhoods as to middle-class areas. Public school parents pressure the state to maintain arts and music programs.

This move from apathy to action, and from disempowerment to empowerment, constitutes a spiritual process, and not only a political one.

The biblical description of human beings as creations in the divine image casts every individual as a partner with God in the work of creation (Genesis 1:26). Many of us give lip service to this notion, while still feeling overwhelmed and disempowered in our day-to-day lives. Through joining with others to take action, we can recapture this feeling of connection to the powerful divine. Within a Jewish or interfaith context, regular discussions of the spiritual dimensions of action can help to remind the group of the divine aspects of this work. These conversations will be especially important if the group becomes frustrated with the rate of change or gets caught up in internal squabbles.

In the Exodus story, it takes a long time for the Israelites to alter their perception of themselves as slaves—at first, they simply shift their loyalties from Pharaoh to God. The internalized slave mentality causes them to whine about their problems and fears, rather than joining together to solve them. Only once they take on a project together—namely, building a *mishkan* (tabernacle) in the desert—do the people begin to contribute their best talents to the effort and start to work together toward a common goal. When the people build this *mishkan*, God promises that the divine presence will dwell among them. God does not wish to dwell inside the building; rather, the community building process that takes place in conjunction with the construction of the *mishkan* is what causes God's presence to become manifest on earth. In our own lives, finding common cause with people inside and outside of our community can similarly make the divine presence felt.

I do not mean to say that there is never a need for visionary leaders, stirring sermons, or ideas ahead of their time. Without a Moses, a Martin Luther King Jr., or a Susan B. Anthony, it might have taken many more years to liberate the Israelites from Egypt, to end the Jim Crow laws, and to grant suffrage to women.[2] But none of these movements could have succeeded on the basis of powerful speeches alone. Real change requires organizing the people to come along—and not only in the sense of agreeing and trusting, but through their active participation and empowerment. While all of these leaders are best known for their public personas, each succeeded only by building a strong organization that harnessed the power of individuals to make change.

GETTING STARTED IN ORGANIZING

Almost all institutions that become involved in organizing do their work in partnership with a local interfaith network or with a coalition of community groups. These organizations typically employ experienced staff organizers, who will take the lead in designing the overall campaign and will work with you to find appropriate and meaningful ways for your community to be involved and to build your own skills. In chapter 6, we talked about finding and creating healthy relationships with these institutions. The discussions there about balancing power and privilege and about clarifying needs and expectations will be especially relevant to developing partnerships with other religious and community groups.

In some cases, individual institutions may also use organizing methodology to make changes within their own institutions. Some synagogues have organized internally to make their buildings more accessible to disabled congregants. In Newton, Massachusetts, a group of teenagers who came together in the context of a synagogue organizing project decided that they wanted to stop their public school's practice of handing out progress reports color coded according to how well the students did. This practice caused intense anxiety for some students, who were deeply embarrassed to be seen receiving a card whose color indicated that they had not done well. The students brought together a group of friends from inside and outside of the synagogue, and together they persuaded the school officials to print all progress reports on the same color paper.[3]

Even when a professional organizer takes the lead in designing a campaign, it will be helpful for each involved institution to understand the outlines and core practices of such a campaign in order to be knowledgeable participants in decision-making processes.

Below, I present the steps to an organizing campaign as though they happen one after another. More often than not, though, many of these steps happen at the same time, and most continue throughout the campaign.

1. Build relationships.

Successful organizing campaigns begin with relationships. Very few people care enough about a cause in the abstract to set aside time from work and personal commitments. If I hear a moving speech about immigration reform, I might be persuaded that the United States needs a new immigration policy. If the speaker gives a pitch for joining a bus full of people heading to an immigration rally in Washington, D.C., I will probably say to myself, "I really should go to that." I might even sign my name to a list of people interested in participating. But a day or so before the rally, I'm likely to find dozens of other things I should be doing instead—finishing a pressing work project, unpacking the last boxes from my move, or spending time with my husband and daughter.

But if my commitment is based not in an intellectual interest in an issue, but in specific commitments to people who are affected by that issue, then I am much more likely to put aside other demands and get on the bus to the rally. If, for instance, a neighbor, a friend, or a babysitter who is struggling with his or her own immigration status asks me to come along, I will have trouble saying no. If I have spent time working on the issue with other members of my synagogue, I will not let them down by backing out at the last minute.

Malcom Gladwell differentiates between the type of activism facilitated by the "weak-tie connections" of social media and those that depend on strong personal connections. By way of example, Gladwell offers two stories of social activism. In one of these stories, twenty-five thousand people respond to a Facebook and Twitter campaign to find a bone marrow transplant for a young man with leukemia. In the second story, which takes place in North Carolina in 1960, four young black men sit down at a segregated lunch counter and refuse to leave without being served. Within four days, they are joined by four hundred others. Gladwell comments:

> How did the [bone marrow] campaign get so many people to sign up? By not asking too much of them. That's the only way you can get someone you don't really know to do something on your behalf. You can get thousands of people to sign up for a donor registry, because doing so is pretty easy. You have to send in a cheek swab and—in the highly unlikely event that your bone marrow is a good match for someone in need—spend a few hours at the hospital. Donating bone marrow isn't a trivial matter. But it doesn't involve financial or personal

risk; it doesn't mean spending a summer being chased by armed men in pickup trucks. It doesn't require that you confront socially entrenched norms and practices. In fact, it's the kind of commitment that will bring only social acknowledgment and praise.[4]

In contrast, he argues, the sit-in, through which participants placed themselves at risk of arrest or physical harm, could never have succeeded through the power of social networks alone:

> One crucial fact about the four freshmen at the Greensboro lunch counter—David Richmond, Franklin McCain, Ezell Blair, and Joseph McNeil—was their relationship with one another. McNeil was a roommate of Blair's in A. & T.'s Scott Hall dormitory. Richmond roomed with McCain one floor up, and Blair, Richmond, and McCain had all gone to Dudley High School.... It was McNeil who brought up the idea of a sit-in at Woolworth's.... Ezell Blair worked up the courage the next day to ask for a cup of coffee because he was flanked by his roommate and two good friends from high school.[5]

Creating the personal connections that will facilitate such strong ties requires spending significant time in face-to-face conversations, such as those discussed in chapter 4. In addition, organizing team meetings might include time for participants to check in about what has happened in their lives since the last meeting, to share personal or professional challenges or successes, and to get to know each other better. Studying religious texts or ideas together also creates a means for participants to connect to their own tradition, to learn more about others' traditions in the context of an interfaith group, and to connect with other group members on a more personal level.

Between meetings, leaders can maintain these strong ties by periodically calling participants, soliciting feedback about how the process is going, and making personal phone calls to hold people to commitments that they have made.

Imagine this scenario: Hannah is a relatively new member of her synagogue. She joined to enroll her daughter in Hebrew School, but she has also begun to get involved in monthly family Shabbat dinners. At one of these dinners, another parent invites Hannah for a cup of coffee and conversation as part of the synagogue's social justice efforts. During their discussion, the two discover a shared concern about the cost of child care in their neighborhood. Hannah agrees to join the group that represents the synagogue in a statewide coalition to increase funding of social services.

The first meeting that Hannah attends concerns an upcoming community event that aims to educate synagogue members about the distribution of tax dollars in the state. The meeting starts with a lay leader facilitating a text study about Jewish attitudes toward money. In the conversation that ensues, group members reflect on their own feelings about money in light of the texts in front of them. Hannah is surprised to learn how many of the other group members share her own anxieties about money.

Toward the end of the meeting, each member of the group commits to what he or she will do before the next meeting. Excited by the energy of the group, Hannah promises to meet with three other Hebrew school parents to talk with them about the campaign.

Over the next few days, Hannah keeps noticing this commitment on her to-do list. But an important work deadline looms, her daughter spends every free moment practicing for a statewide soccer championship, and her father has just fired his newest home health aide. Then, a member of the group calls Hannah to suggest a getting-to-know-you conversation. In the course of their discussion, the two trade stories about the difficulties of balancing work, children, and elderly parents. Reinspired by being reconnected to her motivations and by her renewed personal connection to the team, Hannah resolves to find time for the three coffee dates to which she has committed. Soon, she finds herself on the inviting end. Not all three of her conversation partners decide to get deeply involved in this campaign, but all would like to stay connected to the work and could be called on for future events and actions. They will certainly mention the campaign favorably to other synagogue members if the subject comes up.

As the time for the synagogue education event approaches, each group member commits to bringing at least three others to the event. Hannah calls the three parents she met with to invite them to attend the event with her. She also calls a few other synagogue members she has met through the family Shabbat dinners and encourages them to take part as well. The day before the event, Hannah again calls those who promised to come and reminds them of the upcoming program.

As the campaign continues, Hannah develops closer relationships with other members of the leadership group. They start to have periodic Shabbat dinners together; celebrate each other's birthdays; and continue to share their own passions, concerns, and experiences. With the encouragement of group members, Hannah decides to learn to read Torah and does so for the first time on the Shabbat dedicated to the social service campaign.

Along the way, Hannah also gets to know members of other communities involved in the coalition. She meets people from her synagogue, from local churches, and from community groups who will be affected by any change in the distribution of social service money. She also attends several meetings with state legislators, shares her own experiences and concerns with them, and learns more about the passions that drove them into public service.

Working on this campaign takes up more time than Hannah would ever have thought she would give to the synagogue. But as she learns more and more about the effect of state funding decisions, she becomes increasingly determined to preserve social service funding. Even more importantly, she knows that if she drops off of the committee, she will let down people who have become friends and colleagues.

2. Form partnerships.

Your institution will almost never take on an issue on its own. Synagogues, schools, JCCs, and even Jewish communal institutions rarely have the resources, skills, and savvy to address a large social problem on their own or even to be the lead institution in a campaign. In the majority of cases, then, you will look for community organizations, religious institutions, and established coalitions with whom you can partner. You will also want an experienced professional organizer to guide your work and train your leaders.

A possible exception may arise if your campaign is an internal one, such as an effort to open your school to children with special needs, to green your synagogue, or to persuade your local Jewish Federation to hire unionized cleaning contractors. Even then, consider what types of partnerships and training can help you to conduct your efforts effectively and successfully.

Chapter 6 includes more in-depth discussion about strategies for finding and cultivating partners, both for organizing campaigns and for other types of social justice projects.

3. Research and plan.

Before you begin your campaign, you will need as much information as possible. As I have mentioned, you will need to identify the target of the campaign, to understand his or her interests, and to find the people who have influence over him or her. In addition, you will need to be able to answer questions about the costs and benefits of what you are advocating, the factors that have produced the current situation, and the potential results of the change you are proposing.

As I mentioned in chapter 4, when I lived in Chicago, I got involved in a campaign to extend twenty-four-hour train service to the predominantly Mexican and African American neighborhoods on the west side of the city. At the time, all but one branch of the train ran twenty-four hours a day, seven days a week. This branch, which served some of the lowest-income neighborhoods, operated only on weekdays, and stopped between midnight and 6:00 a.m. Neighborhood residents who worked night or weekend shifts, who wanted to go downtown on Saturday or Sunday, or who wished to visit friends and relatives elsewhere in the city would find themselves spending hours taking multiple buses rather than enjoy a quick train ride.

The Chicago Transit Authority argued that it was economically unfeasible to extend service on the line in question. The number of rides on this line, they argued, was smaller than the number of rides on any other train line. With a bit of research, community members learned that the CTA reached its numbers by comparing this five-day-a-week line with other seven-day-a-week lines. But comparing weekday numbers to weekday numbers revealed that the branch in question actually had *more* riders Monday through Friday than other branches of the train system. This research proved crucial in soliciting support for the extended service among Chicagoans outside of the affected neighborhood.

The particular research questions you tackle will depend on the campaign you have chosen and on who else has already investigated the issues involved. Some questions germane to almost every campaign include the following:

- What economic, political, historical, and cultural factors have contributed to the problem we seek to address? What are the forces that make change difficult?

- Does this situation involve an unequal distribution of resources or burdens? Who benefits and who loses?

- Who has the power to make the change we seek? Who has influence over this person? What are this person's interests? How can we persuade this person that agreeing to our request aligns with his or her interests?

- How much will this change cost? Where might this money come from?

- Who are potential allies in this campaign? What community groups, religious communities, elected officials, educational institutions, journalists, or other stakeholders could be involved?

- Who are potential opponents to this campaign? Opponents might be elected officials, business interests, members of your own community, individuals or institutions who stand to lose money if the campaign succeeds, or community members who are ideologically opposed to the goal. Which of these opponents can you persuade to change their position? Which can you persuade to stay quiet? Which must you confront publicly?

4. Define the campaign goal.

You will only know whether you have won your campaign if you start by defining a clear goal that is both possible and challenging to reach. For example, you might say that you want to end hunger. This is a desirable goal, but not one that your institution will achieve this year, next year, or ten years from now. If you identify "ending hunger" as your goal, you set yourself up for an endless series of food drives, appeals for donations to soup kitchens, and advocacy on a range of hunger-related issues. It will be hard to sustain communal interest in a campaign that has such a broad scope of activity, no target time frame, and a near-impossible goal.

You will have better success maintaining engagement about the campaign if you identify one specific issue within the broader area of hunger that you wish to act on. For example, your goal might be persuading your city's school system to offer healthier school lunches, increasing the number of licenses for fresh-produce street vendors in a low-income neighborhood, or raising the statewide minimum wage. You will know that you have succeeded if school lunches change, if affordable vegetable stands appear in the target neighborhoods, or if the minimum wage goes up. Along the way, you can certainly run educational events about hunger, plan volunteer days at a food pantry, and raise money for hunger-related organizations. But all of these events should maintain a focus on the goal. For instance, if you take a group to volunteer at a food pantry, you can talk with participants about how the campaign you have undertaken will change the lives of people who use this food pantry. You can then invite the food pantry volunteers also to join the organizing campaign.

The goal you choose should be lofty enough to excite your community members, but not so large as to be impossible to achieve. You will not want to pour all of your energy and resources into, for example, setting up a single vegetable stand in a low-income neighborhood. Even if you win this campaign, the victory may not feel big enough to celebrate. As I mentioned earlier, you will also not want to pursue a campaign such as "ending hunger," which is too vast to be achievable.

Some organizers argue against undertaking any campaign that cannot be won within a few years. This approach produces more victories and reduces the burnout that accompanies multiyear campaigns. On the downside, pursuing only small-scale and winnable goals mitigates against pursuing large-scale social change. If you do take on a campaign that you do not anticipate winning within a year or two, you should identify, achieve, and celebrate smaller victories along the way. An interim victory might consist of gaining the support of a key elected official, winning a legal ruling that gives you access to important information, or hitting a target of fifty clergy who sign a letter of solidarity.

For campaigns of any duration, identifying a specific time frame for victory helps you to pace the intensity of your efforts and to expect when you might have time for rest, reflection, and evaluation of your actions.

5. Identify the target.

In organizing lingo, the "target" refers to the person who can give you what you want. For example, in a campaign to pass a state bill, the target may be the governor or a key legislator. In a campaign to raise wages for early childhood educators at your synagogue, the target might be the chair of the board. In a campaign to supply more frequent bus service to a low-income neighborhood, the target might be the head of the transportation authority.

In religious contexts, some people feel uncomfortable with the military connotations of the word "target." If you are more comfortable using a term like "decision maker" or "key player," that's fine as well. The essential point is to identify the one person who has the power to green-light the change you wish to achieve. If you think the target is a group, such as the school board, you need to identify the one person within that group who actually needs to approve the decision. This person's power may stem from his or her position (such as a committee chair who determines what gets voted on) or from influence (such as a senior legislator to whom others look for guidance). If you do not know who this person is or the nature of his or her power, then you have little chance of effecting change. If you say, for example, "We want school lunches to be healthier," you need to start by knowing who has the power to change school lunches. Is it the mayor? The president of the school board? The superintendent? The head of the health department? A general call for healthier school lunches is unlikely to produce any change.

In some cases, your campaign might have a few targets. For example, there may be three key legislators whose committees must each approve a bill in order to move it to the floor for debate. Decisions about school budgeting might lie in the hands of the principal and the chair of the board finance committee. But in no case can your target be "the board" or "the state legislature" or "the government." It is impossible to get "the government" to do something; you need to persuade the individual human beings who make up the government to take a certain action. Each such person has a name, title, and office address.

When you have identified your target, you will want to learn as much as possible about the interests and pressures that affect her decision making. Who has personal or political influence on this person? What motivates this person to take on her position, and what are her ambitions for the future? Who could support her or stand in her way?

Depending on who your target is, you may find this information by doing research, or by establishing a direct relationship with him. If, for example, you have taken on a campaign to raise the salaries of early childhood teachers in your synagogue, the target might be the head of the board. This person is a member of your community and quite possibly a friend or relative of some members of the organizing committee. You do not want to create an adversarial relationship with this person. Instead, you should assume that he wants to do what is right but has other interests and pressures (such as producing a balanced budget) that prevent him from raising salaries. In the course of your discussions with this person, you will want to find out what drives him to take part in synagogue leadership. What are his hopes and dreams for the community? What are the competing interests that he is trying to balance? By creating a relationship with this person, you will increase your chances of persuading him that your requests are in alignment with his interests.

Let's say, for example, that the board president shares with you that he is passionate about educating the next generation of Jews; with your prodding, he remembers a particular teacher who really made an impact on his Jewish identity. You might then focus on helping him to understand that paying higher salaries will help to attract and retain the best educators possible. If you learn that the board president seeks out public recognition, you might consider how to help him to be recognized for his leadership in creating a fair wage scale for the synagogue. If you learn that he is primarily concerned with balancing the synagogue budget, you can work with him to create a fund-raising campaign that highlights the need to pay living wages.

In some cases, organizers may have an adversarial relationship with the target. In the transit campaign described earlier, the target of the campaign was the head of the Chicago Transit Authority. At first, the community group leading the campaign requested meetings with this person. When he refused again and again to meet with the group, neighborhood residents began showing up in large numbers to interrupt CTA meetings. At the same time, group members exerted pressure on elected officials with influence over the CTA by inviting these officials to community meetings, making phone calls to these officials, and—in at least one case—staging a protest on the lawn of a council member's home.

In the end, the community won twenty-four-hour train service. Like the theoretical synagogue board president mentioned above, the head of the CTA ultimately complied out of a concern for his own interests. In this case, though, his interests were not public recognition for his own innovative leadership, but rather the desire to stop the loud protests at board meetings and to tame his increasingly negative public profile.

This confrontational approach can sometimes feel out of place in a religious context, where we try to teach positive interpersonal relations. But, as we learn from the biblical example of Moses and God pressuring Pharaoh to liberate the Israelites, confrontational tactics are sometimes necessary in pursuit of a more just world. And even when engaged in confrontation, we should still honor the dignity of our opponents, as the Torah text does by recording Pharaoh's pain at the death of his first-born son and his poignant request that Moses "plead with Adonai your God to remove this death from me" (Exodus 10:17). Still, confrontation does not need to be a default approach, but rather can be turned to if the key decision maker proves unwilling to cooperate with your group.

Many campaigns will probably also have secondary targets—people who have influence over the primary target. For example, a board president might listen to the rabbi or school principal. A junior legislator might follow the lead of the more senior one who mentored her. A mayor might listen to a certain key business leader who has raised large donations for the mayor's campaign. One businessperson might care about the opinions of other businesspeople. Sometimes, the best way to exert pressure on the primary target will be to focus on those who have the power to influence him or her. In order to persuade the secondary target, you will need to assess that person's interests just as you would for the primary target.

In 2001 I spent the summer working on a campaign to raise the wages of janitors in New Jersey. One of the primary targets of this campaign was an Orthodox Jew who employed nonunion contractors to clean the many office buildings he owned. The owner had consistently refused to meet with the union. As a rabbinical student, I was asked to intervene and to speak with this man from a Jewish perspective. I knew that a young, female, Conservative rabbinical student was unlikely to have much sway over a middle-aged Orthodox man.

However, I learned that this building owner sat on the board of an organization headed by a rabbi with whom I had a relationship. I thought that the rabbi might be sympathetic, but he was not yet an ally—I would need to identify his interests. I met with the rabbi and told him about what I had learned from the workers I had met through the campaign. In turn, he shared with me that he had worked his way through college by serving as an elevator operator. He remained deeply grateful to the union he had belonged to then for guaranteeing that he earned enough to pay tuition. The rabbi agreed to make a phone call, and the building owner agreed to the rabbi's request to negotiate with the union. In this case, I realized that I had no power over the primary target but could have some influence with a secondary target who, in turn, could persuade the business owner to change his position.

6. Educate your community.

Through education, you will excite more community members about the issue, help community members to become spokespeople for the campaign, and link the campaign with Jewish text and tradition. In designing an educational program, it is important to start with a clear goal for what participants should gain from these programs. Before inviting a speaker to address the community or organizing a study session on a topic, the leadership team should identify how these programs will advance the campaign as a whole. To ensure that your educational program contributes to the goals of the campaign, start by answering the following questions:

- Who is your audience? What do they already know, and what should they know?

- How will increasing this group's knowledge advance your campaign? Are you trying to garner support for a policy position? Train individuals to speak about an issue? Respond to internal criticism about the issue? Excite members about an upcoming action? Once you have identified these goals, you will be better equipped to design a program that meets these goals.

In general, the community as a whole should have a basic understanding of the campaign goals, the factors that contribute to the identified problem, and the Jewish perspective on the issue. The leadership of the community should have a more in-depth understanding of the campaign, as they will need to speak in support of this campaign both inside and outside of the community. The campaign leaders should have the most information, as they will act as spokespeople for the campaign both internally and externally.

For example, let's say that your community has decided to address inequities in public school funding in your state. Everyone in your community should learn that these inequities exist, that Judaism holds the community as a whole responsible for the education of children, and that your institution has joined a coalition trying to pass legislation that will abolish the current inequities. For the overall community, your education program might include talks by experts on educational funding to speak about the causes and effects of the unequal distribution of money. Members might meet with local grassroots leaders such as parent activists in underfunded schools. The rabbi, cantor, educator, or a knowledgeable layperson might lead text studies in which you look at Jewish sources about financing education. The community might hold a seder or other ritual event devoted to the issue. The rabbi and other leaders might give sermons or talks about why your community has taken on this issue.

Ideally, these educational programs will take place at every level of the community. In a school setting, students might devote some of their social studies or math time to examining and comparing school budgets. The faculty might discuss the issue during their own meetings. Parents might be invited to educational sessions on the topic. In a synagogue setting, educational programs might take place during religious school or at youth group meetings, at Shabbat services, in gatherings of nursery school parents, at special public events, and in sisterhood / women's league or brotherhood / men's club meetings. Ideally, every member of the community will be able to speak at least in broad terms about why your community is tackling the issue, what you hope to achieve, and why this issue is a Jewish one.

To be effective, educational programs must go beyond simply inviting an expert speaker to address the group or asking the rabbi to lead a text study. Community members will need time, space, and the guidance to process what they have learned, to internalize these lessons, and to practice speaking about the issue. A frontal lecture followed by a question-and-answer session rarely accomplishes this goal. Instead, carve out time for small-group discussion and for community members to articulate their positions on the issue in their own words and in the context of their own stories.

The rabbi, principal, board members, and other key leadership need more information than the average member. As authority figures and presumed experts, they may be called on to speak publicly about the issue or to defend the campaign to members or to outsiders. In thinking about how to educate these individuals, consider the top five or ten questions that these leaders might be asked by someone who hears about your community's campaign. For the public school funding campaign, these might include: "How much will it cost to eliminate this inequality?" "Will the schools that currently receive more money suffer?" "Why should Jews care about schools that primarily serve non-Jews? Why should Jews who send their children to day school care about public school at all?" "Will increased funding actually make a difference for failing schools?"

You will want to invest time talking with your community's top leadership about these issues at board meetings, staff meetings, and in one-to-one conversations (as described in depth in chapter 4). One especially effective means of educating this group will be to develop relationships between these leaders and their peers in other communities and organizations. The rabbi should meet with other clergy members engaged in the issue. The principal or educators should meet with the faculty of schools affected by the inequalities in funding. Board members should meet with board members of community organizations working on the issue.

Finally, the key leadership of the campaign will need an in-depth understanding of the facts and figures involved. They will need to speak articulately about their personal connection to the campaign, about the Jewish connection, and about why your institution has chosen to get involved. They will need personal connections to members of other communities working on the issue.

The particulars of the education program will differ with each campaign. It is most important, though, that you begin with the question: what does each member of this community need to know about this campaign, and exactly how will this program advance us toward our campaign goal? The rest will follow.

7. Incorporate multiple modes of action into your organizing campaign.

Direct service can also become a component in organizing. Consider service learning, defined as service combined with study and reflection, a means of educating the general community about the issue. For instance, in the course of your campaign, you might involve members of your community in tutoring or reading to children in an underfunded school. This experience will yield needed support for the children while also educating members of your community about the challenges that this school faces.

Advocacy and financial investment techniques may also be useful. In the course of the education campaign, some parents may join a class action lawsuit related to the issue. Lawyers and policy experts in your community may involve themselves in drafting legislation. The bar/bat mitzvah class can raise money to donate to an organization that works on educational equity. The youth group can solicit donations of laptops to give to schools that need them.

For example, in 2007, Central Reform Congregation (CRC) in St. Louis, Missouri, learned that health-care coverage was a priority issue for their membership. The synagogue decided to join a statewide coalition working to pass a bill that would guarantee health-care coverage to all state residents. The synagogue, together with other coalition members, pursued a number of different avenues to passing this bill. These included meetings with state legislators, recruiting other religious leaders and congregations to the cause, participation in rallies, and educational efforts aimed at building popular support for the bill. While the legislative campaign moved forward, CRC continued to send volunteers once a week to work in a local health clinic that serves the uninsured. By participating in regular service, synagogue members maintained personal connections with people in need of health care and reminded themselves week after week of the need for legislative change.[6]

8. Take action.

You have identified the campaign, formed strong relationships among those involved, done your research, identified a target, found partners, and educated your community about what you are doing. Now, you will harness the power of your community to encourage your target to make the change you want.

All of the action you take should move you a bit closer to your goal. Let's go back to the public education example. Your coalition wants the state legislature to change school funding regulations so that schools in low-income neighborhoods receive their fair share of support. You have determined that the governor and two key state senators have the power to push this change through. The question now is how to persuade these elected officials to support the bill. There are a number of ways to put pressure on these officials. Some possibilities include:

- Asking members of your community to write letters or to call these officials

- Taking a delegation from your community to meet with these officials or their staff

- Inviting these officials to attend a public meeting at your institution, in which you call on them to support the bill and ask for their public commitment

- Engaging constituents of each state senator in calling, writing to, or visiting his or her own elected representative

Some of these activities, such as writing letters or making phone calls, involve a low level of commitment. Following an educational event, you can ask audience members to write letters, sign petitions, and even make cell-phone calls on the spot. Other activities, such as visiting the state capitol, involve a much higher level of commitment. Participants will need to take a day off from work or school, practice speaking about the issue and their connection to it, and possibly speak to elected officials for the first time in their lives. It is best to create multiple opportunities for engagement, at various levels of commitment, in order to involve as many members of your community as possible.

You will notice that many of these activities are similar or even identical to the kinds of activities used in an advocacy campaign. The essential difference in an organizing campaign is that you spend time building the relationships necessary to involve significant numbers of people in a sustained effort to make change. While an advocacy campaign may involve asking for letters once, an organizing campaign will get hundreds of people to write letters, make phone calls, and visit their elected officials in a coordinated way.

A NEW ELEMENTARY SCHOOL FOR NEW YORK

Central Synagogue, a large and wealthy synagogue on the East Side of Manhattan, learned through a one-to-one conversation campaign facilitated by Just Congregations and Manhattan Together that ensuring quality public education would be essential to keeping its members in the city. Before the recent financial crisis, a large percentage of families in the community sent their children to private schools. Now, with less income, more and more parents wanted to enroll their children in public school. As a result, even the best public schools in the area were overcrowded, and many children entering kindergarten did not receive a place in the school in their district.

Members of the organizing team realized that the best way to alleviate pressure on existing schools would be to open a new elementary school. They began scouring the East Side for appropriate sites. Eventually, they discovered an empty school building that a Jewish day school had planned to lease before cutting its budget in the wake of the economic collapse. Central Synagogue members worked with the day school and with the city to broker a deal that would allow a new public school to open in this building. This was the first new school in ten years to open on the Upper East Side. Following the campaign, the city asked Central Synagogue to help negotiate school redistricting. While the synagogue elected not to participate, the invitation demonstrated that the city now recognized the power of this religious community.[7]

Among interfaith organizing networks, one of the most popular and powerful actions is known as an "accountability session." The coalition invites a select group of people—usually elected officials—to a public meeting about the issue at hand. The group then mobilizes as many people as possible to attend this meeting. Packing a room demonstrates to the public officials the power of the organizations and institutions represented to mobilize their constituencies. Usually, each institution commits to bringing a certain number of people. In turn, individual leaders within each institution's leadership commit to their own turnout goals.

Accountability sessions are highly ritualized events, in which each person plays a designated part. Generally, the action begins with an introduction or prayer by one of the religious leaders present. A lay leader announces how many people are in the room. Another lay leader presents a report based on the research that the group has done. People affected by the issue at hand tell their own stories. The elected officials in attendance are introduced and asked to commit to taking a certain position on the issue. These officials usually are not permitted to give long speeches; instead, they are asked for a yes or no answer to the question of whether they will support the coalition's position.

Some people find accountability sessions to be overly confrontational and even disrespectful to the elected officials present. It is important to remember, though, that by the time these actions take place, the major work has already been done in the course of meetings leading up to the action. The elected officials already know what questions they will be asked, and they will probably not attend unless they plan to commit to the group's request. These actions serve the purpose of making the elected official's commitment public, of building excitement and a sense of accomplishment among coalition members, and of ritualizing a victorious moment in the campaign. In addition, the actions allow the entire community to unite around a shared accomplishment. This positive feeling can give the community the energy to move forward with the next phase of the work. Some people who came to support a friend or just wandered in to see the excitement may be so energized that they join the campaign.

Like religious rituals, accountability sessions involve drama but few surprises. When we attend a Jewish wedding, we usually know what will happen. There will be rings, blessings, and the breaking of a glass. We certainly do not expect a *chuppah* collapse or a surprise interruption by a spurned partner, à la *The Graduate*. And yet, the ceremony is dramatic, even without being surprising. Though the rituals may be familiar, they also gain new meaning through their enactment by each new couple. And something really happens—the couple really are transformed from unmarried to married. Similarly, in an accountability session, the audience knows what will happen. But the drama of watching events unfold can excite the group and motivate continued action. And the ritual's performance really does cement the public figure's commitment and his or relationship with the organization.[8]

9. Maintain relationships.

At every point in the campaign, you should be maintaining relationships with team members, elected officials, professional and lay leadership of your institution, coalition partners, and other key figures. As the work continues, and as you encounter challenges, frustrations, and burnout, these relationships will help you to sustain your commitment to the work. Team members will support one another through the ups and downs of the work, form sacred spiritual community, and encourage each other's leadership and personal growth. Sustaining relationships with individuals affected by the issue will help everyone in the group to maintain a focus on the end goal, rather than get caught up in the day-to-day grind of the work.

Maintaining relationships means scheduling regular one-to-one conversations with these individuals (as described in chapter 4) and asking each member of your organizing team to devote a certain amount of his or her time to these conversations. You will also want to stay in constant contact with members of your group through follow-up phone calls, in-person meetings, and e-mails before and after every meeting or event.

THE POWER OF THE ORDINARY

Through organizing, we harness the power of ordinary individuals to make extraordinary societal change. Organizing differs from other modes of social change in its focus on relationships, leadership development, and strategically planned campaigns. It almost always seeks to produce some structural or institutional change in the form of law, policy, budgetary allocation, or the like. Organizing campaigns can include direct service, advocacy, *tzedakah*, and investment as components or complements on the way to the structural change goal. In some cases, organizing will lead a community to pursue these other modes of social change. In other cases, participation in these modes of social change will motivate a community to begin organizing.

I hope that the discussion above will be helpful in thinking about whether to bring organizing to your community. I do not, however, intend this chapter to be read as a foolproof recipe for organizing, any more than I would want to be operated on by a surgeon who had learned her trade only from a textbook. Running a good organizing campaign takes training and a lot of practice. Seasoned organizers will have a feeling for when to focus on relationship building, when to hold an action, and how to inspire the organizing team to take on the next challenge. They will understand the art and the science of these skills and activities. They will be able to train your leaders and correct course when things aren't working. The best way to learn organizing skills will be to join a local organizing network, to attend training, and to learn from experienced community organizers.[9]

Organizing is hard. It takes time, money, sustained energy, and an ability to stay focused on long-term goals. But the rewards are great. Through organizing, we can develop new leaders; create strong relationships across the boundaries of religion, race, class, age, and ethnicity; transform the world in accordance with our deepest passions and dreams; and build supportive spiritual communities that live out their values in prayer, study, and action.

Conclusion

Where Justice Dwells

In the course of this book, we began with halakhic, theological, and historical questions of why and where Jews should do social justice. We then moved to the principles of social justice and the nuts and bolts of how to do social justice in our own communities, whether these be synagogues, schools, Hillels, independent minyanim, JCCs, camps, or even informal communities. Now, let's take a moment to imagine what our Jewish community might look like if we really infused these social justice ideals with every aspect of our Jewish lives.

On an institutional level, we will succeed in creating communities that live out Jewish values through a holistic, integrated practice of Judaism. The budgets of these institutions will allow for investment in social justice, for paying workers a living wage, and for promoting family-friendly work environments. Prayer services will highlight liturgy that reflects justice themes. Rituals, such as blessings and holiday celebrations, will inspire and support the pursuit of justice. Leaders in social justice activities will receive public honors and praise. Educational programs for children and adults will probe current issues through the lens of Jewish text, history, and tradition. Community members will engage in ongoing service, advocacy, and organizing work connected to issues that reflect the community's concerns and passions. When staff and lay leaders speak about the community, they will tell stories about what the social justice efforts have accomplished. Through social justice work, our institutions will form lasting partnerships with other religious communities and communal organizations, and they will be able to call on these partners when issues arise that specifically affect the Jewish community.

This does not mean that these communities will be all social justice all the time. In strong communities, individuals will visit each other in the hospital, bake a lasagna for someone who has just had a baby, and make sure that there is a minyan during shivah. Rabbis will pastor to those grappling with difficult life events. Children will study for their *b'nai mitzvah*. These communities will boast meaningful prayer services and passionate study sessions. Members will celebrate positive milestones together, and comfort those in need of comfort. These practices and support systems will be enhanced by placing social justice at the center of communal life. The existence of a shared mission will be the impetus for ensuring that the community stays together and that it stays strong.

On a personal and communal level, the creation of these institutions will change how we think about Judaism and the Jewish community. In chapter 1, I mentioned the experience that I often have when I tell a stranger that I am a rabbi. If Jewish, this person immediately starts apologizing for his or her bacon eating, lack of synagogue attendance, and dating of non-Jews. While we immediately identify ritual practice as "religious," many of us have ceased being surprised when we hear reports of Jews who identify as religious mistreating their workers, laundering money, cheating on taxes, or refusing to turn on the heat in apartment buildings they own. When we create an expectation that Jewish communities will be involved in social justice, we will stop thinking about religion as adherence to a set of ritual practices limited to the home and synagogue, and we will take on (or more accurately, return to) a much broader definition of religion, which also includes ethical behavior and engagement in creating a more just world.

This change will not come easily. It will require our communities, leaders, and institutions to devote significant time and money to social justice. It will mean sitting down with members of our communities to craft a vision of the impact that we wish to have on our cities and towns, our states, our country, and our world. It will mean gathering the courage to tell each other stories about our fears and hopes and to listen to the stories of others. It will mean using these stories to identify our shared passions and to choose service projects, *tzedakah* commitments and investments, and advocacy and organizing campaigns based on these passions.

We will need to come face-to-face with our own power and to build partnerships and coalitions that harness and hone our power for good. We will need to look at our texts, our history, and our rituals as sources of wisdom and inspiration for our social justice work. Within our communities, we will need to have challenging, messy, and insightful conversations about how these texts, history, and rituals can guide our engagement in current events. And we will need to act on the courage of our convictions and to commit to the work in the long term. We will have to be prepared for the frustration that often comes with ongoing work on a seemingly intractable social issue.

But we will also celebrate our victories, our new (and seasoned) leaders, our direct and indirect contributions to improving people's lives, and the strengthened community that we have built together.

The title of this book, *Where Justice Dwells*, refers to the rebuke of the Jewish people with which Isaiah begins his prophecy: "Alas—she has become a harlot, the faithful city that was filled with justice, where righeousness dwelt—but now murderers" (Isaiah 1:21). Isaiah's description is brutal. In this fallen city, "every head is ailing" (1:5), the land is "a waste" (1:7), and God rejects sacrifices and petitions.

These images are cruel, but perhaps no worse than the language often used to describe our own world: "It's hopeless," "Things are just going to keep getting worse," "There's nothing we can do." This kind of talk cuts off social justice efforts before they start or keeps us working only on the most immediate and easily understood symptoms. Through a quirk of Hebrew grammar, the phrase "where righteousness dwelt" in Isaiah's prophesy can also be read as a statement about the future: "*Tzedek* [righteousness or justice] will dwell there." This ambiguity poses a challenge to the reader: instead of accepting the dismal state of affairs, the reader is forced to think about how to transform this wasted city into a place where justice will dwell. In fact, a few verses later, Isaiah does promise a brighter future: "You shall be called City of Righteousness, Faithful City" (Isaiah 1:26).

When we look around the places where we live, it is easy to focus on the negative, on the instances of injustice and on the absence of righteousness.

But even in the most dreary circumstances, we must retain hope that someday, "justice will dwell there."

I started this book with a discussion of the importance of committing to "our places," whether these be the places we live or other places to which we feel a deep connection. Through making such a commitment, we begin—either literally or figuratively—to dwell in these places in such a way as to make justice dwell there as well.

In the course of this book, I have discussed ways to build strong communities that integrate social justice work, prayer, learning, and care for one another into a vibrant and holistic Jewish practice. In such communities, we can already say, "Justice dwells here." Building these just and powerful spiritual communities enables us to make our places "cities of righteousness, faithful cities."

Organizational Resources for Social Justice

AMERICAN JEWISH WORLD SERVICE

http://ajws.org

American Jewish World Service (AJWS) is an international development organization motivated by Judaism's imperative to pursue justice. AJWS is dedicated to alleviating poverty, hunger, and disease among the people of the developing world regardless of race, religion, or nationality. Through grants to grassroots organizations, volunteer service, advocacy, and education, AJWS fosters civil society, sustainable development, and human rights for all people, while promoting the values and responsibilities of global citizenship within the Jewish community.

AVODAH

www.avodah.net

AVODAH: The Jewish Service Corps strengthens the Jewish community's fight against the causes and effects of poverty in the United States by engaging participants in service and community building that inspire them to become lifelong agents for social change whose work for justice is rooted in and nourished by Jewish values. Participants in its service corps program live out and deepen their commitments to social change and Jewish life through a year of full-time work at anti-poverty organizations in Chicago, New Orleans, New York, and Washington, D.C.

HAZON

www.hazon.org

Creates healthy and sustainable communities in the Jewish world and beyond through transformative experiences for individuals and communities; thought leadership in the fields of Jewish and environmental knowledge; and support of the Jewish environmental movement in North America and Israel.

JEWISH COMMUNITY ACTION

www.jewishcommunityaction.org

Jewish Community Action's mission is to bring together Jewish people from diverse traditions and perspectives to promote understanding and take action on social and economic justice issues in Minnesota.

JEWISH COUNCIL FOR PUBLIC AFFAIRS

www.jewishpublicaffairs.org

Serves as the representative voice of the organized American Jewish community in addressing the principal mandate of the Jewish community relations field, expressed in three interrelated goals: to safeguard the rights of Jews in the United States and around the world; to dedicate ourselves to the safety and security of the State of Israel; and to protect, preserve, and promote a just American society, one that is democratic and pluralistic and that furthers harmonious interreligious, interethnic, interracial, and other intergroup relations.

JEWISH COUNCIL ON URBAN AFFAIRS

www.jcua.org

The mission of the Jewish Council on Urban Affairs is to combat poverty, racism, and anti-Semitism in partnership with Chicago's diverse communities.

JEWISH FUNDS FOR JUSTICE

www.jewishjustice.org

Jewish Funds for Justice (JFSJ) was founded to affirm the historic commitment of the Jewish people to work for social and economic justice in the United States. From community investing to grant making to service learning, each of its approaches is guided by Jewish values and inspired by Jewish tradition. As of 2011, JFSJ is in the process of merging with the Progressive Jewish Alliance to form a new national Jewish social justice organization.

JEWISH ORGANIZING INITIATIVE
www.jewishorganizing.org
The Jewish Organizing Initiative (JOI) develops the next generation of Jewish leaders and helps them gain the organizing skills and experience to build powerful Jewish and community organizations to create a just world.

JEWISH WOMEN'S ARCHIVE
www.jwa.org
The mission of the Jewish Women's Archive (JWA) is to uncover, chronicle, and transmit to a broad public the rich history of American Jewish women.

JEWISH WORLD WATCH
www.jewishworldwatch.org
Jewish World Watch (JWW) is a hands-on leader in the fight against genocide and mass atrocities, engaging individuals and communities to take local actions that produce powerful global results.

JEWS FOR RACIAL AND ECONOMIC JUSTICE
www.jfrej.org
Pursues racial and economic justice in New York City by advancing systemic changes that result in concrete improvements in people's daily lives. Engages individual Jews, key Jewish institutions, and key Jewish community leaders in the fight for racial and economic justice in partnership with people of color and low-income and immigrant communities.

JEWS UNITED FOR JUSTICE
www.jufj.org
Leads Jews in the Washington, D.C., area to act on shared Jewish values by pursuing justice and equality in the local community.

JUST CONGREGATIONS

http://urj.org/socialaction/training/justcongregations

Just Congregations is an initiative of the Union for Reform Judaism whose primary goal is to engage and train Reform synagogues in congregation-based community organizing, while simultaneously strengthening the congregations.

KESHET

www.keshetonline.org

Keshet is a national grassroots organization that works for the full inclusion of gay, lesbian, bisexual, and transgender (GLBT) Jews in Jewish life. Led and supported by GLBT Jews and straight allies, Keshet offers resources, trainings, and technical assistance to create inclusive Jewish communities nationwide.

MAZON

http://mazon.org

Founded in 1985, MAZON: A Jewish Response to Hunger is a national nonprofit organization that allocates donations from the Jewish community to prevent and alleviate hunger among people of all faiths and backgrounds.

NATIONAL COUNCIL OF JEWISH WOMEN

www.ncjw.org

The National Council of Jewish Women (NCJW) is a grassroots organization of volunteers and advocates who turn progressive ideals into action. Inspired by Jewish values, NCJW strives for social justice by improving the quality of life for women, children, and families and by safeguarding individual rights and freedoms.

NEW ISRAEL FUND

www.nif.org

The New Israel Fund (NIF) is the leading organization committed to equality and democracy for all Israelis. It is a partnership of Israelis and supporters of Israel worldwide, dedicated to a vision of Israel as both the Jewish homeland and a shared society at peace with itself and its neighbors. NIF strengthens organizations and leaders that work to achieve equality for all the citizens of the state; to realize the civil and human rights of all, including Palestinian citizens of Israel; to recognize and reinforce the essential pluralism of Israeli society; and to empower groups on the economic margins of Israeli society.

ON1FOOT
www.on1foot.org
On1Foot, a project of American Jewish World Service, is an online database of Jewish social justice texts designed to support and promote the teaching of social justice in the Jewish community.

PANIM
http://panim.bbyo.org
The PANIM Institute of BBYO's mission is to train and inspire a new generation of teens committed to service, advocacy, and philanthropy focused on issues that make a difference in the world, and to the Jewish values that support civic engagement.

PROGRESSIVE JEWISH ALLIANCE
www.pjalliance.org
The mission of Progressive Jewish Alliance (PJA) is to engage Jews of diverse backgrounds to learn, lead, and act in their communities to create a more just and equal society. Its vision of social transformation is rooted in shared Jewish values and realized through partnership with local and national allies. As of 2011 PJA, now based in California, is in the process of merging with Jewish Funds for Justice to form a new national Jewish social justice organization.

RABBIS FOR HUMAN RIGHTS–NORTH AMERICA
www.rhr-na.org
Founded in 2002, Rabbis for Human Rights–North America (RHR-NA) is an organization of rabbis from all streams of Judaism that acts on the Jewish imperative to respect and protect the human rights of all people. Grounded in Torah and our Jewish historical experience and guided by the

Universal Declaration of Human Rights, we advocate for human rights in Israel and North America.

RELIGIOUS ACTION CENTER
www.rac.org
For fifty years, the Religious Action Center of Reform Judaism (RAC) has been the hub of Jewish social justice and legislative activity in Washington, D.C. As the D.C. office of the Union for Reform Judaism, the RAC educates and mobilizes the Reform Jewish community on legislative and social concerns, advocating on more than seventy different issues, including economic justice, civil rights, religious liberty, Israel, and more.

REPAIR THE WORLD
http://werepair.org
Repair the World works to inspire American Jews and their communities to give their time and effort to serve those in need. It aims to make service a defining part of American Jewish life.

REPAIR LABS
http://repairlabs.org
RepairLabs, an initiative of Repair the World, develops resources and strategies for Jewish volunteer engagement and service learning.

URI L'TZEDEK
www.utzedek.org
Uri L'Tzedek is an Orthodox social justice organization guided by Torah values and dedicated to combating suffering and oppression. Through community-based education, leadership development, and action, Uri L'Tzedek creates discourse, inspires leaders, and empowers the Jewish community to create a more just world.

Notes

PART ONE: ENVISIONING A JUST PLACE

1. Don Isaac ben Judah Abarbanel, for example, kept calculating that the Messiah would come in just one more year. See Eric Lawee, *Isaac Abarbanel's Stance towards Tradition* (Albany, NY: SUNY Press, 2002), 55, 127–168.

1. WHY JEWISH SOCIAL JUSTICE?

1. Most traditional commentators on the story of Amalek agree that we no longer know who descends from the tribe of Amalek and that this command therefore no longer applies.

2. Jill Jacobs, "Work, Workers, and the Jewish Owner," Rabbinical Assembly, May 2008, www.bjpa.org/Publications/details.cfm?PublicationID=8697.

3. The phrase "it was good" is repeated at the end of almost every day of creation in Genesis 1. At the end of the sixth day, on which human beings are created, God declares that "it was very good" (Genesis 1:31).

4. Peter Singer, "Should This Be the Last Generation?" *New York Times*, June 6, 2010.

5. The Talmudic text uses the word *adam*, which can refer either to humanity as a whole or to a single human being. It is therefore possible to read this argument as one about the creation of humanity as a whole or about whether it would be better for each individual person to have been created. The commentators differ on how to read the word *adam*. The *Tosafot* understand *adam* to refer to each individual human being and explain, "'It

would be better for a person not to have been created'—this refers to before a person's birth, when it is not known what will happen to this person. But when a person is just, he is happy, and happy is the generation of which he is a part" (BT, *Avodah Zarah* 5b). But the Maharasha seems to assume that the conversation is about humanity in general, as he contrasts the suggestion that humanity should not have been created with God's declaration, upon creating humanity, that this creation was "very good" (BT, *Makkot* 23b).

6. The challenge of using the kabbalistic notion of *tikkun olam* for the purposes of social justice, as I discussed in *There Shall Be No Needy: Pursuing Social Justice through Jewish Law and Tradition* (Woodstock, VT: Jewish Lights, 2010), 34–36, is that it is not clear whether there will be a place for human beings in this perfected universe.

7. Hannah Arendt, *The Origins of Totalitarianism* (New York: Meridian Books, 1958), 23.

2. PLACE MATTERS

1. I have taken the phrase "place matters" from the title of the seminal work by Peter Dreier, John Mollenkopf, and Todd Swanson, *Place Matters: Metropolitics for the Twenty-First Century* (Wichita: University Press of Kansas, 2001).

2. See, e.g., Rivash (Rabbi Isaac ben Sheshet Perfet, Barcelona/Algiers, 1326–1408), 475, and Joseph Caro (Spain/Tzfat, 1488–1575), *Beit Yosef, Choshen Mishpat* 163:5.

3. See, e.g., Rema (Moshe Isserles, Poland, 1520–1572), *Choshen Mishpat* 163:1.

4. *Arukh HaShulchan, Yoreh De'ah* 251:4.

5. *She'elot u'Teshuvot Chatam Sofer* 2:231.

6. The Rabbis of the Talmud, in general, allow any commandment to be violated for the purpose of saving a life. The three exceptions are murder, certain illicit sexual behavior (such as incest), and idol worship (BT, *Sanhedrin* 74a); that is, a person who is compelled under threat of death to one of those three things should martyr him- or herself rather than violate the law in question. There is significant debate among later rabbinic authorities about whether this requirement applies only to demands that a person

break the law in public or whether a person must also martyr him- or her-self rather than perform any of these acts in private.

7. The Leiden manuscript reads, *T'chiyenah ir va'ir*, "These cities shall live, each city," instead of *T'hiyenah ir va'ir*, "Thus shall it be with these cities, each city." The Leiden version makes Aborodimas's interpretation significantly clearer; according to this manuscript, the word "live" appears in the biblical text itself. Still, the playful interpretation of the verse does not solve the larger moral issue that Yehuda raises.

8. The question of whose life takes precedence echoes another famous Talmudic case. In BT, *Bava Metzia* 62a, the Rabbis imagine a scenario in which two people are traveling through the desert. One of the people is carrying a flask of water with just enough water to sustain one person. Whoever drinks the water will live; the other person will die. If both people drink half the water, both will die. The Rabbis conclude that the owner of the water should drink it, explaining that the biblical command to ensure "that your brother shall live with you" (Leviticus 25:36) means that one should first save one's own life—after all, in order for your "brother" to live with you, you must be alive yourself. In neither the story of the well in the city nor that of the flask in the desert does the Talmud attempt to determine the relative value of the lives of the people in question.

9. Peter Singer, *The Life You Can Save: Acting Now to End World Poverty* (New York: Random House, 2009), 3–5.

10. Peter Singer, *Writings on an Ethical Life* (New York: Harper, 2001), 123.

11. Singer, *The Life You Can Save*, 160–162.

12. For more on this concept, see Bernard Williams, "Against Utilitarianism," in *The Moral Life: An Introductory Reader in Ethics and Literature*, ed. Louis Pojman (New York: Oxford University Press, 2000), 252–264.

13. *She'elot u'Teshuvot Chatam Sofer* 2:46.

14. *She'elot u'Teshuvot Chatam Sofer* 2:234.

3. THE IDEAL CITY

1. *Avot d'Rabbi Natan, nusach* 1, chap. 1; cf. BT, *Sanhedrin* 59b.

2. Ibid.

3. See, e.g., *Avot d'Rabbi Natan*, *nusach* 1, chap. 1; BT, *Shabbat* 88a; and *Midrash Tanchuma*, *B'reishit*.

4. While many interpretations, especially Christian ones, understand the sin of Sodom to be homosexuality (hence the term "sodomize"), the biblical text emphasizes the violent nature of the sexual act that the townspeople wish to impose on the visitors. There is no indication that this text intends to vilify homosexuality in general—only violent gang rape.

5. See, e.g., Jeremiah 8.

6. *Orchot Tzaddikim, Sha'ar HaNedivut.*

7. Some manuscripts of the Talmud list "water" instead of "a butcher." This variation is eventually adopted by Moses Maimonides in his authoritative code of Jewish law (*Mishneh Torah, Hilkhot De'ot* 4:23).

8. See, e.g., Menachem Meiri, *Beit HaBechirah* on BT, *Sanhedrin* 17b, Soncino translation.

9. Ibid.

10. See, e.g., Ya'akov Hertz of Brody, *Yeshuot Ya'akov* on *Seder Eliyahu Zuta* 16.

11. Meir (Ish Shalom) Friedmann, *Me'ir Ayin* on *Seder Eliyahu Zuta* 16.

12. For statistics on the composition of LA's bus ridership, see *Metro Quarterly* 22 (Summer 2008): 12. For an analysis of the inadequacies of the bus system, see Eric Mann, *A New Vision of Urban Transportation: The Bus Riders Union's Mass Transit Campaign* (Labor/Community Strategy Center, 1996), and Richard A. Marcantonio and Angelica K. Jongco, "From the Back of the Bus to the End of the Line," in *Human Rights: Journal of the Section of Individual Rights & Responsibilities* 34, no. 3 (2007): 10.

13. See, e.g., BT, *Sanhedrin* 98a, and JT, *Terumot* 8:4.

14. Setha Low, *Behind the Gates: Life, Security, and the Pursuit of Happiness in Fortress America* (New York: Routledge, 2003), 230–231.

15. Ibid., 232.

16. For the clearest discussion of these concepts, see Emmanuel Levinas, *Otherwise Than Being: Or Beyond Essence* (Pittsburgh: Duquesne University Press, 1998), chap. 4.

17. Robert Pollin, Mark Brenner, Jeanette Wicks-Lim, and Stephanie Luce, *A Measure of Fairness: The Economics of Living Wages and Minimum Wages in the United States* (Ithaca, NY: Cornell University Press, 2008), 14–15.

18. Many of us living in the United States, Canada, Israel, or other Western countries are not accustomed to thinking of the government as primarily a dangerous force (although some communities today do experience a great deal of friction with police and other authorities). The early Rabbis, living under Roman occupation, worried that any Jew seen with the king or another governmental official might intentionally or accidentally pass on some information that would result in harm for the community.

19. For a fuller discussion of the phenomenon of *takkanot hakahal*, see Menachem Elon, *Jewish Law: History, Sources, Principles* (Philadelphia: Jewish Publication Society, 1994), 2:477–879.

20. See, e.g., Chatam Sofer on BT, *Beitzah* 39a.

21. See, e.g., Moshe Isserles in *Darkhei Moshe, Choshen Mishpat* 163, and Rema on *Shulchan Arukh*, loc. cit.

22. See also *Maggid Mishneh* on Maimonides, *Mishneh Torah, Hilkhot Sh'khenim* (6:4), and Joseph Caro, *Beit Yosef, Choshen Mishpat* 163:3.

4. STORYTELLING FOR SOCIAL JUSTICE

1. Robert Cover, "Nomos and Narrative," *Harvard Law Review* 97, no. 4 (1983): 4–5.

2. Ibid.

3. Hannah Arendt, "Isak Dinesen (1885–1962)," in *Reflections on Literature and Culture* (Palo Alto, CA: Stanford University Press, 2007), 270.

4. For a more extensive discussion both of my experience at The Jewish Theological Seminary and of Jewish perspectives on housing issues, see Jacobs, *There Shall Be No Needy*, introduction and chap. 6.

5. Jerome Bruner, *Making Stories: Law, Literature, Life* (Cambridge, MA: Harvard University Press, 2003), 64–65.

6. Adriana Cavarero, *Relating Narratives: Storytelling and Selfhood*, trans. Paul A. Kottman (New York: Routledge, 2000), 92.

7. Martha Minow, "Stories in Law," in *Law's Stories: Narrative and Rhetoric in the Law*, ed. Peter Brooks and Paul Gewirtz (New Haven: Yale University Press, 1996), 36.

8. Joan Biskupic, "Ginsburg: Court Needs Another Woman," *USA Today*, 10 May 2009.

9. See, e.g., the discussion of what *b'rakhah* (blessing) to say when drinking water to quench one's thirst (BT, *Eruvin* 14b) and the question of whether a torn tefillin strap can be sewn together (BT, *Menachot* 35b). Commenting on the latter discussion, Rashi and *Tosafot* disagree about whether "go out and see" is used only to confirm a prohibition (Rashi) or may also be used to support a leniency (*Tosafot*).

10. Doe v. Miller, 405F.3d 700 (8th Cir. 2005).

11. Keith H. Basso, *Wisdom Sits in Places: Landscape and Language among the Western Apache* (Albuquerque, NM: University of New Mexico, 2006), 38.

12. Ibid., 6.

13. My description of this fictional domestic workers campaign is based on the successful campaign by Jews for Racial and Economic Justice and Domestic Workers United to pass a domestic workers bill of rights in New York State. This was one of the most successful Jewish social justice campaigns I have seen—the Jewish participants clearly identified their self-interest, and the two groups worked together for years to win the legislation.

5. CREATING AN INTEGRATED JEWISH LIFE

1. The best known of these researchers is Stephen G. Post. See, for example, *Altruism and Health: Perspectives from Empirical Research* (New York: Oxford University Press, 2007) and *Why Good Things Happen to Good People* (New York: Broadway, 2008).

2. See also *Orchot Tzaddikim, Sha'ar HaNedivut*.

3. For a discussion of contemporary applications of *mussar*, see Ira Stone, *A Responsible Life: The Spiritual Practice of Mussar* (New York: Aviv Press, 2006); and Alan Morinis, *Everyday Holiness: The Jewish Spiritual Path of Mussar* (Boston: Shambhala, 2007). Both of these authors also run organizations and

websites devoted to the practice of *mussar*: www.mussarleadership.org (Stone) and www.mussarinstitute.org (Morinis).

4. I am grateful to my friend and colleague Rabbi Lisa Goldstein for influencing my thinking on *mussar* and social justice.

5. *Birkot HaMitzvot Umishpatehem.*

6. Union for Reform Judaism, "The Blessing for Giving Tzedakah," http://urj.org//learning/teacheducate/childhood/shabbat//?syspage=article&item_id=2387.

7. Written by participants in "With All Your Possessions: Judaism and Economic Justice" class, 1996, Reconstructionist Rabbinical College, Wyncote, PA, taught by Rabbis Toba Spitzer and Natan Fenner.

8. See Augusto Boal, *Games for Actors and Non-Actors* (New York: Routledge, 1992).

9. Judith Gelman, "Paying Living Wage—One Synagogue's Experience," March 28, 2008, www.ameinu.net/perspectives/america.php?articleid=409, and e-mail correspondence with Rabbi Fred Dobb.

10. For a fuller discussion of Judaism and health care, see Jacobs, *There Shall Be No Needy*, chap. 7.

11. The experience of Adat Shalom is supported by the research on the effect of living-wage legislation. In general, business costs do not go up, largely because turnover (and therefore training costs) decreases and productivity rises. See, e.g., Christopher Niedt, Greg Ruiters, Dana Wise, and Erica Schoenberger, "The Effects of the Living Wage in Baltimore" (Johns Hopkins University / Economic Policy Institute, 1999); David Reynolds et al., "Impact of the Detroit Living Wage Ordinance" (Wayne State University, 1999); David Fairris et al., "Examining the Evidence: The Impact of the Los Angeles Living Wage Ordinance on Workers and Businesses" (Los Angeles Alliance for a New Economy, 2005); Mark Brenner, "The Economic Impact of Living Wage Ordinances" (University of Massachusetts, Political Research Economy Institute, 2004); David Reynolds and Jean Vortkamp, *Impact of Detroit's Living Wage Law on Non-Profit Organizations* (Center for Urban Studies & Labor Studies Center College of Urban, Labor and Metropolitan Affairs, 2000), 2.

6. PARTNERSHIPS AND POWER

1. Abraham Joshua Heschel, "What We Might Do Together," in *Moral Grandeur and Spiritual Audacity: Essays*, ed. Susannah Heschel (New York: Farrar, Straus & Giroux, 1996), 298–299.

2. Emmanuel Levinas, *Totality and Infinity*, trans. Alphonso Lingis (Pittsburgh: Duquesne University Press, 1969), 74.

3. J. J. Goldberg, *Jewish Power: Inside the American Jewish Establishment* (New York: Addison Wesley, 1996), 4–6.

4. I. L. Peretz, "The Golem," trans. Irving Howe, in *The Penguin Book of Jewish Short Stories*, ed. Emanuel Litvinoff (New York: Penguin, 1979), 15–16. Thank you to my partner, Guy Austrian, for teaching me to read this story as one about silent power.

5. Paul Kivel, *Uprooting Racism: How White People Can Work for Racial Justice* (Gabriola Island, BC: New Society Publishers, 2002), 6.

6. A research report by the National Bureau for Economic Research finds, "Job applicants with white names needed to send about 10 resumes to get one callback; those with African-American names needed to send around 15 resumes to get one callback" (Marianne Bertrand and Sendhil Mullainathan, "Are Emily and Greg More Employable than Lakisha and Jamal? A Field Experiment on Labor Market Discrimination," NBER working paper no. 9873, 2003, http://papers.nber.org/papers/w9873. See also Michael Luo, "Whitening the Resume," *New York Times*, December 5, 2009.

7. Betty Smith, *A Tree Grows in Brooklyn* (New York: HarperPerennial Modern Classics, 2006; originally published 1943), 18–19.

8. On the history of Jews and whiteness, see Karen Brodkin, *How Jews Became White Folks and What That Says about Race in America* (New Brunswick, NJ: Rutgers University Press, 2002), and Eric L. Goldstein, *The Price of Whiteness: Jews, Race, and American Identity* (Princeton, NJ: Princeton University Press, 2006). Much has been written on the history and legacy of postwar racism in housing. Two excellent starting points are John F. Bauman, Roger Biles, and Kristin M. Szylvian, eds., *From Tenements to the Taylor Homes: In Search of an Urban Housing Policy in Twentieth Century America* (University Park: Pennsylvania State University Press, 2000), and Kenneth Jackson, *Crabgrass*

Frontier: The Suburbanization of the United States (New York: Oxford University Press, 1985).

9. James Baldwin and Randall Kenan, *The Cross of Redemption: Uncollected Writings* (New York: Random House, 2010), 136.

7. SACRED WORDS: ENGAGING WITH TEXT AND TRADITION

1. Rabbenu Yonah on *Mishnah Avot* 3:2, as printed in *Mishnat Reuven: Masekhet Avot im Perushei HaRishonim*, vol. 2 (Jerusalem: Mossad haRav Kook, 2009), 19–21.

2. For a fuller discussion of labor rights in Judaism, see Jacobs, *There Shall Be No Needy*, chap. 4.

3. See Jacob Katz, *Ma'ariv B'zmano U'shelo B'zmano*, in *Divine Law in Human Hands: Case Studies in Halakhic Flexibility* (Hebrew) (Jerusalem: Magnes, 1998), 175–200.

4. Mordechai on *Avodah Zarah* 813, quoted in Elisheva Baumgarten, *Mothers and Children: Jewish Family Life in Medieval Europe* (Princeton, NJ: Princeton University Press, 2004), 144.

8. DIRECT SERVICE

1. Moses Maimonides, *Sefer HaMitzvot Shoresh* 1.

2. *She'elot u'Teshuvot Chatam Sofer* 2:231.

3. See, e.g., the series of stories in BT, *Ketubot* 67a–b.

4. Interview with Barry Glass, Telem.

5. Randy Stoeker and Elizabeth A. Tryon, *The Unheard Voices: Community Organizations and Service Learning* (Philadelphia: Temple University Press, 2009), 9.

6. Interview with Alison Hirsch, cofounder of the Columbia Hillel clothing pantry, 2010.

7. Ariel Kaminer, "Three Steps to Making Smart Haiti Donations," *New York Times*, January 22, 2010.

8. Lior Etziony, "Haiti Journal: Volunteering on My Own," Jewish Telegraphic Agency, January 22, 2010.

9. Susan Dominus, "To Feed the Hungry, Keep the Can, Open a Wallet," *New York Times*, December 12, 2009.

10. Stoeker and Tryon, *Unheard Voices*, 26.

11. See, e.g., *A Matter of Survival: Volunteering By, In, and For Low-Income Communities* (Points of Light Foundation and Annie E. Casey Foundation, 2000).

12. Some useful books to help with these discussions include Susan Benigni Cipolle, *Service Learning and Social Justice: Engaging Students in Social Change* (New York: Rowman and Littlefield, 2010); and David White, *Practicing Discernment with Youth: A Transformative Youth Ministry Approach* (Cleveland, OH: Pilgrim Press, 2005).

9. GIVING AND INVESTING MONEY

1. *B'reishit Rabbah* 16:2; cf. *Sh'mot Rabbah* 35:1.

2. Yechiel Epstein, *Arukh HaShulchan, Yoreh De'ah* 247.

3. See, e.g., *Shulchan Arukh, Yoreh De'ah* 256:5; *Sefer Kolbo* 82; *Arukh HaShulchan, Yoreh De'ah* 247.

4. One might argue that since the distribution of *tzedakah* can be a life or death matter, these decisions should considered to be like capital cases, which require a court of twenty-three. However, requiring twenty-three judges may result in endangering the lives of the poor, who may die waiting for the court to make its decisions. For a longer discussion on this, see R. Yitzchak ben R. Moshe of Vienna (ca. 1180–ca. 1250), *Sefer Or Zarua, Hilkhot Tzedakah* 2.

5. *Tosafot* on BT, *Bava Batra* 8b.

6. See, e.g., *Shulchan Arukh, Yoreh De'ah* 249:1 and Rema there; *Maharil, Hilkhot Rosh Hashanah*; Shakh on *Yoreh De'ah* 249:1; and lengthy discussion of this question in Eliezer Waldenburg, *Tzitz Eliezer* 9:1.

7. Louise Story, "A Big Salary with a Big Stipulation: Share It," *New York Times*, November 12, 2007.

8. Matt Fellowes and Mia Mabanta, "Banking on Wealth: America's New Retail Banking Infrastructure and Its Wealth-Building Potential" (Brookings Institute, January 2008).

9. Federal Trade Commission, "Payday Loans Equal Very Costly Cash: Consumers Urged to Consider the Alternatives," March 2008, www.ftc.gov/bcp/edu/pubs/consumer/alerts/alt060.shtm.

10. Charles McGray, "Check Cashers, Redeemed," *New York Times*, November 7, 2008.

11. Isaac Meir Kahan, *Ahavat Chesed, G'milut Chasadim*, chap. 9.

10. ADVOCACY

1. Rivash, *She'elot u'Teshuvot* 251.

2. Interview with Alex Weissman, December 2010.

3. An organization with a budget of $500,000 may spend up to 20 percent of its budget on advocacy and lobbying. Organizations with larger budgets may spend 20 percent of the first $500,000 and 15 percent of the remaining budget on direct lobbying (defined as direct requests to legislators to support or oppose a bill), up to a total of $1 million. Additional money may be spent on grassroots lobbying, which includes publishing op-eds, giving sermons, or otherwise trying to influence public opinion. Many areas of work, such as publishing research papers, do not count as lobbying for the purposes of the law. For more information, see www.independentsector.org/charity_lobbying.

4. See, e.g., Douglas M. Bloomfield, "The AIPAC Two Aren't the Only Ones on Trial," *New Jersey Jewish News*, March 5, 2009; David Levy, "So Pro-Israel That It Hurts," *Haaretz*, March 24, 2006; and Goldberg, *Jewish Power*, 225–226.

11. COMMUNITY ORGANIZING

1. See, e.g., Saul Alinsky, *Rules for Radicals* (New York: Vintage, 1989), 89–91; Michael Walzer, *Exodus and Revolution* (New York: Basic Books, 1986); and Arthur Waskow, *The Freedom Seder* (Washington, DC: Micah Press, 1970).

2. In this statement, I am consciously echoing the Haggadah's statement that if not for divine intervention, modern-day Jews might still be slaves in Egypt. However, I am conscious that there is no historical evidence that the Israelites ever were slaves in Egypt. For me, the story of the Exodus is religiously true, regardless of what the historical facts may be.

3. Interview with Barry Glass of Telem, December 2010.

4. Malcolm Gladwell, "Small Change: Why the Revolution Will Not Be Tweeted," *New Yorker*, October 4, 2010.

5. Ibid.

6. E-mail correspondence with Rabbi Susan Talve.

7. Interview with Cantor Angela Warnick Buchdahl, December 2010.

8. For more on the ritualization of these actions, see Stephen Hart, *Cultural Dilemmas of Progressive Politics: Styles of Engagement among Grassroots Activists* (Chicago: University of Chicago Press, 2001), 100–101.

9. Some organizations that run training include Industrial Areas Foundation (www.industrialareasfoundation.org), PICO (www.piconetwork.org), DART (www.thedartcenter.org), and Gamaliel (www.gamaliel.org), all of which are faith-based networks; Midwest Academy (www.midwestacademy.com), which runs training for all kinds of community organizations; and Center for Third World Organizing (www.ctwo.org), which takes a race-based approach to social justice. Reform synagogues should contact Just Congregations (http://urj.org/socialaction/training/justcongregations); Reconstructionist synagogues should get in touch with the Jewish Reconstructionist Federation (http://jrf.org); and others can contact Jewish Funds for Justice (www.jewishjustice.org).

Suggestions for Further Reading

Alinsky, Saul. *Rules for Radicals: A Practical Primer for Realistic Radicals*. 1971. Reprint, New York: Vintage Books, 1989.

Bakke, Ray. *A Theology as Big as the City*. Downers Grove, IL: Intervarsity Press, 1997.

Bobo, Kim, Steven Max, and Jackie Kendall. *Organizing for Social Change: Midwest Academy Manual for Activists*. Santa Ana, CA: Forum Press, 2001.

Chambers, Edward T. *Roots for Radicals: Organizing for Power, Action, and Justice*. New York: Continuum, 2004.

Dorff, Elliot N. *The Way Into* Tikkun Olam *(Repairing the World)*. Woodstock, VT: Jewish Lights, 2005.

Dreier, Peter, John Mollenkopf, and Todd Swanstrom. *Place Matters: Metropolitics for the Twenty-first Century*. 2nd ed. Lawrence: University Press of Kansas, 2004.

Freedman, Samuel G. *Upon This Rock: The Miracles of a Black Church*. New York: HarperCollins, 1993.

Georgi, Dieter. *The City in the Valley: Biblical Interpretation and Urban Theology*. Atlanta: Society of Biblical Literature, 2005.

Gornik, Mark. *To Live in Peace: Biblical Faith and the Changing Inner City*. Grand Rapids: William B. Eerdmans, 2002.

Harper, Nile. *Urban Churches, Vital Signs: Beyond Charity Toward Justice*. Grand Rapids, MI: William B. Eerdmans, 1999.

Hart, Stephen. *Cultural Dilemmas of Progressive Politics: Styles of Engagement among Grassroots Activists*. Chicago: University of Chicago Press, 2001.

Heschel, Abraham Joshua. *Moral Grandeur and Spiritual Audacity: Essays*. Edited by Susannah Heschel. New York: Farrar, Straus & Giroux, 1996.

Jacobs, Jane. *The Death and Life of Great American Cities*. New York: Random House, 1993.

Jacobs, Jill. *There Shall Be No Needy: Pursuing Social Justice through Jewish Law and Tradition*. Woodstock, VT: Jewish Lights, 2010.

Northcott, Michael, ed. *Urban Theology: A Reader*. Herndon, VA: Wellington House, 1998.

Piven, Frances Fox, and Richard A. Cloward. *Poor People's Movements: Why They Succeed and How They Fail*. New York: Vintage Books, 1977.

Rose, Or N., Jo Ellen Green Kaiser, and Margie Klein, eds. *Righteous Indignation: A Jewish Call for Justice*. Woodstock, VT: Jewish Lights, 2008.

Sacks, Jonathan. *To Heal a Fractured World: The Ethics of Responsibility*. New York: Schocken, 2007.

Schwarz, Sidney. *Judaism and Justice: The Jewish Passion to Repair the World*. Woodstock, VT: Jewish Lights, 2006.

Solinger, Rickie, Madeline Fox, and Kayhan Irani, eds. *Telling Stories to Change the World: Global Voices on the Power of Narrative to Build Community and Make Social Justice Claims*. New York: Routledge, 2008.

Thompson, Becky. *A Promise and a Way of Life: White Antiracist Activism*. Minneapolis: University of Minnesota Press, 2001.

Tonna, Benjamin. *A Gospel for the Cities: A Socio-Theology of Urban Ministry*. Translated by William E. Jerman. Eugene, OR: Wipf and Stock, 1982.

Toulouse, Mark. *God in Public: Four Ways American Christianity and Public Life Relate*. Louisville, KY: Westminster John Knox Press, 2006.

Walzer, Michael. *Exodus and Revolution*. New York: Basic Books, 1985.

Warren, Mark R. *Dry Bones Rattling: Community Building to Revitalize American Democracy*. Princeton, NJ: Princeton University Press, 2001.

Index

About Jewish Lights

People of all faiths and backgrounds yearn for books that attract, engage, educate, and spiritually inspire.

Our principal goal is to stimulate thought and help all people learn about who the Jewish People are, where they come from, and what the future can be made to hold. While people of our diverse Jewish heritage are the primary audience, our books speak to people in the Christian world as well and will broaden their understanding of Judaism and the roots of their own faith.

We bring to you authors who are at the forefront of spiritual thought and experience. While each has something different to say, they all say it in a voice that you can hear.

Our books are designed to welcome you and then to engage, stimulate, and inspire. We judge our success not only by whether or not our books are beautiful and commercially successful, but by whether or not they make a difference in your life.

For your information and convenience, at the back of this book we have provided a list of other Jewish Lights books you might find interesting and useful. They cover all the categories of your life:

Bar/Bat Mitzvah
Bible Study / Midrash
Children's Books
Congregation Resources
Current Events / History
Ecology / Environment
Fiction: Mystery, Science Fiction
Grief / Healing
Holidays / Holy Days
Inspiration
Kabbalah / Mysticism / Enneagram

Life Cycle
Meditation
Men's Interest
Parenting
Prayer / Ritual / Sacred Practice
Social Justice
Spirituality
Theology / Philosophy
Travel
Twelve Steps
Women's Interest

Ingram Content Group UK Ltd.
Milton Keynes UK
UKHW032004240323
419071UK00001B/7